Spirit and Psyche

Spirit and Psyche

A New Paradigm for Psychology, Psychoanalysis, and Psychotherapy

Victor L. Schermer

Foreword by Kenneth Porter

Jessica Kingsley Publishers
London and New York

First published in the United Kingdom in 2003
by Jessica Kingsley Publishers Ltd
116 Pentonville Road
London N1 9JB, England
and
29 West 35th Street, 10th fl.
New York, NY 10001-2299
www.jkp.com

Copyright ©2003 Victor L. Schermer

Library of Congress Cataloging in Publication Data
Schermer, Victor L.
    Spirit and psyche : a new paradigm for psychology, psychoanalysis, and psychotherapy / Victor L. Schermer ; foreword by Kenneth Porter.
        p. cm.
    Includes bibliographical references and index.
    ISBN 1-85302-926-2 (pbk. : alk. paper)
    Psychoanalysis and relegion. 2. Psychology and religion. 3.
Psychotherapy--Religous aspects. I. Title.

BF175.4.R44 S34 2002
616.89'14--dc21   2002034080

British Library Cataloguing in Publication Data
A CIP catalogue record for this book is available from the British Library

ISBN 1 85302 926 2

Printed and Bound in Great Britain by
Athenaeum Press, Gateshead, Tyne and Wear

For Suzanne

and to

James S. Grotstein, MD – beloved mentor and friend,
a psychoanalyst of rare courage and vision

and

John C. Sonne, MD – psychoanalyst, family therapist,
and dear friend who taught me that life is broader
and wider than any theory.

He who sees the Infinite in all things sees God; He who sees the Ratio only sees himself only.

William Blake (from 'There is No Natural Religion,' 1698)

Contents

PART II: Spirituality and Psychological Healing

Addendum and Exemplification

Foreword

At the turn of the last century a number of critical events occurred in the realms of spirituality and psychology that were destined to change the shape of generations to come. The World Parliament of Religions in 1893 introduced Eastern and Western religions to each other in an organized way for the first time in the history of the United States. A mere two years later Freud published his first work in psychoanalysis. And in the following decade (the first of the new 20th century), three pioneers of psychological investigation began to publish their work: the American psychologist William James, the Swiss analyst Carl Jung, and the Italian analyst Roberto Assagioli. James, Jung, and Assagioli all presented models for the integration of spirituality with psychology.

In a certain sense, the next century was commentary. Throughout the century, but especially starting in the 1960s, Eastern spiritual teachers flocked to America. Psychoanalysts and psychologists increasingly began to integrate their teachings, as well as those of the Judao-Christian tradition, into traditional psychotherapy. And psychoanalysis itself slowly developed into traditions of increasing flexibility and sophistication. As a result of these movements, in recent years there have been a host of attempts to move forward in the integration of spirituality and psychotherapy.

Often, however, these attempts have been personal, anecdotal accounts, or theoretical accounts by non-clinicians. The field has lacked sufficient attempts that are both theoretical and clinical to integrate these two realms of human endeavor. Into this void, Victor Schermer's excellent book comes to provide much needed clarification and food for thought.

Schermer, a practicing psychologist in Philadelphia, comes well suited to his task. A trained psychoanalytic clinician, he also brings to his work years of personal experience on a spiritual path, in addition to much experience as a staff psychologist in a substance abuse rehabilitation unit run according to twelve-step principles. His book is a careful attempt to bring the spiritual into psychotherapy not as window dressing, but as a core, integral part of the healing process.

The book opens with a thoughtful review of modern developments in science, a review of Eastern thought, and a careful examination of the history of psychoanalysis, including modern developments – object relations theory, self psychology, Kleinian analysis, developmental psychology, relational psychoanalysis and intersubjectivity – from a spiritual perspective. There is much here of interest, such as an understanding of Judas' betrayal of Christ and its connection to 'God anxiety,' or Schermer's analogy between the infant's experience of the mother as container or transformational object and the adult's capacity for surrender to, and union with, the divine.

Schermer then goes on to the heart of his book, the concept and development of the psychospiritual self – the inner core of the self seeking union with the divine, needing oneness, infinity, and the mysterious Other, and striving for purity, innocence, and wholeness. A thought-provoking map of the ego, true self, psychospiritual self, ineffable subject, and God is then followed by a section on psychotherapeutic treatment, which considers the spiritual basis of traditional treatment, patients' narratives, consciousness in the patient and therapist, therapy as spiritual practice and as spiritual journey, the therapist as mystic, and therapy as mutual meditation. The book closes with an extended discussion of twelve-step recovery work as a psychospiritual path.

One of the advantages of Schermer's book is that he does not shy away from stating his positions even when they might provoke controversy, and in fact makes clear that one of the intentions of his book is precisely to stimulate further dialogue. Thus, an interesting question is whether the spiritual core of ourselves as humans should be conceptualized as part of the 'self,' whether conscious or unconscious, at all. Many – especially those heavily influenced by Eastern mystical traditions – would argue that it is precisely the self, the personality, or what is called in spiritual traditions the ego, that in fact is the crucial barrier to our experiencing within ourselves the deepest aspects of who we truly are. Similarly, at one point in the book Schermer muses whether it would be possible to live without a 'self' at all, and concludes that it might not be a viable project. Buddhists, Hindu swamis, Sufis, and Taoists would strongly demur. They would claim that it is precisely seeing through the illusion of the self that is the path to the divine.

In line with this, although Schermer includes much information from the Eastern spiritual traditions that will be of great interest to Western clinicians, his book is most deeply informed by the Western, Judao-Christian theistic tradition of the spiritual self yearning for contact with the divine. In this regard, however, the book will serve a balancing function, as much of the psychospiritual literature in recent decades has in fact been written from the Eastern perspective.

In considering a book we often do not take into account what might be called the tone of voice of the author. In this regard Schermer's approach is unusual. He manages to be both scholarly and intimate, theoretical and personal, so that the reader might often feel that Schermer is actually talking with him. This style manages to embody the very point that Schermer is making in the book, that the spiritual, the 'most real,' is not a realm separate from the rest of life, but permeates each aspect of our existence. This same quality is apparent in Schermer's clinical case examples, which reveal him to be a skilled, insightful, caring, and moving psychotherapist.

One additional note — those readers whose interest in spirituality and psychotherapy is aroused by this book may also wish to visit the work of the spiritual teacher A. H. Almaas, one of the few writers to integrate spirituality with psychology whom Schermer does not discuss. Almaas' Diamond Approach, as exemplified in his teachings and many books, offers a particularly human and profound integration of mystical spirituality with Western psychology.

Western culture continues to evolve. Many of us, psychotherapists and non-therapists alike, have found that in the quintessential American pursuit of happiness, spirituality may be the golden key. Certainly our conflict-ridden world could sorely benefit from the oneness and wholeness that Schermer identifies as the heart of the spiritual approach. So as we, our culture and the world continue to develop, we can be grateful for contributions to healing such as this excellent book.

Kenneth Porter
Center for Spirituality and Psychotherapy,
National Institute for the Psychotherapies, New York

Preface and Acknowledgements

This book is the result of, and I trust a fitting contribution to, the convergence of spirituality with developments in psychology and psychoanalysis. The synthesis of religious and spiritual principles with the understanding of psychological development which began over a century ago but remained a 'segregated minority' effort, is now becoming a 'mainstream' preoccupation. While I, for one, have never been steeped in religion or spiritual seeking as such, as a fledgling psychologist I came into contact with humanistic and transpersonal psychology during the 1960s and 70s when, riding the innovative waves of those heady times, I participated in encounter groups, practiced yoga, and studied the work of Alan Watts, Fritz Perls, Abraham Maslow, and others who represented the then 'new psychology' of meditation, the 'here-and-now,' and self-actualization emerging at the Esalen Institute, the National Training Laboratories, and other cutting-edge centers for humanistic psychology. Around that same time, I read with great appreciation the writings of Jung, Fromm, Frankl, Tillich, Buber, and others who wrote about the human condition and psychotherapy from variously Eastern, Christian, Talmudic, Hassidic, and so-called 'pagan' perspectives. I found these humanistic and spiritual vantage points personally inspiring, but, in keeping with my modernist and scientific inclinations, as well as a certain mistrust of religious dogma, a passionate interest in Freudian psychoanalysis soon overtook me.

At that time, Freudian-based psychoanalysis decidedly sequestered itself from spirituality, seeking instead to explain human experience in terms of biological instincts and interpersonal needs within a 'naturalistic' and 'reductionistic' outlook. I pursued my career along these latter lines, and my spiritual interests faded into the background. The humanistic perspective, however, indirectly influenced my first (1987) book, *Object Relations, the Self, and the Group*, co-authored with Charles Ashbach.

During the early 1980s, I endured a personal crisis which my psychoanalytic understanding seemed inadequate to overcome. I began a variety of spiritual explorations and practices in order to 'find myself,' and consciously applying spiritual principles helped me find meaning and purpose through which I emerged with new hope from a period of profound depression and disillusionment. However, I continued my work in psychoanalysis and group dynamics as a scholar and a practicing psychotherapist, making little or no reference to the spiritual changes which had taken place in me. In a way, I was leading two lives, but I was peripherally aware that they were connected.

At that time, I became interested in the work of the British psychoanalyst, Wilfred R. Bion, who startlingly brought mystical ideas into object relations theory. I found his theories brilliant, provocative, and at the 'cutting edge.' Bion's work suggested bridges between my spiritual life and my work.

Then I was recruited as a staff psychologist for an inpatient drug and alcohol treatment program which emphasized a model of addictions utilizing the principles of Alcoholics Anonymous (AA). AA regards chemical dependence as a treatable 'illness' having physical, emotional, and spiritual components, rather than the outcome of a psychodynamic conflict, deficit, or personality type as such. I felt like a duck out of water in this new context but was welcomed and accepted by the staff, and quickly became fascinated with a 'spiritually-based' philosophy of treatment.

During my tenure there, I began to search for connections between spiritual and psychodynamic 'paradigms' of treatment. For example, when a staff member referred to a patient's recovery as a 'resurrection,' or patients explored the need for 'total surrender,' I asked myself what these then foreign notions could mean from a psychodynamic standpoint. I thought of 'surrender' as a parallel to Winnicott's concept of 'total dependency,' and compared 'resurrection' to the personality changes that result from deep emotional insight in psychoanalysis. Numerous comparisons, puzzles, and possibilities arose during the years I worked at that facility. It was a superb learning experience of the sort that leads one to question fundamental assumptions and long-held beliefs.

As the 'New Age' culture took hold, so did spirituality begin to find a place within the naturalistic and reductionist psychoanalytic literature, where it had been taboo for many decades. Psychoanalysts William Meissner, James Grotstein, Nina Coltart, and Michael Eigen, and psychiatrist Mark Epstein articulated views on object relations theory and the psychology of the self that included spiritual perspectives. For the first time, I found a community and a dialogue which brought together the two sides of my life and my work, and I began to think seriously about how spirituality and psychoanalysis could be integrated. After contributing an article on the subject of spirituality and psychotherapy to a professional journal and finding an interested audience, the ideas, however tentative, came fast, and I decided to write a book about it.

The value and validity of the result herein will be for the reader to judge. While I have specialized in and applied object relations theory, self psychology, and other post-Freudian developments in psychoanalysis for over twenty-five years, I claim no expertise about matters spiritual, metaphysical, and theological. I have tried to use my intuition and experience to interpret the spiritual teachings I do know about. Further, I suspect that some will feel that I have overpersonalized and oversimplified some relgious concepts and texts. I beg their forgiveness and hope that they can find some universalities among my musings.

Other *apologia* are owed the reader. My references to religious ideas are confined to Judaism, Christianity, Hinduism, and Buddhism. I wish I could have included Muslim, Native American, Taoist, and other religious systems in my discussions. My only consolation would be to hope that this book will encourage members of diverse religions to join the dialogue by offering their own perspectives on spiritual psychology and psychotherapy.

They say that 'God is in the details.' One seemingly trivial detail proved surprisingly vexing: the use of the third person pronoun (he/she/it) caused me no end of concern. I became acutely aware that there is no adequate way to convey multiple gender in the English language. God, of course, is either poly-gendered or non-gendered, depending on the degree of anthropomorphization we wish to imply. My generic references to persons should be demarcated 'she or he,' but this is cumbersome. I chose to use the conventional 'he' except where gender is a key aspect of the discussion. I hope that women readers will forgive me for what is perhaps a stylistic anachronism and any masculine bias they may detect in my viewpoint. The women's perspective represents a critical 'vertex' for a spiritual paradigm, and women's spirituality is a rich field of its own. It has opened many doors to spiritual understanding that were censored and repressed by patriarchal culture. If I cannot fully represent it, I can nevertheless acknowledge its vital importance.

Case examples play an important role in elucidating the principles put forth in this book. In order to preserve patient confidentiality, I have constructed case examples from my own and others' clinical and consulting experience. All 'patient' names are, of course, pseudonyms; identities and information have been carefully omitted or disguised; and many of the examples are constructed from the narratives of several patients combined into one. Therefore, association of any clinical vignette with a particular individual is purely coincidental. Importantly in this respect, the case studies are meant to be illustrative rather than to constitute concrete evidence of the points being made.

Even a solo effort such as this book owes much to the collective. I am deeply grateful to my patients for sharing their diverse experiences with me and to my colleagues for ideas, support, and inspiration. Conversations with James Grotstein and e-mail correspondence with Michael Eigen were instrumental in setting me on this 'psychospiritual' road, and Jim has been a beloved friend and mentor for many years. My colleagues Yvonne Agazarian, Peter Benda (a political scientist and grant administrator), Phillip Bennett, Harold Bernard, Kit Bollas, Bertram Cohen, Mary Dluhy, Jim Durkin, Raman Kapur, Jeffrey Kauffman, Robert Klein, Lew Krieg, Dianne LeFevre, Malcolm Pines, Cecil Rice, Suzanne Roff, John Sonne, Vamik Volkan, and Corbett Williams (a systems analyst with a deep interest in neuropsychology and the work of Bion) have supported and inspired me in the work I have done. Charles Ashbach, the co-author of my first book, *Object Relations, the Self, and the Group*, was a powerhouse of ideas who 'filled my container' with new ways of looking at the personality and group relations. Gunther Abraham, a great teacher of psychoanalysis, who studied with Donald Winnicott, Anna Freud, and Martin Buber, pointed me in the direction of the work of Melanie Klein, Winnicott, and Bion. Robert Pomerantz mentored me as an addictions treatment supervisor and helped me to find my own voice in that context, and was comfortable but never doctrinaire about integrating traditional and spiritually-based approaches to counseling and psychotherapy. Tom Crane, a gifted administrator, shared with me his own Eastern-based spiritual practice. Robert Foreman, teacher, researcher, administrator, and a pioneer in intensive outpatient treatment of addictions, was the first colleague in my recollection to use the term 'psychospirituality.' I do not know if that term was originated by him, but it was he who first brought it to my attention. The fact that, in merely a decade, 'psychospirituality' has become common coinage says something about the heightened interest in the connection between psychology and spirituality.

Ken Porter, co-founder and Director of Psychiatry of the Center for Spirituality and Psychotherapy at the National Institute for the Psychotherapies in New York City, generously conveyed to me some of his own ideas and perspectives and wrote the foreword to this book. Dan Gottlieb, psychologist, journalist, and host of the National Public Radio program 'Voices in the Family,' has shared my interest in spirituality, presented at three conferences I conducted, and become a dear friend. Dan's own tragic auto accident and his resultant search for meaning and vitality are well known to people in the Philadelphia area. His openness in sharing his experience has affected me deeply. I am grateful to my 'boss,' Jane McGuffin, for her excellent administrative work and for kindly allowing me periodic time off from my clinic duties to pursue my writing. And special thanks are due Jessica Kingsley and her staff for publishing this volume in their distinguished catalog.

And then there are my friends, family, co-workers, my personal physician, Dr Guy Lacy Schless, and my very kind and tolerant past psychotherapists, Edward Gaughran and James Pearson. What can I say? Friends, support persons, and physicianly care are so important to our well-being. I would especially like to honor my father, Matt, who died in 1997, and whose deep humility, love, and openness was priceless and allowed me to lose him with only a little bit of dying in myself.

As you can surmise, I have had mentors but never a guru either in psychoanalysis or spirituality. While following a guru can have its own benefits, I have never been able to follow that path of devotion to a person. I found that I must, however falteringly, find my own inner spirit. My 'guru' is relational – I believe that if we relate lovingly and courageously to each other and are willing to learn from one another, we will find 'the way' that is right for each of us.

God is in our hearts. God is Love. God works through people. God is in I and Thou meeting. Of these things I am sure. As for whatever else I have to say in this book, I present it not with absolute conviction, but with the hope that it may stimulate others to think their own thoughts and look for the mysterious 'unthought known' that is in them and all around them.

Part I

Psychospirituality

CHAPTER ONE

A Paradigm Shift

...the term paradigm is used in two different senses. On the one hand, it stands for the entire constellation of beliefs, values, techniques, and so on shared by the members of a given community. On the other, it denotes one sort of element in that constellation, the concrete puzzle-solutions, which, employed as models or examples, can replace explicit rules as a basis for the solution of the remaining puzzles of normal science.

Thomas Kuhn

Spirituality is the essence of all human experience. It is present even in its denial. The most convinced atheist or existentialist struggles with the meaning and purpose of life even as he perceives life as godless and absurd. Nietzsche, as he negated God, sought to elevate the human spirit. Sartre wrote about 'bad faith' as a failure to affirm existence, even as he said that faith as a principle is undermined by the ultimate absurdity and meaninglessness of our lives. A human being has to find meaning and an ideal to believe in, even in the depths of skepticism and despair. Another existentialist, Camus, wrote, 'In the midst of winter, I found within me an invincible summer.' Where is that summer, if not in spirit?

In the latter half of the 19th century, philosophy and psychology became disillusioned with spirituality. The intellectual and scientific progress that led to 'the modern era' negated our spiritual core. Spirituality was equated with spiritual-*ism*, the belief in paranormal phenomena, and regarded suspiciously by most of the scientific community. Only recently has spirituality come to be considered a legitimate aspect of mainstream psychology and psychoanalysis.

In what follows, I want to explore with you some of the implications of spirituality and religious belief for psychology and psychotherapy. But be forewarned that I am by both nature and nurture an incorrigible skeptic and a scientifically-minded, humanistically inclined individual. So it has been imperative for me to ask a question that will seem unnecessary for those of deeper faith. That question is decidedly modern and postmodern, namely, why must we bring spiritual ideas such as God, a Higher Self, and higher awareness into psychology and psychotherapy, based as these disciplines are and must be, in the natural and social sciences and in the very demands and conditions of our earthly existence? A Jungian psychologist or a devoutly religious person might take the spiritual connection for granted. A latter-day Freudian, modernist, or postmodernist would not. Without having adopted a clear ideological stance, I do find that I gravitate towards the latter points of view, which admittedly embody a certain skepticism and suspicion about human motivation and knowledge.

Like myself, some readers, especially those reared in traditional academic and clinical psychology, may experience this quandary. Although there is renewed interest in spiritual matters in the culture-at-large, such concerns remain beyond the scope of conventional research, theory, and practice, and for good reason. After all, modern psychology is built around the notions that more complex phenomena (mind, learned behavior, cognition) can be explained in terms of the 'simpler' (biology, drives, conditioning), and later development in terms of earlier (adult life as a function of infancy and childhood), and that self-actualizing tendencies are dependent upon first meeting more basic material and social needs (biological and evolutionary determinism; Maslow's need hierarchy; Freud's concept of sublimation in which even the highest creative productions are driven by sexual and aggressive urges). Such reductionism has led to many insights and applications and helped us better to perceive ourselves in the context of biological and cultural evolution.

Furthermore, it is often held that a belief in God, or that there is present in human beings a striving towards the apprehension of a Reality beyond everyday experience, is founded upon metaphysical speculation that has no place in a scientific approach. Research data yield truths that no amount of metaphysics can access. The logical positivists question whether the assumption of realities that transcend sense impressions and logic can have any meaning whatsoever. Finally, as a democratic principle, shouldn't psychology be kept distinct from religious beliefs, so that anyone, regardless of his faith or lack thereof, can have equal access to assessment and treatment? Shouldn't we offer treatments that transcend religion and culture? Isn't this egalitarianism consistent with both a democratic society founded on religious freedom, and a search for universal methods and theories that apply to all human beings?

These are important arguments against bringing spirituality into the social sciences, and they have served well as anchors for psychology, psychiatry, and psychotherapy since the 19th century, when these fields separated themselves from philosophy and theology as separate disciplines based on empirical research. Today, however, we see a renaissance of spirituality in the New Age movement, the widespread interest in meditation practices, spiritual readings, and attendance at workshops, and a trend towards incorporating spirituality in holistic medicine and health, alternative therapies, stress management, and daily life. Some rigorous scientists have joined the bandwagon, contending, for example, that quantum theory implies cosmic consciousness (Young, 1976), and that higher states of awareness can be documented and classified (Tart, 1972; Wolman and Ullman, 1986; Combs, 1995), are beneficial to health and well-being (Benson and Proctor, 1985; Benson and Stark, 1996), and positively impact upon mental health (Levin and Chatters, 1998). By and large, though, 'hard-nosed' scientists continue to seek chemical and biogenetic explanations of behavior, materialistic explanations of events in the universe, and neurotransmitter research to advance the use of drugs to treat mental illness. As well they should. But what place could God or spirit have in a world of electrons, mu mesons, and complex organic molecules?

The one striking exception to the spiritual skepticism that has pervaded psychology has been Jungian analytic psychology, which has always emphasized the spiritual aspect of the self, the numinous and archetypal within the psyche. The long delay in incorporating spirituality into mainstream psychology is partly attributable to the rift that developed between Freud and Jung in the early days of psychoanalysis. Freud insisted on the importance of biological instincts such as the sex drive, while Jung held that the rock bottom of the psyche consisted in the collective historical experience of the human race, which included spirituality in the form of what he later called archetypes, inherited templates which included intimations and perceptions of gods, goddesses, and other spiritual entities. Splitting from the Freudian camp, Jung distinguished between the instinctually based personal unconscious and the archetypal collective unconscious (Hayman, 1999, p.207). Even though he emphasized the spiritual realm, Jung himself played a role in maintaining the isolation of spiritually-based psychology from its secular scientific counterpart by maintaining this artificial division of the mental life. In my view, *the fundamental spiritual element of psychology is not the archetypal realm as such, but life as it is lived, the actual individual journey from birth to death.* Spirituality consists in both existence and essence: in the way that biological and sociocultural imperatives and collective images are integrated in man's attempt to sort out the problems of life and existence. This requires both a naturalistic developmental perspective *and* a mythic archetypal viewpoint working in tandem as complementary and paradoxically related opposites. Thus, to an extent, this book may be thought of as an attempt to heal the schism between Jungian- and Freudian-based schools of psychoanalysis and between spiritual/religious and naturalistic views of human mind and behavior.

Until a few years ago, I was among the vast majority of working psychologists who deliberately kept spiritual ideas apart from their scholarly work, research, and psychotherapy, precisely on account of the above principles. My own primary focus was on the psychodynamics of development, relationships, and groups. I was, and continue to be, interested in how object relations, i.e. interpersonal relations and their corresponding mental conflicts and representations, influence emotional development. I sought to treat patients for whom early attachments and relatedness had become derailed. While I read with interest the work of those who offered a combined psychological and spiritual outlook, such as William James, Carl Jung, Martin Buber, Viktor Frankl, and Erich Fromm, I felt that such perspectives should not be incorporated into my work because I sought naturalistic and social scientific reference points for treatment and had found, in secular object relations theory and self psychology, frameworks which were rich in implications, experientially rich and convincing, and useful. Further, I did not think it appropriate to impose my own spiritual beliefs or skepticism on my patients. So, in my work at least, I remained agnostic.

In time, however, several forces converged to lead me to believe that the interpersonal and object relations frameworks were insufficient, that ignoring spiritual concerns represented a serious omission. Here is how I came to that realization.

The first major professional challenge to my scientific skepticism about spirituality came from extensive work in addictions treatment. In a facility strongly influenced by the principles of Alcoholics Anonymous, I witnessed significant healing of patients with substance abuse disorders and trauma occur through means which, while they did not require a supernatural explanation, could only be described as spiritual, in the sense of a significant change in beliefs, attitudes, and personality which involved higher consciousness and/or a faith in God. I witnessed patients who had received poor prognoses by the mental health system and been labeled as 'recidivists,' 'borderlines' and 'sociopaths' develop full, rich, ethical, and socially oriented lives. None of these changes could have been predicted or expected by a reductionist model which emphasized biological drives, or which held, as did Freud, that the personality is established by five or six years of age.

Second, my interests expanded to include a fascination with Eastern thought, meditation, and states of consciousness. Although at the time I did not see the potential of such practices to treat mental illness and addiction, I met a few therapists who did, and I began to consider that such disorders constituted an alteration in consciousness which could be corrected through meditative experiences and spiritual renewal.

Third, psychologists and medical practitioners were increasingly delving into spirituality and devising theories compatible with a modern scientific orientation. For example, Herbert Benson (Benson and Proctor, 1985; Benson and Stark, 1996), a Harvard physician, is a dedicated scientific researcher who is obtaining rigorous empirical evidence of the health benefits of spiritual practices, rather than relying, as do many of the New Age medics, on personal anecdotes and testimonies which could easily be distorted.

Fourth, in my work as a group and family therapist, I learned of systems theories and the importance of context which led me to believe that straightforward push/pull cause and effect models were insufficient to account for human motivation, emotion and behavior. If we examine biological, social, and ecological systems in widening circles of interaction, we move beyond simple causal connections to the spiritual depth of biological, social, and ecological processes (Capra, 1997). Similarities can be found among spiritual teachings, living systems theories, and modern relativity, quantum, and chaos/complexity theories, all of which go well beyond ordinary cause–effect relationships (Capra, 1975; Wilber, 1998, 2000; Zukav, 1979) to realms of paradox, mystery, and realities beyond the senses. Not incidentally, Jung himself developed a strong interest in quantum theory and its possible relationship to what he called 'synchronicity,' the conjunction of events based upon archetypal resemblances (Hayman, 1999, pp.406–417).

Finally, what seemed to bring these diverse spheres of influence together for me was the work of a psychoanalyst, Wilfred Bion, who developed an extraordinary rationale for linking spirituality to my first and constant passion, object relations theory. Bion (1897–1979) was a brilliant and seminal thinker who, although he sometimes spoke and wrote in difficult and obscure metaphors, arrived at new formulations which allow psychoanalysis to incorporate a much wider perspective than before. Starting out from philosophy and the study of scientific method, Bion was ultimately led to a mystical view of the mental life.

Because the impact of these combined experiences formed the basis for this book, I will discuss each of them in the course of introducing some of the themes which I will explore as a foundation for what I call a 'psychospiritual paradigm,' a way of thinking about and doing psychology, psychoanalysis, and psychotherapy which integrates spiritual principles with psychological models of the mind and behavior. My intention is to bring spiritual understanding into conjunction with science-based ideas regarding the mind and its development, particularly as regards the dilemmas and disorders which patients bring to psychotherapy.

In so doing, I want to offer a perspective through which it is possible to establish a dialogue about how spirituality, the study of the self, and our knowledge of the mind and relationships can be integrated. As I have already mentioned, I come to this task from a psychoanalytic object-relations and self-psychological perspective. However, I hope that my ideas will also be relevant to other psychotherapeutic approaches, whether ego psychological, cognitive, behavioral, existential, gestalt, or others. I am trying to understand how human development emerges from a spiritual center, or perhaps epicenter, with the other epicenter being the need to survive and grow in a difficult world.

Importantly – and this may ruffle the feathers of some of my spiritually devoted friends and colleagues – I take no position on matters of extrasensory perception, the supernatural, and paranormal phenomena. On such matters I remain a friendly agnostic, neither ruling them out nor naively believing that they are proven realities. Indeed, I am hardly qualified to take a position about the supernatural and esoteric. Moreover, questions about their validity abound in the scientific community, despite the revival of enthusiasm about them. I don't preclude their possibility, and I believe that experiences of and beliefs in supernatural occurrences, whether they are 'real,' or imaginary constructions, can be mind-expanding in some ways and are worthy of serious study. For example, Jung's synchronicity, the meaningful concurrence of events in our lives, even in contradiction to conventional notions of causality, seems to me to be an important component of human experience. Exactly what that means in terms of physical as distinct from psychic reality is as yet an open question. Spirituality is an area where imagination and reality converge in what Winnicott called the 'transitional space,' and much that we today consider real was once a gleam in someone's eye. The fact that an experience is uncanny doesn't bear upon whether it is real or imaginary, only that it is in some way surprising and difficult to account for.

Rather than pursue paranormal phenomena, however, I am undertaking here a humbler but indeed complex and difficult task, namely to consider possible connections among several areas of study and practice: traditional psychotherapies, psychoanalytic theory, general systems theory, altered states of consciousness, developmental psychology, and spiritual beliefs. I believe that the integration of these disciplines will be the thrust of what could ultimately lead to new formulations of human nature in the 21st century.

It is exciting that, after a period of disillusionment with religion, science has developed understandings which give the spiritual life new credence. In my view, this convergence calls for a psychological paradigm in which spirituality is a central component. A paradigm offers a kind of aerial view of what scientists in a particular field do and believe. The philosopher Thomas Kuhn held that the sciences operate through a set of norms, procedures, beliefs, and values which are accepted by the scientific community. Kuhn's statement in the opening quotation for this chapter defines the 'paradigm' for a particular science as both the set of general operating principles and rules, and the set of specific beliefs and practices that characterize the day-to-day work of scientists. Thus, classical physics was predicated on the belief that measurements of time were independent of the observer and could be made with whatever degree of precision the measuring instrument permitted. Modern physics holds that the location and velocity of the observer play major roles in measurement, and that there are absolute limits to the precision of any given measurement. Thus the 'new physics' not only includes new theories and laws, but also is based on an entirely different paradigm than classical physics. Similarly, most psychologists and psycho-therapists operated on the belief that religious and spiritual explanations of experience had no place in the study of mind and behavior, because such explanations were neither logical nor material. The new psychospiritual paradigm assumes that many experiences and behaviors do require such explanations.

Indeed, the basic premise of this book is that, given the diverse and often contradictory streams of thought and research which link spirituality and psychology, it would be useful to formulate some basic principles and 'puzzle-solutions' which could lead to an integrative paradigm that suggests areas for future study and investigation in psychology and psychoanalysis. Importantly, such a paradigm is already evolving in an exciting way. Discussions are taking place at many levels and in all quarters of contemporary thought. My goal is to suggest a particular way of thinking about how we can bring together and integrate the diverse elements in the dialogue.

In order to develop such a paradigm, it is necessary to define spirituality as a psychological (as distinct from metaphysical or theological) construct. So let us begin.

Spirituality, the core sense of self, and the journey

Through the ages, the term 'spirituality' has acquired multiple meanings and connotations, only some of which fit within a depth psychological framework as such. A useful definition will turn out to be both universal and personal. Psychology is a field which links objectivity and subjectivity, and any definition of spirituality will have both objective and subjective components.

Very importantly, in defining spirituality as a psychological process, I want to avoid the Thomistic and Cartesian implication that mind, body, and spirit are separate realms. In my view, they form an inseparable unity. The 'soul,' from a psychological standpoint, is simply the essence of who we are, not an entity which has an existence independent of our body. I wish to avoid any implication that there are spirits floating around looking for bodies to inhabit; nor do I hold to the Cartesian duality of mind and body as distinct entities. Rather, mind evolved in bodies, and mental events are 'emergent phenomena' resulting from physical and chemical events of the endocrine and neurophysiological systems. The soul somehow arose from the evolution of the molecules of DNA which are the building blocks of living cells. This unitary point of view is a key to bringing spirituality clearly into the realm of the natural and social sciences.

I view the separation of mind and body as a spiritual malaise which afflicts our world. Only by recognizing the inherent unity of mind and body can we hope to achieve a spirituality which is genuinely healing for human beings. Divorcing body from mind and spirit leaves man estranged from himself and his origins. This division is a source of our collective neuroses and psychoses. Spirit, matter, and energy are one. To know this is liberating and leads to wholeness. Even as the mind/body unity contains the possibility of suffering and death, it is also the source of joy and ecstasy. The unity of body and spirit is a key premise of the paradigm which I advocate.

Spirituality and the sense of self

That said, the psychospiritual paradigm holds that *we are all possessed of a divinity within*. It is inherent in human nature to have valid experiences which transcend mundane reality, and we can access these experiences both in everyday life and through dreams, literature and the arts, meditation, peak experiences, and altered states of consciousness. Humankind is innately possessed of a sense of mystery and awe. We need our spirituality as much as we need food, sex, and other biochemical imperatives. William Blake (1698) articulated such a view of spirituality over two hundred years ago, in the height of the Age of Reason, and it still holds today. He viewed all religions as emanating from a common source within, and found spirituality to be present in art, poetry, and other 'soulful' expressions of our humanity.

Thus, the paradigmatic definition of psychospirituality must be not metaphysical, but within the context of an embodied, distinctly human psyche. Spirituality is an aspect of our sense of self, a self which is present in nascent form at birth and develops through the life cycle. The paradigm seeks to explore the dimensions of that spiritual component. From the standpoint of self, spirituality is defined as *a capacity and a motivation for living fully within the context of being and faith, based upon an urge to experience infinitude and something or some One beyond the confines of our everyday perceptions of ourselves and the world*. That is, spirituality is that aspect of our psyche which is always reaching for union with the mysterious and the beyond.

Even if we can't describe that otherness – perhaps *especially* if we can't describe it but continue to seek it – we are in a spiritual mode. A Talmudic scholar once said, 'Just when you know who God is, that's what He isn't.' Eastern thought respects silence and emptiness. Spirituality is not a system of beliefs as such; it is a quality of living, being, and experiencing which involves an awareness of the infinite, the ineffable, and the indescribable.

In the new paradigm, spirituality is not – as it has generally been considered – an 'add-on' to our basic drives and energies, but an integral part of them, informing and structuring them. That is, spirituality defines both our existence and our essence, and is not merely a religious doctrine or pursuit or a supplement to our basic needs. Deprivation and hunger, for example, may be experienced on both physical and spiritual levels. A person can feel spiritually hungry and deprived even when well fed, and conversely, a bowl of rice and some vegetables can be a feast of the gods for a person whose mind is calm and who is in a state of grace. A late friend who was a Redemptorist monk used to stand on a street corner at night with his friends, gesture with his arms to those around him, to the earth, and to the sky, and say, 'Where is the church? Where is God?' God isn't in a particular place or a particular belief. He, She, or It is everywhere, every place, every experience, and that is because spirituality resides in us as an inherent capacity and structuralizing agent of our minds. Spirituality is not external or peripheral. Rather, it resides within the core of our being and our emotional lives.

The spiritual journey

If spirituality is central in this way, then it must connect to our sense of self in every activity at every moment in time. Since self evolves and develops, the new paradigm requires a way of thinking about self as an evolving spiritual experience in 'real time.' The self, as it were, is perpetually on a journey. Spirituality sets in motion growth experiences that subjectively feel as if we are taken on a ride or asked to walk along a path of which we have faint glimpses, occasionally with major epiphanies, often portrayed as a journey of the soul. We each get a sense of this journey in our dreams, in experiences with others, in major life events and trauma, and in spiritual awakenings where we view life from a radically new perspective. It is as if there is something Other in our experience that carries us along, prods us to explore, and encourages us to move in certain directions. Perhaps we self-create this Other because it is the only way we can assimilate certain aspects of ourselves. We may perceive a pattern, a destiny, a fate, a meaning, in the course of the journey, or we may conclude that it is absurd or mysterious. The periods of doubt and confusion are just as important to our spiritual journey as the times of clear perception and belief.

It is not necessarily the case that spiritual experience must manifest a design or plan. To live amid our confusion without denying it may at times be the closest we come to a higher state of awareness. For example, one of the most intriguing and controversial pieces in the history of jazz is John Coltrane's *Meditations* (1965). Coltrane, like Duke Ellington, saw his music as a spiritual journey (Porter, 1999). On first listening, *Meditations* sounds disturbingly like chaos incarnate. Some listeners never go beyond that stage – even Coltrane's ardent fans were known to shamelessly leave the auditorium at some of his avant-garde performances. After repeatedly listening to Coltrane's recording of *Meditations*, however, one begins to hear gems of unearthly beauty, power, and transcendent reality. Perhaps, like Coltrane's improvisational power, the spiritual life is a complex concatenation of design and chaos, construction and destruction. It is certainly portrayed that way in the Old and New Testaments, in Hindu texts, and elsewhere.

From a psychological standpoint, religious texts and practice as such, while they may be sacred, are not in and of themselves psychospiritual. Rather, they serve the functions of marking the journey, finding elements in it common to the collective, and representing it symbolically. Obvious examples are Moses' and the Jews' journey in the desert, Christ's Stations of the Cross, the story of Shakti and Shiva (about the integration of the masculine and feminine in our nature), and Siddhartha's experiences leading to Enlightenment. The confluence of story, myth, and ritual, as Joseph Campbell (1949, 1997) has elaborated, is where the journey is given cultural form, stirs up the deep within us, and brings us together in a sacred space.

The lessons of clinical experience

Before I continue exploring the psychospiritual paradigm, I must make a diversion in order to share from my own experience how the nature of psychotherapy as a spiritual journey gradually became impressed upon me in my work with patients. These epiphanies of my own journey as a psychotherapist suggest the relevance of spiritual selfhood to the hard-nosed and goal-oriented reality of the treatment process. What really convinced me of the importance of spirituality as a practical tool and an essential aspect of psychology was the work I did on the unit of a drug and alcohol treatment center. There, I encountered for the first time the active and conscientious use of spiritual principles in psychotherapeutic treatment. Furthermore, such treatment was highly effective for a significant number of patients, more effective than conventional, non-spiritually oriented approaches. When a theoretical or technical framework produces major positive outcomes, it must be taken seriously.

The role of spirituality in the treatment of alcoholism and addiction

In the late 1980s and early 1990s, I worked as a staff psychotherapist in a twenty-eight-day inpatient alcoholism rehabilitation unit and founded an outpatient program there. These programs were largely based on the principles of the self-help support group, Alcoholics Anonymous (AA), which includes an emphasis on spiritual development. Prior to that, I served for ten years in an eclectic outpatient substance disorder program which emphasized the more traditional psychotherapies, including behavior modification, transactional analysis, Glasser's 'reality therapy,' and psychoanalysis. The differences in outcomes between the AA-based approach and the traditional techniques were astonishing to me. It led me to question everything I had learned in my graduate studies and psychoanalytic training. (I haven't jettisoned these latter, however, but found that I needed to add a dimension to my understanding of what is effective in treatment.)

In the traditional treatment program, with the exception of a few hardy and insightful patients who benefitted from in-depth treatment to the extent of a major personality change, we therapists had to be satisfied with small gains. A significant number of patients were able to curtail their substance use. However, their overall pattern of living, which included social isolation, depression, overreacting to minor frustrations, and difficulty pursuing a substance-free lifestyle, persisted despite the reduction in substance use. In sum, their sense of self and identity were insufficiently transformed to heal the overarching life pattern. This limitation existed even when treatment, in some instances, was sustained for as long as three to five years. Although the improvements were modest, they saved many lives, and I have no regrets about the work I did at that time. Yet, I often felt as if we were putting on a tourniquet to control a hemorrhage, but that the wound itself did not seem to heal.

In striking contrast, the AA-based program, enhanced by the protective net of an inpatient community, led to genuine changes in attitude and personality, in some cases within a few days after admission, and in others more begrudgingly towards the end of the twenty-eight-day period. Patients' defenses lowered, and receiving intensive support and encouragement from the staff, they became more receptive to the 'conversion' experience described by the psychiatrist Harry Tiebout (Alcoholics Anonymous World Services, 1943, pp.309–319) with respect to AA members. That is, they adopted whole new, spiritually-oriented ways of thinking, feeling, and acting that were compatible with a sober, socially constructive lifestyle. I learned from meeting with many of these patients a year to three years after treatment that, for many though by no means all, these gains were sustained and expanded, primarily with the help of attendance at Alcoholics Anonymous and Narcotics Anonymous meetings. I remembered that in graduate school at the University of Pennsylvania, a professor of physiological psychology and a respected researcher, Phillip Teitelbaum, said that psychological research was questionable unless it showed a large, macroscopic effect. Small, even though significant, differences might easily be due to forces outside the experimenter's ability to control. The changes in the patients in the AA-based program were great enough for anyone to see without subtle statistical tests: renewed family life, a sense of hope and faith, improved self-esteem, restored careers, access to a greater range of feelings, and an increased ability to establish intimacy with others.[1]

I began to ask myself what therapeutic factors (Yalom, 1995) might account for these changes. The following fell easily into place:

1.   The treatment took maximum motivational advantage of the desperation of the patients, who for the most part were in a downhill slide from substance dependence which adversely affected every aspect of their lives. Their extreme suffering made them ready for change, and this readiness was consciously exploited in treatment. They were not 'strung along' in analysis until insight occurred, but rather were told almost unmercifully to surrender their crumbling beliefs and adopt new ones.

2.   The patients were consciously encouraged and offered the tools to adopt a new way of life with new identifications and beliefs, ways of dealing with emotions, and acknowledgement of their own manipulative tendencies and other obstacles to good character.

3.   When receptive, the patients were 'adopted' by the highly supportive AA network, where loneliness was alleviated, help was readily available on a continuous basis, and characterological development was emphasized. Yalom's (1995) therapeutic factors of universality (sharing a common problem), mutual identification, instillation of hope, altruism, and group cohesiveness are well known to group psychotherapists and are strongly manifest at the AA meetings.

Then there was an additional element which AA members and the treatment team called 'spiritual awakening.' AA advocates no religion as such, but it does recommend that the alcoholic follow spiritual principles and it refers to a process of 'spiritual development.' The alcoholic at the inception of treatment is 'spiritually bankrupt,' that is, has lost his or her sense of a larger purpose, feels hopeless and ashamed, is disconnected from others and the flow of life itself, and feels inwardly damaged. A remedy is needed, and this nostrum consists of a 'spiritual awakening.'

As I pursued my work at the inpatient facility, I asked myself what a spiritual awakening could mean. I tried to boil it down to its essence for treatment purposes. Clearly, it went beyond the sudden epiphany and moment of truth and was a prolonged and multidimensional experience. I found that the following ingredients of spirituality were important for recovery from alcoholism and addictions:

1. overcoming a self-centered, narcissistic orientation towards living based upon self-protective fear

2. yielding an obsessive belief in omnipotent control of one's existence, and instead striving for a life devoted to something greater than oneself and 'going with the flow' of that which is good, nurturing, and transcendent

3. reconnecting with one's fellows

4. addressing one's shortcomings and making reparations for small and large injuries done to others

5. helping others as a way of strengthening one's own healing process.

These are dynamics which can be understood within a non-theistic framework, but they are also a part of our spiritual heritage. I came to believe that when people with addictions could find ways to implement these basic precepts, they stood a much greater chance of sustained recovery and an enhanced lifestyle than could otherwise be accomplished. Their awakening was more than a brief epiphany: it was a kindling of consciousness to new levels of experience.

The specifics of this spiritual awakening varied quite a bit from patient to patient. One might in fact remain a 'non-believer' and seek greater union with his or her compeers and the cosmos. Another might turn to religious practices. Still another would seek new ways of understanding, such as through meditation or a study of spirituality as it expresses itself in a variety of teachings. While spirituality appeared to be an essential ingredient, the spiritual path was an individual matter.

Thus, I concluded that the spirituality necessary for healing was not identical with any specific religion or professed set of beliefs, but rather a set of qualities that could be developed within any individual who sought them. I further saw that such spirituality has a meaning which is compatible with a scientific framework and can be put to good use in psychotherapy. These recovering alcoholics and drug addicts had, I concluded, undergone a journey of the spirit which led them to a better place in their lives and which could be studied scientifically. One of the staff members at the facility referred to that process as a 'resurrection.' I could begin to see that a term with such profound spiritual significance might also provide an empirical descriptor of full recovery from alcoholism. Thus, I began to suspect that spiritual concepts could serve explanatory purposes for phenomena that were puzzling within conventional psychotherapeutic frameworks.

Spirituality in treating grief, loss, and trauma

After my tenure in the addictions program, I devoted two years to work with patients who suffered from AIDS. At that time, the course of AIDS could not be slowed significantly as it can now. The prognosis then was rapid decline and certain death. Many were further faced with multiple traumatic losses: the death of close friends and whole communities afflicted by the AIDS epidemic. Thus, AIDS inevitably meant profound, multiple, and complex psychological traumata and loss. Since that time, I have worked in mental health clinics and in private practice where I became increasingly interested in trauma and loss as aspects of other emotional illnesses such as depression, anxiety, personality disorders, and psychosis (Klein and Schermer, 2000; Schermer and Pines, 1999). As with addictions, so with trauma and loss: I found that spirituality played a significant role in healing. A few examples will illustrate this confluence of spirituality and psychological healing of traumatic loss.

I worked with a young gay AIDS victim in the office and later, as he became increasingly disabled and bedridden, in his home and, finally, at a hospice. This man went through great physical pain and the loss of his ability to function. He became disillusioned and angry at the medical profession, sometimes for good reason. He felt helpless and victimized. As I helped him to work through his grief, he became more receptive to accepting his fate, living more fully in the present, and growing closer to friends and to his lover. A breakthrough occurred when, knowing he was dying, he contacted his estranged father and met with him after several years of absence. They wept, reminisced, and embraced each other. His father supported him to the very end. His death was bathed in love and reconciliation.

I was at bedside with this patient a few days before his death. He was relaxed and at peace. He discussed his feelings about dying and said, 'I'm OK, because I know there's got to be something better than this world.' His statement was infused with a mixture of realism with a belief in a state of being that transcended the earthly plane.

This patient stood in stark contrast with another who was frightened, ashamed, angry, and helpless to the very end. He became increasingly alienated from others, and was often scapegoated by them – they perceived his behavior as clownish, hysterical, and insincere and excluded him from their inner circles, which further justified his feelings of rejection. He was anxiously preoccupied with himself and made relentless demands on others. Having no sense of purpose or convictions about a world beyond his own narrow existence, he felt 'alone and abandoned in a hostile world' (Horney, 1994). He died as he had lived, feeling betrayed, shamed, and rejected. Clinically, he suffered from a 'personality disorder with borderline and narcissistic features.' He may have experienced sexual trauma in adolescence which contributed to this disorder.

Neither patient could be said in any sense of the word to be religious. But the former was able to transcend his circumstances to achieve a larger perspective, and this transcendence gave him peace and alleviated some of his symptoms and pain. The latter was unable to grieve and grow emotionally from a devastating experience. I believe that he lacked access to his spiritual interior and could not embrace a wider perspective. It was painful to see how he shut himself away from any opportunity to find connectedness and meaning in his life despite the considerable amount of love and attention he did receive from caregivers.

Some trauma are, unfortunately, the iatrogenic result of treatment rather than the disease itself. I treated a woman whose medical treatment was, literally, shocking. She suffered from a serious heart condition which meant that it could stop beating at virtually any time of the day or night. To prevent sudden death, cardiac surgeons had implanted a small mechanism inside her chest. (A larger version of this in the form of two hand-held electrodes is often used in cardiac units and by emergency workers to revive a patient in cardiac arrest. It applies a shock to the heart muscles, which reactivates their pumping mechanism.) She could be walking around her home, on the street, or riding public transportation and suddenly receive an electrical shock to the heart muscle. As a result she developed conditioned fear and anxiety to whatever she saw and wherever she was. Eventually, she was left, when without a companion, confined in fear to one or two rooms of her home.

Over a period of several months, I helped her regain some of her autonomy and mobility by teaching her cognitive and behavioral techniques to reduce her anxiety. She learned techniques to de-escalate the anxiety response that had hampered her. First, she ventured to do her local shopping, which she considered a major victory. Then she learned to re-navigate her neighborhood. Finally, she was able to take public transportation and come to sessions on her own.

At the end of treatment, she thanked me for the help I had given her. With a glowing expression on her face, she thanked me for helping her negotiate her world again, but, more importantly, she stressed, to regain her faith in herself and in God. That was hardly my goal. Indeed, God and religion never entered into her treatment. I was surprised and moved by the fact that renewed spirituality was her most valued gain.

The work of psychologist Therese Rando (1993) on traumatic loss supports such clinical observations. She has studied and described a quality she calls 'transcendence,' which enables clients to access parts of themselves which help them move beyond the helplessness, shame, guilt, anger, and grief that are triggered by a traumatic event. Psychologists have always known that 'resilience,' the ability to utilize adaptive coping mechanisms in response to dramatic life events, helps traumatized individuals. Now we see that transcendence, the willingness to surrender, let go, and get outside of the fray, is a quality that helps in recovery from trauma and loss.

Of course, the way of transcendence, or how and to what one surrenders, is important. Surrendering to transcend involves:

1.   full acceptance of one's condition

2.   the recognition that one cannot address trauma with material and personal resources exclusively

3.   the faith that *there is something intangible but good in oneself and the world that, if it does not provide cure, will still allow one to maintain one's true self and deeper values.*

It is important that psychologists and psychoanalysts study what it is within a person that enables him to maintain or restore such a transcendent perspective. I call the component of the personality that is capable of transcendence the 'spiritual self.'

As in the case of addictions, what these experiences with trauma and loss show is that an inherent spiritual quality resides within each person and that it has healing potential. Part of the task of the psychotherapist is to help the patient access this core, and, where it is deficient, strengthen it. I believe that virtually every human being is equipped with spiritual selfhood within his or her innate potential, and nurtured by 'good enough' care in infancy and childhood. (Exceptions might be tyrannical dictators and psychopaths, for example. Their core spiritual self could be said to have been aborted or else perverted towards malevolent ends.) For various reasons, however, within any of us the spiritual self can become split off, repressed, and denied, and the therapeutic problem is to enable access to it by the conscious mind. For reasons we will explore throughout this book, access to the spiritual self can evoke profound anxiety, so that, while we may know it 'through a glass darkly,' it often terrifies us to meet it 'face to face.' This is why both spiritual seeking and intensive psychotherapy can be adventurous, sometimes tortuous, journeys.

The core sense of self and its spiritual essence, while it is a source of communion and community, is nevertheless private and personal. D. W. Winnicott, a founder of the British Independent School of psychoanalysis, referred to an 'incommunicado core' within the self, implying the importance of private experience within the developing mind (Winnicott, 1963b). I see linkages between early object relationships, the sense of self, and the spiritual life. As I considered such matters, connections began to form between what we know about the spiritual life, and current concepts in science, psychoanalysis, and psychotherapy. I looked to such concepts as ways to build spiritual bridges to psychotherapy, where therapy could be seen as a deeply personal spiritual journey. As I have emphasized, to view psychology and psychotherapy in this way requires nothing less than a paradigm shift, a radical alteration of our basic concepts, procedures, and 'puzzle-solutions.' Whereas previously spirituality was merely peripheral to the self and its treatment, now it becomes its center. But is such a conception of treatment scientific? I think that, over the last century, scientific theory has expanded to a point where that question can be answered in the affirmative. The next chapter is about some of the specific concepts of modern science which I find useful in negotiating that paradigm shift.

Endnote

1 In keeping with the scientific critique implicit in this book, I do not mean zealously to imply that Alcoholics Anonymous is a new 'religion' that is effective for all alcoholics, or that it is the only approach that works. I want to suggest that when it is effective, it results not only in abstinence from alcohol (symptom reduction) but also in significant global changes in psychosocial functioning (personality changes) that are difficult to attain via conventional therapies with this population. I do not contend that AA is either a panacea or a harbinger of a new era of treatment. But I do believe that it is a very powerful force in recovery from alcoholism and that its spiritual principles play a major role.

CHAPTER TWO

Newer Perspectives in Science, Psychology, and Medicine

Albert Einstein, in a letter to Freud, said that solving the problems of psychology is more difficult than solving the problems of physics. Because the mind is so complex, multifaceted, and elusive, it takes considerable time for psychology and psychotherapy to 'catch up' in sophistication with the other sciences. When I first began my undergraduate studies of psychology in the early 1960s, most theories of human learning and development harked back more than two centuries to the Age of Enlightenment (the 18th and early 19th century) and the Renaissance and Restoration periods that preceded it, when humans and the universe were believed to behave like machines. Back then, the cosmos was described by Newton and others as a vast clockwork or a set of 'billiard balls' (matter, atoms) set in motion at some remote time, and everything we observed in nature and man reflected the position, speed, and direction of these billiard balls as they collided with each other and went off in directions that a few mathematical equations could predict. The universe was portrayed as cold, hard, mostly empty, and completely predictable. Some said that 'God' set the balls in motion and then just watched. Similarly, Descartes hypothesized that the 'mind' was located in the pineal gland in the brain, and yet a different sort of entity from the material world. God as 'first cause' and mind as observer were separated from the mechanistic universe in an uneasy dualism.

With the advent of relativity and quantum theories at the beginning of the 20th century, the Enlightenment view of the world as an elaborate machine was profoundly challenged. But when I began my training, psychology was still using the 'billiard ball' theory applied to behavior and learning. Tiny atoms of behavior or 'mental' associations could be 'chained' in sequences to compose the more complex ideas and personalities we observe in daily life. Ivan Pavlov, Clark Hull, B. F. Skinner, pioneers in the fields of 'classical' and 'instrumental' conditioning (learning by association and by outcome), and a host of others did minutely detailed research on animals and humans to test various hypotheses about how the cognitive and behavioral balls collided and connected. Likewise, Freud's theory of 'psychic determinism' assumed that each mental event was connected to others by the same laws of force and energy that applied to physics and chemistry (Amacher, 1965).

During that time (the 1950s/1960s and before), the one exception to this framework was Gestalt psychology, a point of view which held that 'the whole is greater than the sum of its parts.' Pattern perception and the organization of parts into wholes went beyond billiard ball 'units' to levels of organization and phenomenological 'fields' that had special features of their own. Spirituality might be understood in the Gestalt framework as a higher level of organization. But even within Gestalt psychology the building blocks were, as Freud held, biochemical needs and drives, like hunger, sex, reproduction, and aggression. There was little or no mention of spirituality as such.

Therefore, when I first heard the West Coast intellectual guru and psychologist Alan Watts speak, I thought he was an oddball. (He himself was partly responsible for that image, because, as I recall, he walked out on the stage in a flowing robe, shaking a baby's rattle!) Watts was one of the first to import Eastern thought into Western psychology. At the time, his ideas about higher states of consciousness were far outside of the mainstream. They were intriguing ideas, but mysterious and unquantifiable! So I went happily along with the standard reductionistic, mechanistic ideology. My early forays into encounter groups, meditation, and yoga rarely entered my thinking as a working psychologist.

All that has changed for me, as it has for many psychologists. Today, we are no longer bound to the mechanistic mold. We have found in the physical and natural sciences newer frameworks which allow complex peak experiences and altered states of consciousness to be a part of man's everyday bread, and even for the possibility of a God-consciousness present in every atom and electron and neutrino in the universe. The four scientific perspectives which most interest me in this respect are living systems theory, quantum theory, chaos/complexity theory, and space/time as defined in relativity theory. Without going into anything like the detail that each of these frameworks deserves, I will now discuss why, in my view, each of them offers a sophisticated rationale for a paradigm in which the spiritual life is an essential part of the human condition. I hasten to add that the proponents of these theories do not necessarily incorporate spirituality into their thinking. Their theories can be interpreted in ways which make no mention of the spiritual dimension. I am simply arguing that these theories have the scope, reach, and complexity that can provide a rationale for a spiritual understanding of the human psyche, if we choose to do so.

Living systems theory

Ludwig von Bertalanffy (1968) was a biologist who realized that living systems functioned by very different laws from the mechanical interactions of billiard ball atoms. For one thing, he noted the obvious: that living systems, unlike atoms, can and do reproduce themselves. (It is possible, of course, that by this time, physicists have posited the existence of subatomic particles that reproduce themselves!) Indeed, self-reproduction seems to be one of the primary defining capacities of living systems. For another, he observed that not only are the parts organized into wholes, but the wholes and parts have features in common which he called 'systems isomorphisms.' Isomorphic means 'similar in form and process.' Thus, each cell takes in and metabolizes nutrients just as the digestive system takes in and digests food, the mind takes in and digests information, and groups take in and influence members. The processes of internalization and transformation occur in all living systems. Furthermore, von B, as he was affectionately called, was struck by the fact that organisms are self-orienting and self-governing: they don't respond mechanically to the world around them, but follow their own built-in tendencies. A frog leaps when it sees a fly, a cow flaps its tail wildly, and a human – capable of cultural learning – gets a fly swatter, a hand-held tool. Each organism is responding in a way that is consistent with its own structure. As its own 'God,' it self-creates. That is, an organism contains within itself the genetic 'blueprint' both to construct itself and to orient itself to its surroundings. In an Aristotelian sense, it is its own 'final cause,' and theologians have often argued that God is the final or ultimate cause of the universe. Some researchers (cf. Maturana, 1980) use the term 'autopoiesis' (self-positing or self-poising) to describe this self-governing characteristic of living beings.

For me, living systems theory suggests that we are not merely driven by basic biological urges like hunger and thirst as such, but that each level of functioning is equally important to all the others and has similar properties to all the others. We are not so much drive-directed organisms as we are hierarchically organized beings, with each level in the hierarchy being equal in importance. For example, being filled and empty, separate and one, withdrawing and attacking, are aspects of all human systems and subsystems. So, in this view, spiritual hunger is just as real and significant as the hunger for food. Separateness and oneness with the cosmos is as manifest and significant in development as the sperm's propulsion towards an ovum. Making creative and artistic 'babies' is just as important as making real babies. These systems all mirror each other in definable ways. Each evolved for a purpose. We are not reducible to those systems which may have evolved earliest, such as physical hunger and thirst. I attended a lecture (the 2002 Dean's Forum at the University of Pennsylvania) by J. Craig Venter, one of the prime movers of the human genome project, which strives to decipher the entire genetic code. Venter made clear that genetic structures are not aimed simply at 'drive reduction' but encode complex strategies of adaptation at all levels of organismic functioning.

Furthermore, contrary to the belief that children compliantly or rebelliously learn spiritual principles from adults with their capacity for mature thinking, decision-making, and ethical responsibility, living systems theory permits us to assert that infants and children are themselves spiritual beings. The pediatrician T. Berry Brazelton once said that 'Babies are competent executives:' they *intiate* interactions with others – a startling revelation of videotapes of mother–infant interactions. Although it is pure speculation at this point, one can consider that babies not only relate to significant others, but that they experience rudimentary spiritual entities in their dreams and in the context of their relationships. One can further surmise that they may seek preverbal meanings of what their existence is all about, for example, that they can become depressed if they lose a certain faith in the dependability of things. Living systems theory allows for this possibility: the various stages of development have similar, isomorphic features. I exploit this belief that spirituality is present at birth in my concept of the spiritual self and its origins in the 'pristine ego.' (See Chapter 8, 'The Psychospiritual Self.')

Quantum theory

Quantum theory is based on two ideas. One is Einstein's formulation, fully accepted today, that waves and particles are complementary manifestations of the same vibrating electromagnetic phenomena and, further, that matter and energy are themselves interchangeable. Matter is visible, hard, and inert, but energy is invisible and insubstantial, like spiritual essences. Deepak

Chopra, the holistic medicine guru, holds that we are as much spiritual (invisible energy) as corporeal (material) beings (Chopra, 1990). Relativity theory further holds that just as matter and energy are one, so are time and space. This formulation lends credence to the Buddhist notion that an 'empty mind' is the highest state of consciousness, for when mind-as-empty-space becomes paradoxical and multi-dimensional, the dichotomies of matter and energy, time and space, vanish, as they do in relativity theory.

Second, Heisenberg's formulation of the 'uncertainty principle,' a fundamental theorem of quantum mechanics, states that the velocity and position of entities such as electrons cannot be measured with equal precision. Thus, many events in the universe are, in principle, unpredictable. The early philosophical interpretations of the uncertainty principle implied that there is no design in the universe, hence no God with a plan. But today we can turn this notion of randomness on its head, and say that the uncertainty principle allows for miracles to be an everyday event, because, in some sectors at least, events can occur spontaneously in inscrutable ways. We can also say that there might be consciousness present in these areas we can't see into. Furthermore, some cosmologists and information scientists, utilizing a quantum theoretical perspective (Lockwood, 1989; Seager, 1991) hold that our universe is what it is because it evolved for us to be and that there may be alternative universes in which we don't exist! It is possible that we reside in a universe in which consciousness is an integral part. These ideas, although as yet largely untested, make our depictions of gods and God seem, not unlikely but, rather, overly simple and insufficiently radical. Imagine a God with black holes, other worlds, a dark side, multiple personalities, and who is and is not at the same time. Well, actually, the Jewish Cabalistic tradition sees God in just that way (Sidlofsky, 1999). And cosmologists, who are hard-nosed scientists examining the esoteric equations of physics, portray the universe as such a God, with the cosmos no longer consisting of inert particles colliding in empty space, but a complex of matter, energy, and information in dialogue with the very human beings it has created. It now strikingly appears that the universe, rather than being a straightforward mechanical device, bears a resemblance to the living self! Our scientific understanding has taken us full circle, from a universe in which we, our existence, our planet, were at the center, to the Enlightenment view in which we represent small, insignificant manifestations of chemistry on the surface of a little ball whirling in space, to the modern and postmodern perspective in which our presence, our form, our selfhood, our gods, are an integral part of and a mirror for the universe itself.

Chaos and complexity theory

The fact that the universe does not always function like an orderly, mechanical device, and has aspects that are disorganized and hard to predict, led to the development of chaos theory (Gleick, 1987) and complexity theory (Waldrop, 1992), which attempt to bring understanding to events at the interface of organization and disorganization. We know, for example, how difficult it is to predict the weather. Conceivably, even if improbably, a butterfly aloft in Los Angeles could stir the molecules of air in such a way as to trigger off a snowfall in the Sierra Nevada Mountains. Such events in which small changes trigger large ones, sometimes called the 'butterfly effect,' are unusual, but possible. The meteorological reality of the butterfly effect is well known in the Miami area, where changes in the atmosphere of the Everglade swamps can trigger sudden storms in that city. Chaos and complexity theory describe events in which small interactions converge to create large effects in a process called 'cascading,' as when a series of small movements of a snow bank cascade and produce an avalanche.

Chaos and complexity theories describe the universe in ways that parallel spiritual texts. For example, the universe has places that are relatively random (like interstellar dust, perhaps) and organized (like stars and planetary systems). The organized parts are called 'fractals,' and each fractal, like each star, is similar to all the others. The Bible, as well as Hindu descriptions of 'the eternal wheel' of the cosmos, offers a similar picture: each human being contains God within himself: we each are fractals of God. Furthermore, in the Bible, God intervenes at times when communities verge on chaos and when His Laws are violated. God ejects Adam and Eve from Eden when they cause 'trouble in Paradise' by violating His order to refrain from partaking of the apple of the knowledge of good and evil. Jonah is swallowed by a whale because he refuses to do God's Will. God creates chaos in response to disobedience: He calls for war, famine, and epidemics when nations disobey His precepts. It is as if the human universe tends towards chaos that is 'pock-marked' by God's 'fractal' efforts to restore his design by a series of divine interventions. Further, God uses chaos (plagues, floods) to punish wrongdoings, and offers clarity and serenity as a reward for following His leadership. A religious sanctuary can be a fractal of peace and spiritual orderliness in a world inclined towards chaos. We feel closest to God in times and places of peace, silence, and clarity. But God is also present in the chaos and complexity that frighten us. Those who dare to seek Him in that frightful cauldron are often those who expand the limits of the knowable.

Similarly, Hindu texts portray the cosmos as a place of alternating creation and destruction which are part of the eternal cycle of life and death. Human biology and the human mind have components of creation and destruction. For example, we chew food to break it in bits. The stomach breaks down the bits chemically, and in the liver the chemicals are re-structured into metabolites useful to the body. Further, animals and humans create babies and destroy prey and enemies. The mind creates ideas, then breaks them down by analysis, and finally creates new ideas by synthesis. The dialectic between creation and destruction, organization and chaos is present in all living systems.

Our spiritual life operates along lines of creation and destruction. The apex of creative insight and renewal is self-transformation: 'revelation' or 'resurrection' leading to a new way of being and understanding. At other times, our lives are shrouded in mystery: we live within the 'cloud of unknowing' (Wolters, 1978). 'Blind faith' is called for. It is no accident that spiritually evolved individuals have often reported periods of chaos and upheaval in their lives. Moses and the Jews traveled the desert in search of their homeland after they were nearly destroyed by the Egyptians. Jesus threw the money-lenders out of the Temple: a symbolic act challenging the old order that had become corrupt and hypocritical. William Penn lived a life of debauchery before practicing devotion, ethics, and peacemaking. Periods of chaos often precede spiritual growth.

Chaos theory also suggests that there are many ways to observe and measure the same event. Consider the length of the Atlantic coastline. From the vantage point of an airplane or space satellite, we obtain one estimate. However, if we were foolish enough to use a tape measure on the ground we would obtain a much longer total distance because we would include each bay and inlet in our measurement. There would be little or no correlation between the large-scale measurement and the more detailed one. So, how long is the Atlantic coast? It depends entirely on your measuring instrument. The process is chaotic, because there is no comparing one measurement with the other. By convention, we measure distances with instruments which are as rough or finely graded as the distance we are trying to measure. So we would all choose the aerial view of the coast, not the microscopic one. Yet, the geologist studying coastal erosion would seek a finer grade of measurement.

Similarly, chaos theory can help account for the proliferation of religions, some with many deities, others with One (Judaism), still others with the One divided into Three (Christianity); some sects of Buddhism with none; some ancient religions (as in Homeric Greece) with multiple gods; some with the god(s) inhabiting a different space from humans (heaven and earth; within the village and in the distant mountains); within time and outside of time (Jesus incarnate and the Father eternal); some with God as masculine, some feminine. Think about it. If you were meandering around Greece, you might find a goddess behind a bush (Aphrodite? Diana?); a god on a mountain who made lightning (Zeus); or else a sun-god (Apollo) who reliably drove his chariot across the sky. But if you were escaping Egypt and wandering through the desert, God might approach you with a firm voice and tell you 'I am Who I am!' so that your tribe could have strong leadership. As a poor man or woman in Jerusalem and threatened daily by abusive Roman soldiers you might see God in a compassionate Christ who came to redeem you. And if you were a Native American, finding solace and survival in the wilderness or on the plains, you could see God as a Spirit present in everything around you. Yet, it's the same God. We all 'feel' that unity even if we differ theologically.

Chaos theory tells us that such varied theologies are an expectable and inevitable part of the way we measure and live in our surroundings. Those who thrive on exploring many different perspectives – the 'seekers,' the anthropologists, the archetypalists and mythologists, and the New Age enthusiasts – will appreciate this complexity. Those whose faith depends on a particular religious orientation will continue to believe that their perspective is more advanced and accurate than the others. They will say that without their specific belief system, things become chaotic, and they will be correct. Jung, after many years of exploring and valuing the varieties of religious experience, from Mithraic to pagan to North African to Buddhist and Hindu, finally returned to the Christian experience inculcated by his father, who was a minister (Hayman, 1999, pp. 401–418). For many people, the mode of belief changes throughout a lifetime, reflecting shifting needs for unity, orderliness, and complexity.

Thus, modern systems and complexity science include a variety of perspectives which have a spiritual quality or spiritual parallels, in contrast with the mechanistic, reductionistic model which portrays the world as a cold, material place in which we humans are buffeted about by matter in motion. Furthermore, developments in science allow us to explore the spiritual aspects of our minds without feeling that we have violated the canons of scientific faith. Michael Polanyi (1974) has asserted that science itself is based on faith: faith in the community of researchers; faith that observations can be arranged in an orderly pattern; faith in scientific progress and advancement. Once again, as I define it, spirituality per se does not necessarily imply the paranormal or supernatural, but rather is concerned with the qualities of human existence and the nature of the universe as we are coming to know them in all their complexity.

For the present purpose, what I am suggesting is that modern science offers an opportunity to build a psychology in which spiritual experience is an integral part of human biology and development, not an epiphenomenal add-on, quite a bit more than a set of societal myths created by civilizations to make their members feel more secure and act more obediently – although organized religions have, unfortunately, been exploited for that purpose. Spirituality is built into everything we do and are. It comes into focus whenever and wherever we begin to see our experience in terms of wholes, patterns, and unities, rather than discrete parts.

Relativistic space/time and the sacred space

Einstein's theory of relativity constituted a revolution in physics in which the Newtonian fundamentals of forces acting on otherwise inert particles yielded to a view predicated upon modifications of time and space, previously thought of as constant. Einstein held that time and space are interchangeable dimensions that can have qualities and shape. This principle of a multi-dimensionally shifting space/time continuum applies equally well to psychology.[1] For example, the space of the therapy room can expand to include unconscious processes. Time can contract so that past and present come together. Mental space can be inert or actively alive, overflowing or empty. Grotstein (1978), discussing 'inner space: its dimensions and coordinates,' noted that mental space is not static, but dynamic. Indeed, it can de-dimensionalize to a psychotic black hole (Grotstein, 1990) in which persona and objects of the mind shrink and fragment, and also expand to include creativity and experiences that transcend everyday time and space.

If relativity theory places a primary emphasis on time and space rather than material particles, a focus on spirituality in psychology reminds us that when two or more human beings meet in depth, that meeting evokes an experience in which God (the Infinite and wholly Other) is present in the space. The place in which such a holy encounter occurs is sacred.

I once spent a week at a New Age retreat called the Feathered Pipe Ranch in Helena, Montana. We learned from the Native Americans there that a part of the ranch, within a grove of trees through which a narrow stream passed, was considered by the Indian tribe of the region to be sacred. They believed that the spirits of their ancestors gathered there. We may or may not believe in ghostly disembodied spirits as such, but we can agree that there are special places in the world which are hallowed, where we experience extraordinary beauty, awe, and respect. A feeling of 'dying' with ecstasy is frequently experienced in sacred spaces and in spiritual awakening and is an aspect of what we mean when we say we must die in order to live more fully. What is dying is not our core, but our conventional view of ourselves and reality, which cannot hold spirituality within their four walls. Spirituality and the sacred space are multi-dimensional.

In the best psychotherapy, the space in which it is conducted becomes hallowed by the experience. It is a place where something extraordinary occurs: one human being encounters another in a helping relationship and an exploration of the soul. Instead of being a bystander helplessly watching someone being victimized, the therapist takes an interest, sometimes a passionate interest, in a stranger who is hurting. In the best treatment, the therapist also makes himself vulnerable enough to realize that his patient's pain is or could be his own. He moves beyond the good Samaritan role to one who is grieving silently for the patient. 'There but for the grace of God go I.' Grotstein has explored this transformation in great depth and detail in his powerful book, *Who is the Dreamer Who Dreams the Dream* (Grotstein, 2000, pp.221–4), where he refers to the therapeutic alliance as a 'Pietà covenant,' likening the therapist's regard of his patient to Mary holding the body of Jesus after the Crucifixion.

In the sacred space of psychotherapy, a marvelous and awesome event can occur: the exploration of a soul and its journey. The veil that obscures the unconscious mind is lifted, and the panoply of hopes, fears, desires, and struggles of a human being come into clearer view.

Thus, the therapy space is sacred, for within it there occurs a shift in time/space coordinates in the context of a special kind of relatedness and openness. For example, the time between childhood and adulthood is collapsed when the patient vividly recalls an early experience. Paradoxically, the present moment is experienced as endless, and the space becomes infinite, invoking the *dramatis personae* of the patient's life, helping to contain uncontainable emotions, holding two people in a kind of suspended animation until a transformation becomes possible.

Thus, the corollary to the proposition that psychotherapy is spiritual is the notion that the total context in which therapy occurs is sacred. To myself and my colleagues, I say: We must find our sacred space again.

My discussion of several modern scientific frameworks constitutes not a unified formulation, but multiple schemata for constructing a paradigm for a spiritually based psychology and psychotherapy. It is not that any one of them explains the human mind as such. Rather, they support the premise that psychologists and psychoanalysts need no longer be hampered by the reductionist outlook of looking for inert 'units' that appear to make spirituality superfluous. Rather, spirituality inheres within the complexity, serendipity, interactions, and shifting dimensionality of the world, and, specifically, of the psyche itself.

Capra (1975), Zukav (1979), and others have suggested that Eastern thought, as distinct from the dichotomous 'either/or' thinking of Western culture, allows for many of the same features of complexity and paradox that characterize modern thinking in physics and biology. As a result, some psychologists and psychotherapists have been attracted to Eastern religions such as Buddhism, Hinduism, and Taoism. This affinity between modern psychology and Eastern thought is the subject of what follows.

Endnote

1   The group psychologist Kurt Lewin (1951) developed an elaborate formulation of group 'topological space' and 'life space' to map the 'force fields' impinging on individuals and groups. The mathematical exactitude he hoped to achieve has never been realized, but the ways in which subjective time and space are determined by context is essential to modern psychology.

CHAPTER THREE

The Impact of Eastern Thought

Ideas from the 'mysterious' Orient have had a profound impact on Western life. Although the evidence isn't clear, it is possible that oriental cultures may have long ago influenced Plato, the Judaic and Muslim prophets, and Jesus. In the 13th and 14th centuries AD, journeys to the Orient were undertaken by Marco Polo and others. Then, in the 19th century, Eastern art and mythology attracted artists like Degas, who applied concepts from Japanese art to his own work. In the early and mid-20th century, writers such as T. S. Eliot and James Joyce utilized myths, imagery, and ideas from many world cultures. Psychologists like Jung and mythologists like Joseph Campbell looked towards pagan as well as Eastern religions for new understanding. Around that time, yogis and Zen masters were invited to America and England and established a following among Western seekers.

In recent years, with the increasing presence in Western countries of teachers, practitioners, and gurus from India, China, and Japan, Eastern religions, traditions, and medical treatments have directly influenced Western spiritual attitudes, meditation practices, religious systems, and medical approaches. Indeed, Western science itself has recently experienced a confluence with Eastern ideas. Capra (1975, 1997), Zukav (1979), and others have found striking parallels between modern physics and Buddhist, Taoist, and Hindu philosophy. The Eastern influence is so pervasive in psychology that recently, in convening a conference on spirituality and psychotherapy, I had a more difficult time finding presenters from a Judao-Christian standpoint than from Buddhist perspectives! Many psychotherapists now see parallels between Eastern meditation and psychotherapy, and they find that Eastern thought carries less of the negative or irrelevant 'baggage' that people bring to therapy from their own religious upbringing, which is sometimes contaminated by the dysfunctional projections and distortions of practitioners, teachers, and families. Eastern thought is valuable partly because it comes to us fresh and unencumbered by the collective neuroses of Western society.

A thorough exposition of Eastern thought would lead to many fertile regions of exploration, but would carry us far afield. At the moment, I only wish to try to distill a few essential ingredients which I feel have important implications for psychology and psychotherapy. They include:

1. the acceptance of difference and paradox within the self and the ability to transcend dualities

2. altered states of consciousness

3. the concept of 'no mind'

4. the unity of body and mind.

Object relations theories and self psychology tell us about the 'way into' pathology, conflict, and psychic wounds. Eastern spiritual teachings suggest a 'way out of' these difficulties and deficits. Psychoanalysis and psychotherapy ordinarily help us *think* our way out of our troubling conflicts, based on what we know about the origins of these dilemmas. In addition, Western therapists use the bond between therapist and patient to help repair the underlying damage wrought by early deprivations, abandonments, and abuses.

Eastern spirituality suggests an alternative route to healing: *non-thought, non-attachment, and emptiness of mind.* We could say that emptiness of mind and its corollary of living totally in the present moment offer the psyche an opportunity to cleanse and restructure itself according to its own natural flow by transcending the memories, anticipations, and distortions which reflect our disturbed attachments of and to the past.

Paradox versus conventional logic

All Western thought is based upon the 'law of contradiction,' that a statement and its negation cannot both be true. Such 'bi-logic' (Matte-Blanco, 1975) has led to vast developments in science, philosophy, and the material quality of life, because of the capacity of analytic thinking to dissect objective reality into functional components and thereby solve puzzles and problems. Unfortunately, bi-logic has nearly killed the human spirit because it murders complexity and connectivity! It is the cognitive equivalent of the Enlightenment 'billiard ball' universe.

THE IMPACT OF EASTERN THOUGHT / 55

By contrast, paradox consists of unresolvable contradiction which leads to 'both/and' rather than 'either/or' thinking. While we begrudgingly admit paradox into our thinking in the arts and literature (which we conveniently house in museums, theaters, and concert halls), we refuse to allow it full admission into our lives. Western thought sees life as an eternal struggle between contradictions within ourselves: good and evil, one doctrine and another, pleasure and pain, material and spiritual, body and mind. Both Freud and Jung held that this set of contradictions was housed in the agency of the mind called the ego. Thus, at a conscious ego level, we are constantly fighting ourselves, and many patients bring into therapy an unfinished task of integrating the different sides of themselves.

Eastern thought holds that bi-logical contradictions emerge from our illusions about 'reality.' Hindus call such illusions 'Maya.' Buddhists feel that such contradictions and the 'either/or' of obsessive thinking cloud our mind and interfere with meditation and concentration. Our natural state is that of unity within the self and oneness with God (some sects of Buddhism avoid positing the existence of a deity, however) and the cosmos. In this state, we experience 'ultimate reality,' are 'enlightened,' and our experience is freed of suffering, conflict, and contradiction. In effect, we transcend the conflicts and illusions of our egos and apprehend a deeper reality without the intermediary of the law of contradiction.

Conventional psychotherapy, whether psychoanalytic, cognitive, or behavioral, strives to make patients aware of contradiction rather than find a way out of it. Western therapy wants the patient to accept 'reality' (Maya), i.e. materiality, temporality, and conformity to social and interpersonal norms, rather than to transcend them. It wants him to see the irrationality of his symptoms and give them up. It wants him to do more thinking rather than less. It wants to strengthen his ego rather than help him overcome it. Admittedly, a wise therapist harbors some reservations and caution about 'critiquing the ego through the voice of reason,' and is thus tolerant of his patients' incompleteness, 'abnormality,' creativity, and spirituality, but, by and large, 'ego strength' has been the criterion that Western therapists have used to define 'successful' outcomes. Conventional psychotherapy is often helpful because it increases social adjustment and functional capacity, but many of those who seek deeper levels of healing find themselves dissatisfied with the outcome of such treatment.

By contrast, Eastern thought encourages not only living with paradox, but thriving on 'both/and' rather than 'either/or,' and leaping into the waters of complexity. It offers practices that encourage relinquishment of ego and struggles with contradiction. It is interested in deeper realities than those necessitated by survival and conventional wisdom. As a result, it offers a basis for a new psychology and innovative therapy goals.

Altered states of consciousness

Eastern spiritual practices, especially those of Tibetan and Zen Buddhism, have led Westerners to the exploration of altered states of consciousness. We all are vaguely familiar with these states, for we experience them when we become totally absorbed in a sports event or a creative project; or when we are deeply relaxed and our problems seem to dissolve for a while. When, for example, we enter a church or a synagogue, or a place of great historical significance, or listen to elevating music, the space or sound itself may cause a temporary trance state that is almost hallucinatory. We 'feel the presence of God,' are lifted into ethereal planes, as in the last movement of Beethoven's Ninth Symphony, encounter ghosts of ourselves, as in a good novel, and so on. In dreams, we create vast new landscapes to live in and people to inhabit them.

It is interesting that Western therapy regards dreams primarily as useful information to further orient the person to the reality of ordinary waking consciousness. Such a 'reality orientation' may be necessary for some patients, particularly those with a tendency towards psychosis, but most people are deficient in something quite the opposite, namely the ability to imagine, to reach new shores inwardly and outwardly, and to find inner wisdom. Our dream life is one place where we dwell in an 'altered state' on a nightly basis. Jung, of all psychologists, most clearly saw dreams as expressions of our spirituality. Indeed, he believed that our dreams were 'written,' not by us (our egos), but by spiritual essences within us representing the entire evolution of human thought and articulated in an archaic language that required 'translation' (Hayman, 1999, p.206).

Thus, the Eastern emphasis on paradox encourages us to find within altered states of consciousness opportunities to accept and explore rather than resolve irrationality, contradiction, symptom, and disruption. We reside 'in' them, and then go beyond them. We needn't work our way 'out of' them. 'Paradoxically,' I will now discuss the possibility of going even further along these lines, of going beyond paradox, even obliterating it, as a 'way' of Buddhist spiritual practice.

The notion of 'no mind'

To obliterate mind in search of transcendence has been, up until recently, foreign to Western ideas and the psychotherapies. For Westerners, 'mind' – the aspect of consciousness and brain functioning that involves cognition, attachments, emotions, and insight – is the very basis of our existence. This is one of the meanings of the Cartesian *Cogito ergo sum* – 'I think, therefore I am.' Thinking and being are equated. If we give up 'mind,' as if that is even possible, we are nothing and nowhere. We fear that nothing will be left of us and that we will become total non-entities. We equate our selves and our personal value with our thoughts, our minds.

Zen Buddhism, on the other hand, teaches that 'no mind' is the clearest, most effective state humans can achieve. Of course such a state is impossible to describe, since there is 'no mind' left to cogitate about it: description implies bi-logic. Nevertheless, attempts have been made by S. Suzuki (1970) and others to convey the experience to Westerners. 'No mind' is a state arrived at through repeatedly letting go of and diminishing the ideas and chatter running through our consciousness. Gradually the mind then appears to empty itself of turbulence, ultimately becoming like a clear lake with no ripples. When one has awakened into such a state, one is freed to live wholly in the direct apprehension of the present moment.

Could such teachings about 'no mind' be fruitfully utilized in psycho-therapy? Some therapists now actively teach Buddhist meditation to their patients. Further, conventional therapists often use techniques that coincidentally approximate to such tenets. In effect, therapists can employ traditional approaches while expanding their use of paradox to help the patient move beyond the law of contradiction that perpetuates symptoms.

The psychoanalyst's non-judgmental stance and evenly suspended attention are examples of the indirect use of 'no mind.' Through this non-committal, pre-interpretative mode of being, the therapist, although he seems very interested in what the patient says, is subtly conveying to him that ideas are not the essence of the work. Rather, both are seeking something so vague and unexpressible that each time 'insight' appears, the therapist expresses doubt. Such benign doubt seems to me not so far removed from what a Zen master does when he poses unresolvable paradoxes called 'koans,' which help the student to jump out of the stream of thought. The therapist's silence is in effect a Zen koan: 'When I am silent, what is it that I am saying to you?' The patient has insufficient information to resolve this paradox. Eventually, he may 'let go' and begin to experience the moment without cogitating about it. In analysis, stopping the flow of cogitation leads to deeper layers of unconscious processes.

Another method of psychotherapy which in some respects approaches a 'no mind' philosophy is what Weeks (1991) and others have called 'paradoxical therapy.' In one such approach, the therapist fully, even exaggeratedly, accepts the very symptom or thought process he is trying to alleviate. A paradoxical therapist, for example, worked with a paranoid patient who was certain that his office was bugged with recording microphones. Instead of questioning this delusion, which would merely have reinforced the patient's suspicion (how can you trust the enemy?), the therapist 'joined' the patient in a thorough search of the office, crawling under the couch, tapping the walls, looking in the hallway. Manifesting the principle set forth in the movie, *The Ruling Class*, that only one delusional person can occupy the same space at the same time, the patient's delusion lost its power.

Milton Erickson (O'Hanlon, 1987; Rossi and Erickson, 1989), a hypnotist and acknowledged master of paradoxical techniques, brilliantly used paradox to treat symptoms. Again, not unlike the Zen master, he put the patient in a position where maintaining the symptom was untenable, because, whether or not he followed Erickson's direction, he had to yield the errant behavior. Interventions were expressed in such a way that either accepting or rejecting Erickson's suggestions meant giving up the symptom! As Jung (1934) earlier pointed out, psychological symptoms are complexes of mental associations that cause undue pain or lead to negative consequences. If the patient can't sustain the thoughts, the complex loses its power.

Cognitive therapy (Burns, 1999; McMullin, 2000), a popular treatment modality today on account of its efficiency (a relatively small number of sessions to achieve symptom reduction) and validation through research, has elements of 'no mind.' Cognitive therapy is firmly based on bi-logic. It encourages the patient to question the rationality of thoughts which have become ingrained, automatic and convincing to him. Through an appeal to logic, cognitive treatment strives to change the 'negative' thinking which perpetuates depression and anxiety into logic-based 'positive' thinking which leads to beneficial mood changes. Thus, for example, a depressed person concludes from the mere fact that it is a rainy day, that 'Life conspires against me. That proves I'm bound to be a failure.' Conscious questioning of these irrational thoughts elevates the mood, as the patient begins to see that a rainy day is just a change in the weather that has nothing to do with his self-worth.

On the surface, this use of logic appears to be the direct opposite of the Zen approach, which wants to omit reasoning rather than strengthen it. An acquaintance of mine went to a Zen master and said, 'I'm such a failure. What can I do about it?' Unlike the cognitive therapist, who would question the patient's logic in thinking he was a failure, the Zen teacher replied, 'The problem isn't that you're a failure, it's that you are not enough of one. If you are going to be a failure, really fail! Get into it!' (Of course the cognitive therapist would say, conversely, that there is logic in implying that failing is a positive act – after all, it is the basis of all learning. One could argue that Zen masters are exceptionally good cognitive therapists! (Cf. Segal, Williams, and Teasdale, 2001.)

It is my impression that the best cognitive therapists paradoxically encourage 'no mind' through their very appeal to reason. In effect, they help the patient to capture and hold the automatic thoughts, the ideas that flash through the mind on a moment's notice. This is precisely the chatter that the Zen master goes after. When such thoughts are subject to scrutiny, they diminish in power and intensity. What I suspect happens with successful cognitive treatment is that the patient not only subjects his thoughts to logical examination, but also begins to unload his mind of intrusive thoughts and to use his thinking in a more precise, focused manner. His mind becomes clearer and more effective.

An empty, clear mind is healthy in that it is relaxed and prepared for whatever happens in the moment, unencumbered by extraneous complexes. But in what sense could the state of 'no mind' be considered spiritual? The answer is that if we live totally in the experience of the moment, instead of cogitating and obsessing about it, not only are our powers increased, but also – in spiritual terms – we are at that moment one with God. God, we are told, is inside us, all around us, eternally present. If so, then when we are totally in the moment, we are also wholly present with God, without the intermediary of our ego. The primary difference between Zen Buddhism and the Judao-Christian God is that the latter views God as a being different from the self, while Zen views the enlightened self as the embodiment of all that Western theology attributes to a holy and sacred Otherness.

Non-attachment

The Buddhist strives for 'non-attachment.' He observes his experience without being involved in it. Pursuing such a practice in various forms – meditation, martial arts, archery, etc. – leads to a 'natural flow' of responses, unencumbered by interfering thoughts and emotions. Further, when one is truly non-attached, one becomes aware, as did Siddhartha, that attachment is the cause of human suffering. I believe that is the reason why many therapists adopt a neutral but empathic, compassionate stance with their patients, seeking transformation while remaining outside the arena of conflict. In a striking instance of non-attachment, one therapist gently said to a suicidally depressed man, 'I'm trying to feel what it's like to be in your condition.' He did not become overwhelmed by or attached to the patient and his emotional state, but tried to join quietly with the patient in a therapeutic moment. The patient reported that the therapist 'passed the test' and was of great help, that had the therapist become upset, or conversely, cold and distant, he would have felt abandoned in his moment of utter neediness. The patient seized that moment of compassionate non-attachment as a chance for a renewed existence.

Everyday attachments are healthy. The Buddha warned against asceticism and advocated the 'middle way' of balance. Problems arise when normal strivings for closeness and love become transformed into crippling dependency and repetitive attempts to control outcomes. Buddhists call normal attachments 'compassion.' A Buddhist teacher would be most dismayed if his student became detached to the point of manifesting an uncaring attitude towards his fellows. What Buddhist 'non-attachment' is really about is detachment from 'thing-ness' and objectification. To genuinely love another is to perceive him clearly as he is in the moment. Thus, Buddhist non-attachment is paradoxically compatible with Judao-Christian agapé, spiritual love.

The unity of body and mind

In a state of 'no mind' and non-attachment, logical distinctions disappear, including those between body and mind, mind and spirit. This unified state of consciousness offers a potential correction to the Cartesian mind–body dualism (mind and body as separate entities), a dichotomy which haunts humankind in the form of an overvaluing of mind and an abhorrence of bodily functions and the 'ways of the flesh.'

The mind–body dualism stems from a false equation of mental activity with existence. Again, 'I think – therefore I am.' Descartes should have said, 'I am conscious, therefore I know that I am.' A computer can think, but it is not conscious. (Indeed, the unconscious mind can think, but doesn't know that it thinks!) Consciousness is a bodily function, centered in the brain. That

it is a bodily function is suggested by the fact that it is at least partially oblit-
erated in alcoholic 'blackouts,' during seizures, and in deep, non-dreaming
sleep. Thought is also a bodily function, but thought is different from consciousness. One can be conscious and not think. The mind–body dualism is
a product of a certain kind of thinking. When fully conscious, fully awake
and alive, our minds and bodies flow together. Ask any fine athlete or
performing artist about that.

The mind–body dualism preceded Descartes by a few thousand years,
and indirectly reflected an alienation from the body as a source of contamination, disease, and evil desires. Historically, the mind–body dualism and
the abhorrence of the flesh may have grown partly out of the ancient need to
maintain health standards. By practicing rituals that prevented disease, early
societies such as the tribes of Israel established rules like the kosher laws that
helped prevent the spread of infections caused by food contamination.
Further, by portraying sex as unclean or sinful outside the institution of
marriage, they could limit inbreeding and sustain social hierarchies and relationships. Gradually, over the course of history, these life-sustaining rules
transliterated to an abhorrence of the body and sexuality, independent of
health concerns. And this hatred of the physical became institutionalized,
for example, in the self-mortifying practices of some Christian monks as well
as the Victorian repression of sexual impulses. Such attitudes of repulsion
towards the body have been reinforced by an insistence that life be asexual
and ascetic, which I suspect stems partly from the subordination of women in
a patriarchal culture. Queen Victoria told her daughter, who asked what to
do when having sex, 'Lie still, and think of England.' Stripped of power,
women (and other minorities) must subordinate their bodies and bodily
pleasure to the state and the status quo.

In homage to the great composer and conductor, Leonard Bernstein, the
violinist Isaac Stern said, 'He had a clean soul.' He didn't mean that 'Lennie,'
as everyone affectionately called him, abhorred the 'flesh' – in fact it is well
known that Bernstein was a very physical, sensual, and sexual person. He
meant that Bernstein was at every moment spontaneous, fully alive, and
uncorrupted. A certain kind of 'cleanness' of body, mind, and spirit is
necessary for the preservation of the sacred space. But that does not imply
separating body (as bad) from mind (as good). It means that the body is a
holy temple, and must be cared for, since it houses and expresses the God
within. This notion of the holiness of the body had all but disappeared from
Western religion, until its recent encounters with non-Western belief
systems.

Eastern religions have always emphasized the importance of the body in spiritual development. Ancient yoga practices evolved on the presupposition that if one had a healthy, well-functioning body, one could actualize one's spiritual life and achieve what we now call higher consciousness through sustained meditation with a minimum of physical discomfort. Martial arts, physical postures, and healing have always been a part of Eastern religious practices. Vedantic religion, in which sexuality is sacred, describes, in the Kama Sutras, sexual practices whose aim is spiritual ecstasy (Mann and Lyle, 1995). The spiritual aspect of Vedantic sexual practices has, of course, been all but lost in recent American popularizations.

Western psychotherapy and medical practice are almost entirely based on the mind–body dualism. In psychotherapy, the mind is treated, while the body is ignored; in medicine, the body is treated as if it had no mind. Thoughts and behaviors are addressed as if they had no relationship to the body. In effect, psychotherapy patients are often treated as if they are disembodied ghosts. In medicine, patients are regarded as machine-like bodies.

In the early days of psychoanalysis, there were attempts to remedy this problem. Freud held that feelings and fantasies about the body were major factors in symptom formation. He tried to change psychology from an exclusively cognitive science of suggestion and persuasion to one which recognized the profound importance of the body in early development, in the oral, anal, and phallic stages, as he put it, with deliberate reference to parts of the body. Wilhelm Reich (1973) developed ways of applying pressure and massage to the body both for diagnostic purposes and to evoke constellations of feelings and memories. He regarded full and complete orgasm as a defining criterion of mental well-being. Such emphasis on the body was largely abandoned as mind and behavior became abstracted from the bodies which produce them and to which they always symbolically refer.

Eastern thought encourages an holistic approach to psychotherapy in which mind and body are treated as a whole. Today, for many patients, this takes the form of supplementing traditional psychotherapy with holistic health practices such as reiki therapy, massage, dance, art, psychodramatic therapy, and acupuncture. But as we become more sophisticated about the mind–body relationship, 'talk' therapists may increasingly learn to touch the patient, dance or sing, sense bodily changes occurring in the session, and lead the patient to a greater state of body–mind unity. I was very moved when a woman psychotherapist told me that she sang a lullaby to a patient who had been emotionally abandoned in childhood. Dance therapists use movement to evoke feelings and resolve conflicts. Some massage therapists use their awareness of the patient's physical state to treat psychosomatic disorders. Grof's (1988) holistic breathwork employs deep breathing to evoke powerful memories, emotions, and altered states of consciousness. The legacies of physical and depth psychological therapies need to be coordinated and integrated to develop a new psychotherapy of body–mind wholeness.

So, my paradigmatic position on the body–mind complex with respect to spirituality is that it is not the body, but the mind–body split, that keeps us from reaching a higher spiritual plane. This split is part of 'Maya' – illusion – an illusion that develops early in life. For example, when we view ourselves in a mirror, we have the illusion that we are looking at ourselves rather than an image. Similarly, when we look at our body we see only its surface, not ourselves. Such a false equation of an objectified, concrete image with the subjective 'I' has been pointed out by the French psychoanalyst, Jacques Lacan (1977, pp. 1–7), who regarded the child's recognition of himself in the mirror as the first objectification of self, the alienation of the self from itself. What the child gains in objectivity, he pays for in the loss of his primal relationship to his physicality and emotionality.

Judaism warns against worshiping 'idols,' physical representations of God such as statues. These 'craven images' obscure the real God or Goddess within, as 'subject.' Similarly, our bodies are just as much within our minds as our minds are within our bodies. The neurophysiologist Thomas Damasio (2000) holds that all thought is linked to bodily sensations and experiences. The yoga concept of the 'subtle body' – the chakras and *pranayama*, the subtle aspect of the breath – reflect this mind–body unity. When mind and body embrace one another, a great energy called *kundalini* is released. This physical release brings us closer to our spiritual nature.

The beautiful and ecstatic evocation of sexual orgasm that climaxes James Joyce's *Ulysses* is a powerful statement of mind-body oneness as it is felt within the soul. Molly Bloom not only experiences sexual delight, she is elevated in her spirit by her raw, uninhibited sexuality. In this moment, she manifests a oneness with her own embodied self. She experiences herself as a total being with a body, mind, heart, and spirit that cannot be separated. Saying, 'Yes, yes, yes,' over and over again, she is fully affirming life and physical ecstasy. The very essence of the human soul is that it is embodied.

Eastern thought has the potential to release us from splits and dualities into an holistic consciousness and a psychological paradigm in which spirituality is at the center of our existence, rather than an appendage or postscript to our embodied being. On account of its emphasis on paradox and multivalent logic, Eastern thought is compatible with modern quantum and systems theories.

Up to this point, I have tried to introduce concepts from Western science and Eastern religion that can facilitate a new way of thinking, a psychospiritual paradigm for psychology. My objective is to begin to build an integrated spiritual, emotional, and developmental formulation of the spiritual self and the life cycle. To move in that direction, I must now rely on perspectives from psychoanalysis and consider the psychodynamic, interpersonal insights of object relations theory and self psychology, under the contemporary umbrella of the intersubjective and relational perspectives. In my opinion, these views, while not phrased in spiritual terms as such, contain the nuclei of concepts which reach towards the spiritual realms. They form the psychological side of the bridge between spirit and psyche. They will provide the basis for a developmental psychology in which spirituality forms an integral component, one which incorporates but expands these viewpoints into a broader, spiritually-centered vision.

CHAPTER FOUR

Building Bridges between Spirituality and Psychology through Object Relations Theory and Self Psychology

The project of linking spirituality and psychology runs the perpetual risk of creating a *deus ex machina* – a 'god in the machine.' That is, the spirit is viewed either as a non-material ghost or a higher-level striving of human beings who are otherwise driven by basic physical necessities and social requirements. Somehow, this externalized 'god,' mind, or soul influences events while remaining outside of and above them. It would be simplistic thus to regard God and spirituality as appendages to a naturalistic view of the psyche. Indeed, Western thought has been characterized by such a bifurcation between a God, soul, and mind supposed to exist in a non-material plane and our embodied, physical being. To repair that rift, we must instead seek a new synthesis, so that spirituality becomes an integral part of a discourse and practice in which spirit, body, and psyche are all made of the same cloth. Such a formulation would constitute a genuine paradigm shift in Kuhn's sense. Theory and practice would then emanate from the perspective of the new, unified paradigm, rather than constitute a postscript to an outdated, billiard ball view of the world.

Ad hoc theorizing rarely works in science. At the end of the nineteenth century, physicists, puzzled by discrepancies in their measures of the speed of light, tried to account for light waves by postulating a hypothetical ether through which the waves were propagated. The data from the Michelson–Morley experiment, showing that the speed of light is independent of the movement of the observer, contradicted this theory and remained a scientific anomaly that could ultimately not be reconciled with the ether theory (Feynman, Layton, and Sands, 1989, 15, pp.3–4). Then

Einstein proposed an entirely new understanding of time and space which accounted for Michelson's and Morley's finding, and revolutionized physics. Similarly, for psychologists, spirituality should not become a super-imposed 'ether' of the mind, but lead towards a radical reconceptualization. Just as with Einstein's theory of relativity, the tools of such a paradigm shift are already present. The problem is to get the pieces of the puzzle to fit into place.

Since, as I have previously suggested, psychology is both a subjective, deeply personal, and an objective science, my own understanding of such a paradigm shift may differ from those of others. By exchanging views on how the new paradigm should be envisioned, we may arrive at a more universal formulation. My own search for the Rosetta Stone which marks the sought-after new paradigm began with my long-held interest in psychoan-alytic theories of object relations and the self. While these theories are rooted in Freud's biological and developmental premises, they also extend their branches and leaves into the sunlight of the spirit. In certain of their branches, they approach the integrative paradigm we are seeking, but they never quite take this step. I try to use them in a leap of faith toward a spiritually-centered viewpoint.

Object relations, the self, and spirituality

The conceptual understanding to which I have gravitated as a clinician and theoretician consists of a combination of object relations theory and self psy-chology, psychoanalytic vantage points which evolved in the latter decades of the twentieth century – object relations theory mostly after 1940 (cf. Guntrip, 1961, 1971; Kohon, 1997) and self psychology after 1965 (Strozier, 2001). Recently, relational and intersubjective perspectives have evolved which incorporate these two approaches within them. The latter are meta-theories which give primacy to subjectivity and interpersonal relations over the 'billiard ball' theory of the psyche as a self-contained aggregate and a closed system.

Object relations theory consists of the developmental investigation and treatment of emotional difficulties emerging in infancy and childhood which may persist through the life cycle. In Great Britain, where it has been at the center of psychoanalytic thought for many decades, it encompasses two major schools of thought: the Kleinian (Segal, 1974), which emphasizes internal processes of phantasies and defense mechanisms, and the British Independent Tradition (Kohon, 1971 [1997]), which highlights the interplay of inner experience with interpersonal relations. For example, Donald Winnicott (cf. Giovacchini, 1990), a leading founder of the British Independent School, held that when the infant receives consistent nurturing and holding, he can develop a sense of 'going on being' and 'aliveness' which propels subsequent emotional development. If disruptions or deprivations are unmanageable in infancy, however, the child grows up feeling acutely vulnerable, depressed, and empty. For Winnicott the spirituality of 'going on being' and 'aliveness' are qualities of the person's 'true self,' just as Tillich (1952) wrote about 'the courage to be' from a theological perspective, and Jourard (1980) understood 'inspiritation' as a sought-after wholeness and aliveness of self.

Object relations theory can help us understand how spiritual feelings and qualities develop from birth. While Winnicott believed that 'being,' 'aliveness,' and the 'true self' have sources in biological functions and impulses, he also saw them as distinctly human qualities on which the quality of our lives depends. In his notion of the 'true self,' Winnicott came very close to the idea of a soul, and he linked 'being' with a faith the infant acquires in the provisions of the mother.

Ronald Fairbairn (Sutherland, 1989), a contemporary of Winnicott, also emphasized the importance of the mother–infant relationship.[1] Challenging both the Freudians and Kleinians, he held that the object relationship is more important to emotional security and growth than the biological drives. Importantly and uniquely, Fairbairn also believed that the infant is born with a purity of spirit, a 'pristine ego' (Ashbach and Schermer, 1987, p.55). Born undefiled, innocent, and seeking relationship, the infant feels endangered when its connection to the mother is disrupted (as it inevitably will be, even with the best of maternal care). The child then withdraws inward, where he creates a world of 'internal objects' and becomes conflicted and divided within himself. Fairbairn's 'pristine ego' suggests an innate purity and innocence, a spiritual core which accompanies us on our life's journey.

Melanie Klein, whose work preceded and inspired Winnicott and Fairbairn, was avowedly Freudian in her basic orientation. She consistently held to the idea that the libidinal and aggressive drives (life and death instincts) propelled all of human development. She portrayed the world of the infant as populated with 'internal objects,' phantasy elements which represented 'good' and 'bad' parts of the psyche, pleasure and pain, the precursors of the struggle between good and evil. The mother's function is to 'contain' these phantasy objects when they are 'projected into' her so that the infant can better manage his emotions and evolve a more benign inner life. Klein's portrayal of development was decidedly non-spiritual, since, unlike Winnicott and Fairbairn, she saw all of mental development stemming from biological necessity. In some respects her ideas presaged those of contemporary biogeneticists. For her, as for Freud, biological imperatives ruled.

Despite her 'biologism,' Klein's perspective is relevant to a spiritual paradigm. Her picture of the infant's inner life was derived from her treatment of children, inferring backwards in time from what they revealed to her in play therapy sessions, and also from her analyses of adolescents and adults, whose primitive phantasy lives were understood by her as derivatives of infancy. She depicted this infantile world as one populated, metaphorically speaking, by demons and angels in conflict. The mother's breast served as a primal God, facilitating through its warmth and nutriments the dominance of 'good' over 'evil,' the victory of love over envy and hate.

Gradually, according to Klein, the child begins to perceive the real, total mother behind the breast, and, recognizing her need-satisfying status, fears harming her with his own destructive impulses. The child develops feelings of guilt and concern, and strives to make reparations for his aggression. His consciousness of real persons and their vulnerability allows the child to enter more fully into the human community. Thus, as in Genesis, the infant is ejected from the Eden of the protective 'breast God' into a legacy of 'depressive anxiety,' the capacity to see others as separate individuals, and his own potential for 'sin.' In effect, Klein suggested that the infant, out of biological necessity, assimilates what I call 'quasi-religious schemata' of itself and the world well before it can learn about religious belief as such. A Quaker friend once said, 'We acquire religion at our mother's breast.' Klein would heartily agree.

In portraying the infant's 'cosmos,' Klein implicitly delineated a process analagous to spiritual development. The child possesses an innate conception of 'good' and 'bad' which he first experiences as pleasure and pain. He encounters a life-and-death struggle to contain the bad 'objects,' just as adults may fear the devil and attempt to keep their demons at bay. Soon, however, the infant becomes concerned with the potential damage his anger, envy, and greed may do to the primary caregiver. He develops a conscience and learns to live in a community with his own and others' mixture of good and bad impulses.

In this formulation, 'God' is a representation of the goodness the child has stored up and then externalized in order to keep himself safe from his own pain and aggression. Melanie Klein's depiction of the infant's mind at times reads remarkably like the Judao-Christian epic of our eternal struggle with Good and Evil and its resolution in the acceptance of our humanness in the light of God, who, for Klein, contains the omnipotence we once believed we and our mothers possessed. Thus, religious analogies and metaphors crop up in Klein's writing, even though she contended that we are products of biological necessity. Her contribution to a spiritual psychology was to see that the cognitive and emotional schemata for spiritual development begin as seeds or nuclei of phantasy in the world of the pre-verbal infant.

The new psychology of the self

In the last thirty years, the study of narcissism (self-preoccupation and self-love) has become a primary interest of psychoanalysts. Freud and Klein, in keeping with conventional religion, regarded the capacity to relate to others and the acquisition of a conscience as the foci of all social development. By contrast, self psychology, inspired by the work of psychoanalyst Heinz Kohut, views narcissism as a normal and healthy aspect of the personality, a perspective which Western religion has frowned upon, given its emphasis on selflessness and altruism.

According to Kohut's self psychology, a child who is appreciated, validated, understood, and 'mirrored' in the form of approval, joy, and empathy, naturally basks in his own demonstrativeness and achievements and will not become spoiled or 'sinful,' but instead differentiates a self which is insulated against many of the blows of rejection, disappointment, hurt, and loss which occur throughout a lifetime. Kohut believed that the capacity to relate to others would emerge naturally if the self were nourished by empathic understanding and responsiveness. He 'resurrected' the self from its lowly position in the psyche as a residue of the id and superego to a 'supraordinate structure' (Kohut, 1977, p.97), i.e. the basis of cohesion and integration of the psyche into a unified whole. Kohut's view of a larger self that is beyond the narrow confines of the conflict-driven ego parallels the immanent manifestation of God in a messianic figure such as Jesus. Through the Messiah, God affirms his empathic relation to us, and tells us that we are like the 'lilies of the field.' That is, our selves derive from Him. Two thousand years later, Martin Buber asserted that God is immanent in all genuine 'meetings' among us.

For the self psychologist, self-interest is a positive quality. It devolves into greed and selfishness not because humans are inherently sinful, but because healthy narcissism has lived in the shadows. Kohut agreed with Carl

Rogers, the founder of client-centered psychotherapy, that humans are not born with bad or evil tendencies, but that their innate goodness can be thwarted by unmanageable frustrations, deprivations, and violations of selfhood. Theologian Matthew Fox, in a book entitled *Original Blessing* (Fox, 2000), countered the notion of 'original sin,' and held that God's infinite love is a basis for a belief in human goodness. It seems to me that Kohut professed a similar belief from the standpoint of a psychiatrist.

Thus, object relations theory and self psychology, although they developed within a secular frame of reference, can give us a picture of how the person's spiritual core evolves from birth. It is this early developing spiritual self which influences how people live and act, even more perhaps than the religious and ethical teachings in which they may later be indoctrinated. Indeed, if religious teachings conflict with the person's own spiritual endowment, he or she may spend a lifetime resenting and rebelling against them or, conversely, trying fruitlessly to conform to them. (Neuropsychologists know that implicit, non-verbal learning is as important as the learning of concepts through language.) As a result, religious people – indeed whole nations with religious traditions – regularly kill (in wars, death penalties, ethnic cleansing, and domestic violence, for example), greedily pursue personal goals at the expense of their fellows (different from healthy competition which does not violate persons), and, as Thoreau said, live out 'lives of quiet desperation.' Something has gone wrong, I believe, in their earliest psychospiritual development. Religious teaching *per se* is not the answer. From an object relations and self psychological perspective, healing the spiritual self at its roots and point of origin is what is required.

Bringing the mystical into psychoanalysis

Wilfred R. Bion was one of the great object relations theorists, a student of Melanie Klein, and best known for his groundbreaking work on group dynamics (Bion, 1959). Following his psychoanalytic training with Klein, Bion became an independent thinker who developed a profound and complex theory of the human mind, which has proved rich with implications for both theory and treatment (cf. Bleandonu, 1994; Symington and Symington, 1996). Bion introduced ideas of mysticism into traditional psychoanalysis, which up to that point had frowned upon them, allowing other analysts, such as Michael Eigen (1998) and James Grotstein (2000), to address spiritual issues from an object relations point of view.

Bion held that when the therapist listens to a patient (or, for that matter, when any of us observes a work of art or responds to an infant's cry) he is a mystic, in that he strives intuitively to ferret out something inherently 'unseen' from the patient. Uniquely, Bion believed that one could discover new features of the human mind through mystical apprehension of the psyche. He referred to such insights as 'messianic ideas' (Bion, 1970, pp. 110, 115–116). He compared psychoanalysis to the experiences reported by such mystics as Isaac Luria (the Jewish cabalist) and Meister Eckhart (the Christian monk) several centuries ago. Luria said that experiences of God were so awesome that they could not be put into words. An anonymous medieval treatise entitled *The Cloud of Unknowing* (Wolters, 1978), was about the darkness and confusion that often precedes the direct apprehension of God. Bion felt that knowledge of the unconscious mind came from such transformative, non-verbal, dark experiences.[2]

In some of his writings, Bion (1970) implied that when the therapist is in transformational contact with a patient's unconscious, he is awesomely in touch with a God principle, which he called 'O' in order to keep the concept open-ended and not relate it directly to theology. For Bion, the experience in the consulting room can and should approximate to a spiritual epiphany, although he remained vague about what that might mean, preferring that we further explore the implications of this idea rather than drawing premature conclusions about it. I explore Bion's work more fully in Chapter 13 on 'The Listening Process.'

With this brief synopsis of several contemporary psychoanalytic perspectives, I have begun building the bridge for the new paradigm on that side of the river where depth psychology and the origins of mental development reside. I will carry this perspective forward in greater detail in Chapter 5, 'Insights from Kleinian Object Relations Theory,' and Chapter 7, 'The Self in Relation.' Then I will offer my own particular synthesis that consititutes a movement toward a new, psychospiritual paradigm.

Endnotes

1   In the era of Winnicott and Fairbairn, the mother assumed primary caregiver responsibility for the infant. Today, the father frequently serves in this role. Grandparents and other family members have always done so. In addition, we now have considerable evidence (Kagan, 1994) that the infant himself brings his own resources and dispositions to the caregiving equation, which we can speculate may include perhaps spiritual or archetypal predispositions. The simplistic notion that the mother is the 'pathogenic' element in emotional maladjustment is no longer tenable.

2   Jung (Hayman, 1999, pp.218, 282) anticipated by a few decades some of Bion's ideas about mysticism, the darkness that precedes insight, and the 'invisibility' of the unconscious. In my opinion, however, Bion's conceptualizations are more rigorous than Jung's and carry less of an implication of spiritualism and paranormal phenomena.

CHAPTER FIVE

Insights from Kleinian Object Relations Theory

I was fortunate enough to begin my clinical training during an especially exciting time in psychoanalysis. Profound insights into the earliest formation of the psyche were being applied to the most difficult, seemingly intractable cases: borderline, narcissistic, and psychotic disorders. Such afflictions limited and deformed the whole personality, leading to frequent states of fragmentation, and sometimes occasioning extended periods of hospitalization. Psychoanalysts like James Grotstein, Otto Kernberg, Heinz Kohut, Herbert Rosenfeld, Harold Searles, and Vamik Volkan were leading us into the dark caverns of these vulnerable personality types and lighting the way for us. The depth understanding of the personality grew at a rapid pace, with great hopes for alleviating the most severe and protracted mental suffering through intensive psychotherapy.

One day, I noticed in one of Kernberg's books a reference to Melanie Klein. No one in the training institute I attended in the 1970s had up to that time mentioned her, even though she had been a force in Great Britain and the European continent since the 1940s. I decided to read her work. My mind was blown by her fearless dissection of the human personality, starting with its earliest origins. When I mentioned her name to one of my teachers, I was met with disdain and the threat of excommunication from the select circle of that instructor's favored Freudian 'disciples'! Undaunted, perhaps even spurred on by his objections, I voraciously digested work by and about her.

Today, Klein's concepts have been integrated into the mainstream of psychoanalytic thought. While her theories have received worthy criticism (King and Steiner, 1991), no one can any longer deny their profound significance for an understanding of the human mind.

As I mentioned earlier, Melanie Klein viewed the nascent personality as a battleground of disparate forces, life and death, 'good' and 'bad,' with the infant developing various strategies for maintaining a predominance of goodness, security, and pleasure in the face of the 'bad objects' fueled by the 'death instinct.' She called the internal dynamics of this struggle for survival of the self against internal and external 'enemies' the 'paranoid-schizoid position.' The paranoid element (fear of attack from 'bad', persecuting objects) stems from the projection of inner pain and displeasure and their feared 'return' as persecutors. The schizoid component involves splitting between 'good' and 'bad' aspects of the self. As the infant discovers that his nurturing comes from a 'real, whole person,' mother, who is sometimes frustrating and depriving, given that she has a life and subjectivity of her own, his focus shifts from himself to maintaining her survival and well-being. Entering the 'depressive position,' the child becomes aware of his capacity to both protect and harm mother. He begins to see himself and mother as capable of mixtures of good and ill, thus entering into an interpersonal world in which the various shadings of 'good' and 'bad' are increasingly tolerated. This struggle to integrate opposing sides of human experience continues throughout the life cycle.

Klein's view of the human personality was not religious in any sense of the word. Her sparse comments on religion were, however, rather supportive, with an implication that religious belief is a necessary and important way of maintaining psychological equilibrium (Grosskurth, 1986, pp.454–5). Remaining within the biological framework of the drives, she nevertheless explored in depth the psychodynamics of good and evil, persecution, envy, guilt, and reparation which are close to the teachings of religious systems. Her depictions of the inner workings of the child's mind resonate with the Old and New Testaments, recapitulating man's relationship first to a transcendent God who created the universe, who judges our loyalty and conduct, and who influences the fate of human beings, and then to an immanent God, personified in Jesus, the embodiment of universal love and peace, whose inherent goodness and compassion is attacked by his children, the flawed human beings whom He has come to heal and redeem. Klein showed how these biblical notions arise quite early in human development. As such, they are not initially acquired in religious teachings, but in the interactions between the infant and his primary caregivers, well before the child has words to express them. (They are similar to Jung's archetypes, except that, for Klein, they do not reflect racial inheritance as much as they are creations of the infant's limited mental repertoire in the context of the earliest experiences and relationships.)

In this sense, religious documents and stories represent 'the return of the repressed,' the forgotten world of our inner infantile life. This is not as heretical an idea as it initially sounds – great philosophers like Plato held that the child is close to the spiritual world from which he has so recently emerged into materiality, and Christ compared the Kingdom of Heaven to the children in the community around him. While Klein would have emphasized the biological and evolutionary basis of childhood experience, her student, Bion, did link the Kleinian understanding to Plato's thought and to religious teachings, noting that the child has 'preconceptions' which are akin to Plato's ideal forms, and citing mystical teachings as ways to access early experience (Schermer, 2001). I shall later suggest that the mystical view calls for a 'spiritual self' which is not inherent in the views of either Freud or Klein. Nevertheless, Klein did imply that ideas of a spiritual nature exist in a primitive, inchoate form in the infant's mind.

In what follows, I would like to develop the notion that the paranoid-schizoid and depressive positions represent, in fact, 'internalized quasi-religious schemata,' systems of mentation which manifest the moral and spiritual struggles that follow us through a lifetime, and for which religion, at its best, serves as a benevolent guide, and at worst, leads man into shame and guilt with 'no exit,' and pits one group against another based on paranoid-schizoid doctrines of 'true' and 'false' belief. My emphasis here will be on the ways in which such schemata are manifest in the difficulties experienced by patients in psychotherapy, and how working out such difficulties can lead to healing.

Internalized quasi-religious schemata: the paranoid-schizoid position

For Melanie Klein, the infant is faced with the problem of regulating his emotions, with limited equipment for doing so. Therefore, he relies on the good auspices of his mother as he perceives and fantasizes about her from an egocentric position focused on his own well-being.

Klein's account of the infant as a greedy, insatiable, self-centered being unfortunately lends itself to the Calvinist notion of 'original sin.' For example, she regarded envy as an emotion that haunts the child from birth, and greed, aggression, and the psychotically demoniacal as qualities inherent in human nature; the infant is an omnipotent, power-usurping 'god' who yet derives much of his power from an external 'God,' the mother, and is thus faced with the constant potential to become a 'fallen angel.' Yet, Klein also allowed for developments where reparation and redemption are possible. I would rather think of her as saying that human beings are 'originally tarnished,' rather than inherently sinful, and she certainly did not follow any doctrine of predestination. Indeed, her case studies are filled with hopefulness that insight could overcome psychological ills.

As a reader, you are invited to read Melanie Klein's own writings (Klein, M., 1977a and b), and the finely crafted explanations of them by her student and brilliant clinician, Hanna Segal (1974). In the portrait of early development that I paint, I strive to remain faithful to her basic ideas, but I transpose them into the domain of our evolving spiritual life.

Klein stated that 'The infant is an intensely embodied person'. (Guntrip, 1961, p.49). That is, he is preoccupied with regulating his bodily functions and level of comfort and discomfort. He does this by crying, sleeping, dreaming, eating, sucking, and eliminating. He quickly acquires a rudimentary schema of his and mother's bodies, a 'psychic reality' which Melanie Klein believed is inhabited by images and phantasies that she called 'internal objects,' examples of which might be images of the food the infant has taken in, the nipple it sucks, its penis or vagina, and so on. We don't know – perhaps can never know – what the infant is actually thinking, but we can infer backwards from the analyses of children and adults that his images and internal objects are larger than life, something like gentle, loyal lions, on the one hand, and devouring, flame-throwing dragons on the other, perhaps even something akin to God and the Devil.

These inner objects are housed in the infant's body, in his skin, which soon becomes a boundary between itself and the world. Some Kleinians, for example Bick (1968), believe that the 'skin frontier' is the fundamental defining element of the self, setting up a distinction between 'inside' and 'outside,' and allowing for contact at the same time as it defines a boundary. (If you touch another person's skin with your hand, you will see that you simultaneously experience a connection both to them and to the surface which keeps you separated from them.) Autistic children, who suffer from profound deficits in the ability to relate to others, seem never to have satisfactorily established a skin frontier, so they experience human contact as overwhelming intrusions into their psyche and tend to withdraw from others. Interestingly, they appear to be less anxious about hard, solid objects, and machines such as computers, than about 'soft' human contact. These objects and mechanical devices provide their own rigid boundary and do not require the child to have one.

The infant finds himself housed in a body/world 'skin,' and he needs both boundaries and openness that are often difficult to manage. He copes with anxiety by dividing experience into 'good' and 'bad,' splitting off the bad from the goodness in order to protect the latter. If mother is sufficiently available, he further expels the badness – the painful, rageful, and overstimulating aspects of his experience – into her for containment.

The combined mechanism of projection by the infant and containment by the mother is called 'projective identification' (Grotstein, 1985; Klein, 1946; Ogden, 1982) and operates as follows: the infant imagines he has put his own badness into mother and is comforted by that phantasy; he begins to notice that when mother 'gives back' the badness (i.e. she responds with nurturance and empathy to her perception of the infant's discomfort), the experience becomes more manageable and acceptable as a result of her holding capacities. Klein called splitting and projective identification the 'defense mechanisms of the paranoid-schizoid position' (Ashbach and Schermer, 1987, pp.38–45). These defenses help the infant manage the complexity and psychic pain of experience, given his limited capacity for thinking and symbolization.

I see a similarity between Klein's description of the infant's mental life and our relationship to God as it is depicted in religious texts. In the Old Testament, Adam and Eve in Paradise, (and perhaps we would say unconsciously envying God's pleasure and knowledge), partake of the apple offered by the serpent. The fig leaf they then wear to cover their genitals symbolises their shame at usurping God and their need for a second skin to cover their psychic 'wound.' Upon their confrontation with Evil (the Fall), they are consigned to initiate a complex kinship lineage, limited and conflicted. In the legacy of their progeny, good and evil are in constant battle. Humans try to manage their lives through their own will, resulting in sibling rivalry, infanticide, fratricide, war, pestilence, floods. God is the 'good, omnipotent, protective Other' who speaks to humans through Moses and informs them that He (God) can contain and transform evil. Man learns that by obeying the Commandments and making sacrifice, he can projectively identify the badness into God for containment (God as protector and redeemer). However, seeking man's development as free beings, omnipotent God perpetually re-delegates the problem of good and evil to men, to teach them lessons (Job; Jonah and the Whale), and humankind gradually learn to live a reasonably good life, given their limited resources, on condition that they maintain faith and trust in God, who is the infinite 'I Am.' Thus, God both contains and helps us to own and grapple with good, evil, and our projection of them into others.

The one inconsistency in this parallelism between the breast as container and the God of Genesis is that the latter is biblically portrayed as male, while the container-breast of infancy is female. However, we do know that earlier versions of God were indeed female, and as cultures evolved into patriarchies, God's maternal role was usurped by men and transliterated in this way (Fromm, 1970, pp.109–188). Furthermore, Melanie Klein held that men experience 'breast' and 'womb envy' (Berke, 1997) just as women envy and want to possess the phallus. Even within patriarchal societies where women are reduced in status, they retain a god-like image at unconscious and symbolic levels. Conversely, in child development, the containment function is partly delegated to the father, who teaches the laws of cultural interaction to the child, and helps him contain the 'badness' through the familial and social context. So the legacy of containment is carried out by both mother and father in different ways.

In infancy and beyond, each of us internalizes schemata of object relations which are then managed by splitting and projective identification in ever-evolving forms, some of which are adaptive, and some maladaptive. As adaptive mechanisms, they help us to grow emotionally and express ourselves creatively. For example, our ability to empathize with another's feelings is a process in which we project aspects of our own self-experience into that person, and then take them back introspectively in a way which mirrors the other's wants and needs. In the arts, we project ourselves, whether as artists or observers, into the work of art, and take back parts of ourselves through our identification with the elements of the artistic production. The artist and the viewer or listener mutually pour a lifetime of experience into the creative work, which seems to take on a life of its own and serves to contain the passions and struggles of both the creator and those who appreciate and learn from it. Thus, through creativity and empathy, we restore the 'container' function and sometimes are genuinely transformed by the experience.

Projective identification plays a role in spiritual praxis as well. One who meditates and prays, in effect asks God to contain parts of himself that are painful and make them good and manageable. Eating chaleh or a wafer and drinking a glass of wine to affirm his faith, he simultaneously 'pours out' his heart and his faith into God, and 'eats and drinks' God into his body and soul.

In their pathological form, however, splitting and projective identification are capable of generating interpersonal conflict and mental illness. Pathological defense mechanisms manifest rigidity and concreteness. They lack resilience and 'shades of gray.' For example, one projects one's 'badness' (shame, guilt, aggression) into another, demonizing that person or group and denying one's own 'shadow.' That mechanism is the basis of scapegoating and religious persecution. The psychotic individual projects major segments of his own fragmented personality into 'defective' containers. He 'goes crazy' because he cannot find anyone or anything to contain and hold his errant thoughts. When we 're-own' our projective identifications as parts of ourselves, we are in a better position to address them, leading to the insight contained in the cartoon character Pogo's famous statement, 'I have seen the Enemy, and he is Me.' Adaptive projective identification consists of a 'feedback loop' in which projections are 'returned' in a way which, paradoxically, strengthens our own internal container.

Spirituality, then, has the potential to develop each person's container function so that God dependency often has the paradoxical effect of making the person stronger internally. The surrender of parts of ourselves and our destinies to an invisible being in whom we have faith can establish a more resilient internal container that depends less on momentary, sensory experience and more on a relationship to an Other that is based upon principles and commitment. The God-transformed container expands and 'dimensionalizes,' and so can help the person to endure, create, and grow.

God's containing function, however, depends on a mutually loving relationship with Him. In my view, religious teachings which emphasize man's 'original sin,' evil propensities, and the need for a God to 'save' him from himself show an incorrect understanding of splitting and projective identification. The function of a loving God-qua-container is to provide shelter from badness and evil by rendering them more manageable and tolerable to an essentially good self who is beloved of God. It is by growing in the sense of our inherent goodness and power that badness and pain become tolerable, and we can then begin to recognize and tolerate the fact that some of the badness we see in others resides in ourselves, and perhaps turn it to good purpose without losing our sense of inherent worth and dignity. Through the God that is outside of ourselves, we learn to find the God within, and vice versa.

Internalized quasi-religious schemata of the depressive position

The child's entry into the depressive position is characterized by two major developments which define our essential humanness. In the depressive position, the child develops the capacity to integrate good and bad representations into a 'whole self' and a 'whole subjective other,' which are flawed, but adequate for interpersonal relatedness. He becomes increasingly aware of mother as a separate person with an agenda of her own. Fearing the capacity of his aggression to hurt her, the child also develops the capacity for concern and feelings of guilt. He is moving from a self-contained, egocentric world of good and bad internal objects and a struggle for survival, to a world in which he is one among many subjectivities, each of whom has her own needs. Now the child begins to integrate within himself the good and bad features of self, thus individuating that self, yet knowing that he needs others in order to survive and thrive. Ejected from Eden (the exclusive dependent relationship to mother), he strives to create a world which contains at least some aspects of that 'lost Paradise.' During this phase, 'God' changes residence from the breast to the parents and then to the child's unconscious, in the structure of the superego – the internal source of guilt and shame which, under optimal conditions, guide the child into right actions and social adjustment.

The depressive position is a milestone in human development. By integrating good and bad extremes into shades of gray, the child no longer needs to adopt positions of over-idealization and devaluation. He begins to accept his desires, limitations, and hostilities, loving himself even with his shortcomings. In addition, he finds that he can make reparation and restitution for misbehavior which hurts the love object, and so survive his human shortcomings and his hate, knowing that those around him, on whom he so depends, can also do so. He experiences 'wholeness' – as opposed to fragmentation and division within the self and between self and others – as a desirable quality.

Entry into the depressive position means that the child can begin to accept and cope with the diverse, complex, and affectively mixed parts of himself and others. He becomes capable of surviving the knowledge that he is 'not-God,' and that he must give up his unique, privileged place in the maternal and familial orbits. He is increasingly able to tolerate frustration and regulate his feelings. Because he is now able to recognize his separateness and the possibility of loss, he enters more fully into the human condition, with its potential for sadness, suffering, and grief, without reverting to persecutory feelings toward self or others. Importantly, his infinite soulfulness is able to find a safe haven in the finite ego-world of family, friends, animals, toys, daydreams, and stories.

During this phase of development, the child hopefully begins to experience a God who judges but is forgiving, understands our humanness, and offers ways of redemption – the monotheistic, loving, and merciful God of the Judao-Christian tradition. Once, I spoke to the Sunday-school class at a Quaker meeting, and I asked the children, 'Why do you think we have a concept of one God, when our ancestors believed in many gods?' A young girl answered, 'So they shouldn't argue!' I couldn't agree more. What a wonderful way of saying that our multiple self representations, previously maintained by splitting, become integrated into a singular self. Quakers, of course, are known for their outstanding legacy of protecting the world through consensual action. Their seeking of consensus, minimization of ritual and paraphernalia, and silent prayer and meditation as a group manifest living the spiritual life in the depressive position. The beatitudes of Christ brought religion into the depressive position in a Roman period of paranoid-schizoid persecution. Mourning, meekness, purity, mercy, peacemaking – these are virtues which develop from an understanding of human suffering and limitation, and a desire to protect others and the fragile environment in which we live.

The dilemmas of contemporary religion stem from two sources: excessive guilt within the depressive position on the one hand, and, on the other, a reversion to the paranoid-schizoid position in which 'personal responsibility' is disavowed or non-existent. In my opinion, which I realize differs from some who place their trust in religous authority, examples of excessive guilt include the provision that bad thoughts are to be excluded from the mind, and the presumption that moral authority such as the Church and its ministers can, as if they are representatives of God, judge and condemn our innermost thoughts. In the depressive position, good and bad thoughts become acceptable and shade into one another. Guilt is experienced, but tempered by mercy and love. Reparation and redemption are always possible. Responsibility rests, in large part, in the individual self.

In the depressive position, cultivating purity does not mean the absence of negative thoughts, but rather possessing the humility to question their power and significance – they are, after all, only thoughts. This is what is meant by kindness. At its best, religions should help us to contain our split-off objects and integrate them within a schema of ourselves as fully human.

Many therapy patients come to treatment with a need to rework their internalized schemata of the depressive position. They live in shame and guilt and are blind to the possibility of reparation and restitution. They therefore feel isolated and alienated from others. For example, Mary Jo came to me in a severely depressed state, and her body was beginning to experience the debilitating effects of her chronic shame and guilt, as she over-ate compulsively and neglected her self care by avoiding social contacts, exercise, proper nutrition, relationships, and other sources of well-being.

Under very difficult circumstances as a single parent, Mary Jo had done an outstanding job of raising her children, who loved her profoundly and yet showed great independence and love of life. She was a beloved member of her community, had a delightful sense of humor, and was a thoroughly responsible citizen. Yet she could not acknowledge these strengths in herself and devoted each therapy session to a litany of self-castigation, contending that she was an incurable, hopeless case. She had been raised by strict and harsh parents and was literally taught to think of herself as a sinful person. This self schema was so rigidly internalized that no amount of positive feedback about herself could convince her that it was wrong. No measure of exhortation, cognitive restructuring, or insight into her past seemed to help her to think differently about herself.

Curiously, what helped her was humor. Periodically peering out of her shell of shame and guilt, Mary Jo would break the ice by telling me a joke, and I could not resist laughing. As a result of such spontaneous mirroring on my part, she began to see herself as human, and her 'bad self' and 'judgmental other' schema began to loosen from its moorings. Her jokes symbolized reparation to me for the heaviness she brought into the sessions. Self-forgiveness now seemed possible. This woman was overburdened by shame and guilt and was blind to the goodness that abounded in her. Her guilt stemmed from the feeling that she had somehow damaged her parents and siblings. Her life was claimed by her guilt, and she lived in a hell of constant self-chastisement. Our mutual humor allowed her, in some small way, to use me as a mirror for self-nurturing, and to begin a process of making reparation to herself – a relief from her by-now self-inflicted purgatory.

Paul, a young adult, had been raised by a loving and devout family in a strict religious tradition. He came to therapy for sexual obsessions which led him into troubled and fractured relationships in which his fantasies about women dominated over the reality of who they were, and which sometimes involved serious risks to his own life and limb. For example, through his computer, he actively pursued women about whom he knew little or nothing. They were 'virtual realities' for him. In one instance, he flew to a foreign country to meet a woman with whom he had briefly corresponded on the internet. His visit and his infatuation ended when he arrived there and found out that she was in the midst of several other affairs, thus putting him at risk for rejection, sexually transmitted disease, and assault by a jealous lover. Several times thereafter, I had to caution this mild-mannered and deeply religious individual about the hidden dangers in such liasons.

Although Paul had difficulty curtailing his romantic escapades, his problem was not the lack of impulse control, but quite the opposite: an internalized quasi-religious schema about women which led to feelings of guilt and failure rather than genuine intimacy. The acting out through the internet helped him to avoid genuine closeness to an embodied woman. In therapy, the two of us examined his religious beliefs in detail, trying to see whether and where there was room within them to see women as whole persons, rather than the extremes of over-idealized, 'perfect' souls on the one hand, versus dangerous, persecutory seducers on the other. We became convinced that such splitting of his concept of women was at the root of his sexual obsessions, since the 'bad' representation stimulated his desire, while the idealization permitted him to experience 'virtual' closeness to them. Underlying his schema of women as containing the best and worst of human nature (like Eve before and after the Fall) were notions of purity and chastity he had acquired at religious services and from his parents long before he could understand them. He had concluded early that a 'good boy' doesn't have sexual thoughts and that spirituality equals chastity. However, he soon encountered a conflict when, in adolescence, he realized that he could not sustain such a self concept among his peer group, for whom masculine prowess was proven by sexual conquests. So he split his concept of women into two separate images, the Virgin Mary and Mary Magdalene as it were, and in this way he was able simultaneously to maintain acceptance within both his adolescent peer group and his religious community.

Therapy aimed to help him to understand the sources of his split image of women and to relate to them as whole persons. By revising and updating his childhood religious understanding to an adult level, he was able to maintain his religious beliefs and yet achieve a degree of intimacy and safety in a relationship with one fairly 'safe' and reliable woman over an extended time period. His internalized quasi-religious schema about the archetypal Holy Mother versus the dangerous seductress possessed the rigidity of paranoid-schizoid dynamics, but it also had the potential to be modified into a more resilient, depressive position schema which allowed for individuation and the possibility of genuine intimacy rather than the relentless pursuit of desire. This is precisely what occurred as he integrated his 'seductress' image of women with his need for a 'beautiful soul.'

Even though Melanie Klein developed the first comprehensive theory of object relations, her work was steeped in Freudian biological reductionism, with all aspects of the mental life seen as derivatives of the life and death instincts, primal urges which Freud (1920) believed were the genetic inheritance of living cells. Some of Klein's students and followers, however, saw the potential of her theory to grasp the relationship between the unconscious mind and the actual interactions between the infant and caregivers. For them, object relations meant 'relationship,' not instinct. It is perhaps no accident that the two major proponents of the evolving British school of object relations had strong religious backgrounds. R. W. D. Fairbairn came from a Scottish Presbyterian home (Sutherland, 1989, pp.31, 88–89), and D. W. Winnicott grew up in a non-conformist Wesleyan religious household, later becoming an Anglican (Rodman, 1990, pp.31–33). Fairbairn was devout, and Winnicott, although he disliked religious dogmatism, was imbued with a strong spiritual legacy. Spirituality carries within it the side of psychology which entails love, union, and oneness, in stark contrast to a biologically based psychology which for over a century implied a struggle for survival and an emphasis on individuality, separateness, and aloneness. In what follows, I would like to suggest how a truly 'relational' psychology, with its emphasis on connectedness, can provide the beginnings of a spiritually based theory of emotional development.

CHAPTER SIX

The Relational Matrix of Infancy and its Impact upon Spiritual Development

Melanie Klein focused attention on the inner psychological world. In so doing, she neglected the interpersonal and social matrix in which the self develops. In Great Britain, others, such as Winnicott and Fairbairn, took up where she left off, exploring the impact of the caregivers, especially the mother, on the child's development. Eventually, their views and those of the next generation of analysts coalesced into what is now called the British Independent Tradition of psychoanalysis, a vantage point which emphasizes the relationship between Klein's focus on phantasies, anxiety, and defense mechanisms and the newer emphasis on relationships with significant others. While the British School does not employ specifically religious or spiritual concepts as such (as does, for example, Jungian theory and practice), its proponents clearly maintain that there are emergent higher-level qualities in the infant's psyche which involve relatedness, meaning, and a search for continuity and oneness.

An example of the spiritual 'edge' in British object relations theory is to be found in Winnicott's notion of 'going on being' (Winnicott, 1956, p. 303). The infant, in his helplessness, vulnerability, and dependence upon a caregiver, needs to hold his fragile self together during times when the mother is not immediately available. If mother's responsiveness to his needs is 'good enough,' i.e. if her nurturing is timely, empathically attuned, and sensitive to the infant's budding self, he will realize the continuity of his existence in time and space, of 'going on being,' instead of feeling fragmented and disrupted, Eigen (1985) insightfully pointed out that such continuity depends upon a rudimentary faith that 'all is well' and that provisions will be available when needed. This inner security, based upon a primal faith in an 'other' who is not visibly present, is precisely what religion and spirituality offer the adult. The faithful are led to trust in an unseen presence, so that the continuity of self is thereby ensured, even when it is alone. It is important, for such inner security and continuity to prove reliable in the face of life's vicissitudes, that it be based on a faith in someone or something beyond the senses. We re-negotiate our 'going on being' through an invisible Other.

Winnicott and his contemporary, Ronald Fairbairn, shed light on a problem that has long haunted Western psychology and religion: the relationship between dependency and self-sufficient autonomy. Modern psychology has emphasized independence and self-sufficiency as goals of development, while religion, on the other hand, has stressed dependency, humility, and obedience.

To fully understand the dependence/independence dilemma, one must grasp its roots in infancy. Winnicott held that the ultimate fear is the prospect of 'regression to dependency' (cf. Little, 1990), with its frightening potential for helplessness and loss of self accompanied by 'annihilation anxiety' (Hopper, 1991, 1997; Winnicott, 1986, pp.243–244). Winnicott strove to offer his patients a renewed and vital healing experience of dependency while being consistently 'held' by the therapist so that the primal self could survive the dependency experience and annihilation fears without disintegration, thereby developing a more resilient and spontaneous core. For example, Margaret I. Little, a psychoanalyst who was analyzed by Winnicott, recalled that during the most anxiety-provoking phases of her treatment with him, Winnicott clasped his hands around hers to indicate his presence and absolute concern while she underwent terrifying re-experiences of abandonment and annihilation that occurred in infancy due to her mother's severe depression (Little, 1990). Winnicott worked attentively and steadfastly with Little almost daily, sustaining her 'going on being' during the regression to dependency. Recalling her analysis, Little remembered how Winnicott's 'holding' allowed her to 'go on being' within the regression and enabled her to 'restart' her sense of self, her spontaneous aliveness, and her creativity on a new basis. Winnicott thus regarded the holding experience of total dependency as paradoxically essential to the development of an independent self.

Our spiritual lives, under optimal conditions, allow us to negotiate 'total dependency.' Whether a Tibetan Buddhist meditating in the Himalayas with minimal sensory stimulation and social contact, or a Jew or Christian experiencing his existential aloneness and then finding a connection to a loving God, we are guided through our helplessness and fear to an experience of oneness which sustains the core of our being. The 'cloud of unknowing' that often precedes the awakening to God reflects the condition of helplessness and anxiety that precedes the arrival of the mother in infancy.

Fairbairn (1952) held that the trajectory of human development led not from dependency to isolated independence but to *inter*dependent, separate selves who are nonetheless connected to one another by our common humanity. Through communal worship and sharing spiritual goals, and through the notion of an omnipresent, omniscient Other, believers find that they can sustain their independent lives while uniting with their fellows.

The British Independent psychoanalyst Christopher Bollas (a Californian and a literary scholar who emigrated to London, where he became a prominent analyst) offers a somewhat different slant from Winnicott or Fairbairn on the infant's dependent situation, by referring to the mother as a 'transformational object' (Bollas, 1987, pp.13–29). For Bollas, the infant is 'bathed' in the mother's caregiving ambience. In this context, with the infant's self not yet fully differentiated from his surroundings, the mother's arrivals, departures, and ministrations are not experienced as coming from a distinct external person, but as alterations in the sense of self.

As a transformational object, mother holds and suckles her baby, attending lovingly to its needs. The infant experiences her holding as a sea change in his own state of being, a 'transformation,' in which he feels more whole, pleasurable, and pleasing, a source and recipient of essential goodness. Similarly, in spiritual experience, we experience such transformations of self without specifically knowing their source. In meditation, we may know bliss, 'peace beyond understanding,' grace. In religious services, we experience awe, ecstasy, protection, and salvation as if we are surrounded by God, by an Other. 'In a moment, in the twinkling of an eye, ...we shall be changed.' Spiritual transformations are partly the legacy of the infant's inner experience of a nurturing surround.

Grotstein (2000, pp.37–59) offers a further perspective on the state of infantile dependence, one which is paradoxical and addresses the problem of so-called infantile omnipotence. How can an infant, so needy and powerless, believe that he is all-powerful, as if he were 'His majesty the baby,' as Freud had said? Grotstein believes that the child is initially protected from dangerous intrusions by his own feelings of omnipotence (all-powerfulness). This self-protective capacity gives the infant a conviction of self-creation (autochthony), as if he birthed himself and is 'God omnipotent' reigning over his little kingdom. Grotstein views omnipotence not as corrupting power, but as an adaptive illusion that leads to later capacities for creativity, assertiveness, and initiative.[1]

The infant, for Grotstein, is necessarily 'autochthonous' (self-motivated, self-organizing), in its cooperative relationship with mother. The research of pediatrician T. Berry Brazelton (Brazelton and Als, 1979) and of the developmental psychiatrist Daniel Stern (1984) supports Grotstein's view. Their videotapes of infants interacting with their mothers show that infants are initiators of spontaneous activity rather than passive recipients of their mothers' ministrations. That is, when babies feel safe and held, they are able to 'self-organize' their interpersonal activity. This autochthonous power to create may be the infantile prototype that is externalized and elaborated into the concept of an omnipotent God who created the universe.

Thus, in Grotstein's view, the infant, in his own mind, is God, the omnipotent One. Stories of the origins of the universe, so-called creation myths like the Scandinavian 'Kalevala' (Pentikainen and Poom, 1999) and the biblical Genesis, recapitulate the infant's own phantasy of 'self as Creator,' as organizer of his own universe. What we experience later as 'God' is a reflection of our authochthonous selves experienced as Other. The Judaic saying, 'God is in our hearts' and the Christian belief in God's presence on earth in human form with whose suffering we can identify, reflect this experience of God as Self, as inside the self, as one with self, as immanent within our being.

I should hasten to add that Grotstein by no means wants to reinforce any simplistic idea that we are all-powerful or all-controlling, as, for example, in the notions that 'might makes right,' and 'only the fittest survive.' Indeed such 'overkill' beliefs in self-control and self-interest at the expense of others stem partly from paranoid projection in response to 'persecutory' danger based upon the notion of dwindling supply. Grotstein is rather referring to our self-organizing potential and our faith in ourselves as competent beings. Although he generally does not speak in frankly religious terms, Grotstein's later writing (2000, pp.127–129) is infused with depictions of the 'ineffable subject,' the unconcealed and pure self which approaches the awesome experience of God that occurs during a spiritual awakening.

In normal development, we are gradually guided by our parents, our emotional wounds, and our own mistakes to a more humble, delimited concept of ourselves. In that context, we experience an external God who allows us to retain a measure of power and creative potential for ourselves. When we meditate, we sometimes attain a state in which God is 'everywhere,' in us, around us, and outside us all at once. At those moments when we are surrounded with an ambience of a 'Higher Power,' we are simultaneously aware of both our limits and our infinitude. This confluence of our smallness and infinite reach leads to the sense of awe and the miraculous, wherein the universe is filled with magic, the seemingly impossible happens, and events coincide in a startlingly synchronous way to create miracles. It is as if such grace comes from the infinite scope of the universe and God. But at the same moment, we feel as if we ourselves have unlimited potential, as if by proxy. We achieve true 'authochthonous' power in this way through our relationship to God as both within and outside of ourselves.

However, contact with the Divine Power can, even as it gives us strength and security, also be a source of anxiety. I have spoken of the annihilation anxiety that results from threats to the self. I now wish to say more about a related state of anxiety that arises from spiritual experience as such, from contact with the divine and the transformational movement towards transcendence. Such experiences pose threats of their own which are similar to, but different from, the dangers to the self that stem from other sources. They pose a further paradox in that such anxiety is in response to overwhelming goodness rather than badness and evil.

'God contact anxiety'

Object relations theory emphasizes the role of persecutory anxiety – the fear of attack by specific internalized antagonists or 'bad objects' – and annihilation anxiety – the dread of the fragmentation and death of the self. Meditators and others who engage in deep or prolonged spiritual practices often report such anxieties in the course of their spiritual development, and descriptions of anxiety states abound in the spiritual literature. Some well-known biblical representations of acute anxiety are to be found in Jonah's engulfment by a whale, Saul of Tarsus flung from his horse by a bolt of lightning, and the New Testament apocalyptic vision of the Day of Judgement and the end of the world. Coming into contact with God is not always a blissful experience. It can be anxiety-provoking – so much so, that I believe the phrase 'God contact anxiety' is warranted.

Anxiety that results from a close encounter with God has to do with a massive threat to the 'meaning context' which sustains the sense of self. The self is, first of all, the seat of conscious awareness, our subjectivity. It requires a meaning context that allows us to feel alive, competent, and righteous participants in an orderly and recognizable universe. The self seeks survival, growth, and immortality not only through its biological base, but also, and importantly, through *meanings* (Janoff-Bulman, 1992). Such meanings are initially simple in structure, consisting of 'signs,' objects which indicate and signify events in the way that a road sign indicates a sharp curve ahead or the availability of 'gas, food, lodging.' For example, the mother's breast becomes a 'sign' of nurturance and soothing for the infant. In the course of development, meanings evolve beyond signs to symbols, metaphors, narratives, and rituals, and ultimately in abstractions, such as theological concepts of God (such as can be found in the writings of St. Thomas Acquinas), the universe (as represented, for instance, in the cosmological 'wheel' of Hinduism), and/or the human community (as manifest in pilgrimages and gatherings for worship). The self is validated and finds expression within these meaning structures. When meanings and subjectivity are threatened, the self experiences annihilation anxiety.

A primal dilemma of the self is that, while it finds consciousness and meaning through the signs, symbols, and other meaning contexts of the external world in which it is 'con-signed' and 'co-signed' to live within a time–space frame of reference, it also has a need to reach beyond the limits of structured meanings to the limitless, infinite subjectivity of God. God is holistic and all-encompassing, exploding and transcending any particular meaning context, so that a direct encounter with His 'light' is blinding and threatens the self with destruction at the same time that it is a necessary nutrient for the self. Self-transformative exposure to this light and surrender to God's will is thus filled with terror, dread, and awe. The ego fears dissolution.

Such a state of terror has been documented by spiritual 'witnesses' throughout the ages. When the self has an encounter with God or Higher Self, it either experiences a 'grace' which allows it to internalize God in such a way that He becomes part of the person's life (a spiritual 'conversion' experience), or else defends in radical and sometimes destructive ways against such an experience. My own understanding of Judas Iscariot, for example, is that he had to betray Jesus, not only for political and mercenary reasons, but to kill the God he had encountered in Christ because that light threatened Judas' fragile sense of self. I would argue that the persona of Judas is not that of the horrific figure that he has often been purported to be. Indeed, with considerable pathos, even Judas among Jesus' disciples is doing God's will, for it is God's will to sacrifice his Son. Judas stands for the 'holy terror' present in Everyman. (We must remember that Jesus forgave him.) The great American poet James Wright (1990, p.84) indeed portrays Judas as a 'saint' who comforts a dying man in the crowd as he remembers with remorse the One he sent to be crucified. We mortals probably betray the 'God with us' every day in a thousand ways, even as we worship Him, in order to maintain our fragile sense of self. We find it supremely difficult to stay in that blinding light and yet go on with our daily affairs and sustain a viable meaning context.

I saw a young man for a consultation shortly after he was released from a brief stay in a psychiatric ward. He had been going about the normal business of the day when he suddenly and with no forewarning experienced an altered state of consciousness in which time, space, and sensory experience shifted abruptly and he 'felt the presence of a powerful Being in the room with me.' The moment was so frightening for him that he went to an emergency room for an examination, thinking that he was going crazy. (He had no history of psychiatric treatment, and recovered completely within a few days.) What he had undergone was what has been called a 'spiritual emergency,' which can occur when people undergo spiritual encounters and transformations (Grof and Grof, 1989). The ego and its meaning context may indeed be annihilated for a short time, leading to a dread like no other. When possible, spiritual awareness should be attained gradually, with guidance, and in a disciplined manner. The self must have time to incorporate 'God presence' into its structure of consciousness and meanings. Sudden psychotic-like experiences and hallucinogen-induced states, for example, are risky shortcuts and cannot be easily assimilated into daily existence; indeed they may cause malevolent transformations of the personality such as prolonged psychoses.

'God-contact anxiety' is an experience of boundaryless intensity resulting from an unassimilated experience with the infinite Other. Persecutory feelings and loss of self are involved, but I agree with the Jungian perspective that such anxiety also reflects the innate presence of an archetypal God (or gods/goddesses) which can only be gradually integrated by the conscious ego. Such a 'godhead experience' deserves a place in our understanding of psychological structure in order to explain the radical transformations and restructuring of consciousness that occur in spiritual awakenings and other deeply transformative experiences. However, when the God presence occurs to a self-system that is not prepared for it, its overwhelming nature can dissolve the meaning context of the ego, leading to severe anxiety which may be mixed with shame, guilt, and other self-denigrating feelings.

To summarize, the British Independent School's studies of the self and its acute vulnerability in the context of interpersonal relations complemented the work of Melanie Klein on internalized object relations. Subse-

quently, through the work of Heinz Kohut (Strozier, 2001), an Aus-
trian-born psychoanalyst who lived and worked in Chicago, the psychology of the self was elaborated into a totalistic frame of reference for theory
and practice. Kohut regarded the subjective self, rather than Klein's 'internal
object,' as the fundamental unit of psychological functioning, and emphasized the self's vulnerability to what he called 'narcissistic injury,' the hurt or
slight one feels when one is shamed or rejected. Mitchell (1988), Stolorow,
et al. (1994), and others emphasized the connection of such vulnerability to
the intersubjective and relational matrix. I will now discuss the implications
of self psychology and related developments, which – as in the case of object
relations theory – are formulated within a secular humanist and
natural/social sciences context, for a spiritually-based psychology.

Endnote

1   Descriptions of the mental state of infants can never, of course, be verified by verbal report.
    Therefore, they constitute, in effect, epic archetypal 'myths' about our origins which are
    utilized by psychoanalysts and students of human nature in a metaphorical rather than literal
    way to understand the subsequent experience of the verbal child and of the adult. Conversely,
    some adult experiences are used to make inferences about the infant's inner world.

CHAPTER SEVEN

The Self in Relation
Vulnerability and Mutuality as Gateways to Healing

Object relations theory has always presupposed a complementary 'self psychology' but viewed the self primarily as a repository of 'objects' (representations of and identifications with significant others) rather than an entity with dimensions and dynamics of its own. Furthermore, although British object relations theory emphasized interpersonal relations, it neglected the *reciprocal mutuality* of interactions – for example, the impact of the child upon the parent, and of the therapist's self experience on that of the patient. The importing of object relations theory from Britain to the United States is what brought 'the self in relation' into full view and led to an understanding of relationship as a two-way street of reciprocal influence. Since I will be discussing my central paradigmatic concept of the psychospiritual self at length in the next chapter, it is important to see what self psychology, intersubjectivity, and relational psychology have contributed to understanding the self and their potential to enhance our grasp of human spirituality.

Kohut's self psychology

Heinz Kohut (1971, 1977) was the first psychoanalyst to consider narcissism, man's inherent preoccupation with and love of self, as a developmental process in its own right. Freud, Klein, and the British object relations theorists viewed narcissism as a normal personality trait, but with the qualification that such self-love should normally be transformed into affiliative love, social interest, and altruistic concern for others. Since, in Freud's view, there is only a limited quantity of 'psychic energy' available for fueling development, some of the energy of self preservation and self-love needs to be deflected outwards for use in the socialization process. Thus, according to Freud, we learn to love others by giving up some of our initially all-pervasive self-love. The Freudian position on narcissism thus embodies the Judao-Christian view that unchecked self-love leads to selfishness, greed, envy, lack of a social conscience, and other undesirable traits.

While there is some truth to this perspective – we have all known people who are so enamored of self that they leave a trail of neglect and abandonment wherever they go – it is also true, as Fromm (2000) pointed out, that love of self can enhance our relationships with others. Self-love can include the 'objects' of one's love within it, and positive regard for oneself is a minimum requirement for genuine care for others. Taking a cue from Freud, most psychoanalysts, however, hold that the individual must yield a substantial portion of his initial narcissism and self-centeredness in order to become a social being. Kohut went against those prevailing winds, and thus began a major controversy.

Interest in Kohut's views began at a time when American culture shifted from a 'hippie' lifestyle which emphasized communal living, love, and peace (of course, the hippie era had a downside of chaotic existence, disregard of material need, and unthinking hero worship as well) to a 'yuppie' climate of acquisitiveness, achievement, and goal-directedness. This shift from group merger and idealism to the relentless pursuit of self-interest called for a psychology that said, 'It's OK to love yourself, focus on your own desires, and pursue personal ambitions.' Many of the self-help books of the last twenty years have therefore emphasized such goals and advised people how to accomplish assertiveness, wealth, and self-love.

Kohut's theory to some extent fulfilled the role of a psychology compatible with the pursuit of self-interest, but on that very account, his work is to some extent misunderstood. For example, Kohut emphasized ideals along with ambitions, and his view of mental health was not focused so much on achievement and self-aggrandizement as upon developing a sense of wholeness and resilience in the face of life's hurts and rejections. He was not advocating an avaricious capitalist lifestyle but rather seeking to heal the damage that was wrought upon many individuals by parents who, while they may have been well-intentioned and devoted, had failed to empathize with their child's inner self. One legacy of such empathic failure was a generation of high-achievers who paradoxically felt empty and fragmented, reflecting a loss of self-cohesion which no amount of external success or validation could remedy.

It is a fact that narcissism has received bad press from Western religion. As the book of Genesis suggests, religion sees all of man's troubles stemming from his usurpation of God's power and seeking greedily to fulfill his own desires. The twist that Kohut applied to this, by now formulaic, understanding of human nature was that the culprit wasn't narcissism itself, but rather frustrated and injured narcissism. He felt that if narcissism were allowed to develop in an atmosphere of empathy and support, it would naturally become tempered and shaped into healthy ambitions and ideals, reinforcing rather than interfering with altruism.

Kohut believed that the parental 'mirroring' of the child's self-love would lead the child into healthy relationships with others. (In this respect, Kohut followed in the footsteps of the eighteenth-century philosopher Jean-Jacques Rousseau, who held that man, in a 'state of nature' was inherently good, and that civilization's task was to facilitate this goodness.) For example, he felt that the narcissistic rage which the child feels when rejected or refused gratification would naturally be tempered by parental understanding and empathy. Protracted hate and resentment, he held, were products of injured narcissism, not an expression of an innate aggressive drive. Similarly the arrogance, grandiosity, and relentless self-seeking we see in the narcissistic personality disorder is, for Kohut, a way of compensating for an underlying deficiency or psychic wound, not a product of overindulgence.

Kohut, unlike those Freudians and Kleinians who consider narcissistic expressions to be a resistance to treatment, therefore recommended that the therapist accept and mirror the patient's grandiosity and accept even an illusory idealization by the patient. By reflecting empathically with the patient on the inevitable slights and failures that occur in the sessions, Kohut believed that the patient's grandiosity would naturally give way to a balanced self-appraisal, a process which he called 'transmuting internalization,' i.e. a transformation of the self in the direction of genuine self-esteem based upon realistic self-assessment.

A patient, whom I shall call Josh, came to me stressed and 'falling apart...' He worked as an entertainer, in a job which required that he be the constant center of attention. He was in pursuit of a woman whom he described as 'perfect,' beautiful, and sophisticated. However, her interest in him did not relieve his feelings of inadequacy and shame. Reflecting on his childhood, he recalled that his mother was kind but possessively used her son to meet her own needs and salve her emotional wounds. Josh's father was cold and critical, and emotionally unavailable. Josh always had to prove himself to both parents, and no matter what he accomplished, he felt like a failure. His mother, fearing abandonment, would 'rescue' him from his failures but not reward his successes.

Using a Kohutian approach, I listened with understanding as Josh told me about his anxieties and discomforts, his feelings of rejection, his headaches and indigestion, and his difficulties pleasing his girlfriend. Soon he began to tell me that I was 'the greatest therapist in the city,' and one of those 'incredible doctors' like his pediatrician, capable of amazing cures. At first, I was flattered by his compliments, but he was so repetitive and insistent on this point that I soon tired of his demonstrativeness and praise. I began to explore with him why it was that he needed me to be a therapist who was so extraordinary and without any apparent shortcomings. Instead of the painful insights which one would expect from a hurting person exploring his own soul in deep psychotherapy, Josh, who had theretofore felt like a dismal failure, began praising *himself.* He had reversed the idealization from me to himself. At this point, his self-estimate was magically transformed. He was now 'marvelous' in his work, the best dressed man in his community, and a fantastic lover, all of which contrasted sharply with his self-abnegating demeanor in previous sessions.

At this juncture, I knew that I was dealing with what Kohut called the 'grandiose self,' a compensatory overestimation of self, so I worked very hard to sustain empathy with his frustrated narcissistic strivings. I reflected his statements of greatness benignly and with compassion. In time, in this atmosphere of understanding, Josh began to realize that he didn't need to be perfect in order to receive acknowledgment and nurturing, and his view of himself became more realistic. He explored his feelings of shame and vulnerability as they occurred in a variety of situations. His symptoms subsided as we saw together how many times he had been hurt by his father's criticism and unavailability and his mother's view of him as an extension of herself. In treatment, his narcissism shifted from deficient to exaggerated to accurate self-appraisal and a sense of being a whole person.

Kohut's views on narcissism not only imply a more generous and empathic way of approaching treatment (I should also say by qualification that I find Kohut's technique helpful with some, but not all, patients), but are deeply relevant to an understanding of man's spiritual nature. While Melanie Klein's insights suggest how spiritual struggles begin in infancy and are manifest later in the person's religious beliefs and life conflicts, Kohut's perspective suggests a different way of thinking about the relationship between man and God than the traditional interpretations. I will now try to apply Kohut's theory to the Old and New Testaments to show what I mean.

It is an understatement to say that religious texts are laden with contradiction and paradox. In fact, I think that, like a Zen koan, paradox is the vehicle through which revelatory texts elevate us to a higher state of consciousness. One of the paradoxical dualities that recurs throughout the Bible is the way in which narcissism is portrayed alternately as valued and decried by God. For example, the Jews are chosen by God as a wonderful, valued people whose narcissism has been injured repeatedly by evil social forces. God idealizes the Jews, and asks them to idealize Him. He offers them prosperity, victory over their enemies, and most importantly His love. He sees them as 'made in His image.' What more narcissistic relationship can there be than this one?

At the very same time, God puts the Jews through their paces. He tests Abraham to see if he is faithful enough to sacrifice his son for the sake of his beliefs. He sends Job one misfortune after another to see if his faith can withstand these blows. He induces a whale to swallow Jonah until he becomes penitent enough to fight God's battle. He asks the Jews to practice the Ten Commandments, which clearly involve putting the welfare of others above self-interest. He requires that they engage in practices such as circumcision, avoidance of certain foods, and animal sacrifice to show their humility and their deference to Him. In other words, God takes his beloved people down a few notches – injures their narcissism – in order to forge their souls and their devotion to Him.

So God, so to speak, is both an 'object relations' God and a 'Kohutian' God. He inflicts conflicts and challenges which help the children of Israel to master their persecutory objects and to move into the depressive position of concern for others. But this life of deprivation and discipline is compensated by His mirroring of their specialness and their infinite potential.

How do we resolve this paradox? In one sense, it can't be resolved at all. The message of the Bible, indeed of life itself, is that we have to live with this duality, which alone promotes growth and development. Similarly, parents need to mirror and encourage their children's self-strivings while admonishing them when they transgress ethical values and social norms. All of us, in addition to realistic self-assessment, need to love and appreciate ourselves deeply, and receive adulation. The comedienne Carole Burnett, who is known to be a generous and charitable individual, once said, 'If you got it, flaunt it!' Nelson Mandela, who has devoted his life to, and made great sacrifices for, the freedom of his people, has said that we fear our own light more than our darkness, our self-potential more than the possibility of failure. So, God loves us in both ways: mirroring our narcissism and challenging our self-centeredness. God is One, while man is a dualistic being with the potential for oneness. Man needs dualisms in order to grow.

There is, however, another way to view this duality from the perspective of narcissism. Let us for the moment relinquish our tendency to give narcissism a bad name. Let us empathize with God's dilemma in creating the Universe. He produces a beautiful, pristine world, and looking upon it, He feels lonely. (God's loneliness and need for mirroring and idealization is often ignored by theologians, while children often intuit this truth.) Plants and animals are insufficient to soothe and nurture Him. So He creates humans as self-conscious subjectivities to mirror and idealize Him. He is content, until they, by virtue of their God-like and God-given capacities to self-reflect and choose, begin to fail Him. At that point, He intervenes to help his chosen people become good mirroring and idealizing 'selfobjects' again. The apparent contradiction between narcissism and altruism can at least partly be resolved by seeing that God Himself is narcissistic! If we could view our relationship to God as mutually empathic, we would perhaps be less threatened by Him and more able to fulfill our trajectories of ambitions and ideals, our destinies, with less conflict and feelings of inadequacy and defeat.

In a book entitled *An Answer to Job* (Hayman, 1999, pp.410–414), Jung questions the traditional idealization of God, and considers the Judaic God, Jaweh, to be profoundly and ontologically 'tarnished,' i.e. possessing both good and evil traits. Cabalistic thought (Berke, 1996) postulates that when God withdrew from the world after creating it, he left pieces of Himself scattered in the cosmos, and that this fragmentation is the source of evil in the world. It is man's duty to combat evil by seeking wholeness. I am here stating a milder contention – not that God and his works contain evil, but that God has a side of neediness and vulnerability which allows Him to empathize with us, and draws Him to us. If you will, this is God's feminine, maternal side, the aspect which modern patriarchal society has shunted aside.

The New Testament and the coming of Jesus thus represent one attempt to repair the rupture that occurred between man and God. (It will surprise some Christians to find that there are other attempts, including psychoanalysis itself, various forms of spiritualism and spiritual seeking, and re-interpretations of the scriptures by Jewish scholars.) We all know that the idea of a Messiah originated in Judaism and is explicit in the Old Testament.

Messianism implies redemption through the arrival of God in human form. There are many psychospiritual implications of the messianic view, for example, the restoration of hope, and the notion that God is in our hearts, inside us all, God made immanent and manifest. This principle is essential to the concept of a psychospiritual core which I shall take up in the next chapter. Another is the Buddhist/Hindu striving towards enlightenment. Eastern religions emphasize a transcendent state of mind over and above a Western theology of conflict and struggle. The messianic view reaches its apogee in the presence of Jesus, a man/God who exemplifies the 'transcendent position' (Grotstein, 2000, pp.300–302).

What I wish to focus upon here is the relationship of messianism, and in particular Jesus, to narcissism.

Jesus is an important starting place for understanding the relationship between narcissism and charisma, the character trait which entails attraction and appeal to others. Jesus' charisma was paradoxical. On one level, the historical Jesus was in his time one of the *least* charismatic leaders in human history. His ideas and his martyrdom, not his charismatic personality, led to his mass appeal centuries later. Jesus, like many other great rabbis and religious prophets, was a humble and simple man who wore the plainest clothing and spoke in uncomplicated language. He demanded nothing of anyone, and insisted at all times that it is the Father who is deserving of reverence. His disciples were a small group of men and women, most of whom were culturally marginalized and/or of the lower social classes. He died hated by the masses, relegated to near oblivion for two hundred years. His insights, healing power, and unconditional love did, however, have charisma for a very small group of followers. Their frequent guilt at failing him partly reflects the narcissistic injury and shame they felt at not measuring up to his ideals. (There were also times when the masses flocked to hear and see Jesus, but that was on account of curiosity about his remarkable healing power, not his charisma.) Here was not a man who charmed and attracted the populace, but one whose thinking was morally advanced and misunderstood, appreciated by a precious few.

Despite his utter simplicity and humility, there are two respects in which Jesus represents healthy narcissism and charisma. The first is His extraordinary manifestation of human love, and the second is His mass appeal over an incredible and unprecedented period of two thousand years following his death (and resurrection and ascendance, if you are Christian).

With respect to the first, I see Jesus as a preacher of healthy narcissism. His unconditional acceptance of mankind represented a new validation and mirroring of the human spirit. Furthermore, He manifested a merger of the self with God in a way that is similar to the way that healthy narcissism represents a merger of the self with the mirroring and idealizing selfobject. His views on grief ('Blessed are those that mourn ...') and on universal peace and love, are eternal teachings about how to cope with loss, hurt, and affliction without projecting blame and returning the hurt into others. The miracle cures he affected were examples of the self's capacity to heal. His examples of 'the little children' and 'the lilies of the field' as instances of how to be in God's light were not prescriptions to be dependent, helpless creatures, but of how to bask in God's love instead of complicating life.

Jesus' posthumous mass appeal – unprecedented in human history – stems partly from his martyrdom, but Jesus' legacy is unique among martyrs. His promise was that out of His wounds and death would come wholeness and redemption. In healthy narcissistic development, the need for external validation ('mirroring' and 'idealization') is gradually transformed into a self that is whole and able to cope with hurt and rejection. Kohut's concept of 'transmuting internalization' (Kohut, 1971, p.55) implies that something or someone external is internalized into the self, transformed from outward 'object' or 'thing' into 'mind stuff' and 'spirit.' Jesus' resurrection symbolizes such a perennial transformation.

Unfortunately, the reverse all too often happens. In addictions and compulsions, in doctrinaire belief, in acquisitiveness and greed, spirit (the inner core of our being) becomes externalized into objects and possessions, momentary stimulation and attainment, illusory victories, and so on. The person feels increasingly 'empty' as he pursues such externals because they don't 'fill' his spirit.

Christians, like all of us, come to religion and spirituality partly on account of this 'hole' in their being: they want to fill the hole with 'being whole' (narcissistically integrated). In this respect, we all are drawn towards the promise of wholeness, which gives its provider and prophet great charismatic appeal as a 'selfobject,' someone whom we identify with and idealize. But if we seek wholeness in the external trappings of religion, instead of that spirit which already resides within ourselves, then we merely perpetuate the cycle of narcissistic injury and narcissistic rage that we are trying to heal.

So, my message is: love your own narcissism, and transform it into love of your spirit and love of your true self. Love yourself in everyone, and everyone in yourself. In the next chapter, on the psychospiritual core, I will try to suggest how an expanded concept of the self allows development in this direction to occur. But self psychology contributed to two additional perspectives: intersubjective and relational psychology, which also have implications for a spiritual understanding, and the complete picture requires their inclusion.

Intersubjective and relational psychology

Object relations theory and self psychology, both originally linked to an individualistic, biologically-based Freudian frame of reference, have sired broader perspectives within psychoanalysis in which the self and its 'objects' are seen as social constructs (Gergens, 1991; O'Leary, 2001) and mutually created 'intersubjective' experiences (Stolorow, Atwood, and Brandchaft, 1984). Rather than focusing on the individual, these perspectives emphasize the interpersonal context and regard the individual's inner world as derivative of what transpires among persons.

There has been an accumulation of evidence from developmental research (Lichtenberg, 1983) suggesting that the infant's self is engaged with significant others from birth and creates itself (self-organizes) out of relational experience. Therefore, we have come to see the self as an emergent structure which evolves from the interactions with primary caregivers. This does not mean that the self lacks a being or structure of its own, but that it defines and equilibrates itself through relationships. The relational and intersubjective psychologists therefore view psychotherapy in terms of the intersubjectivity of patient and therapist, with attention to the contributions of both their subjectivities to the course and outcome of treatment. The relationalists and intersubjectivists take the insights from object relations theory and self psychology, both of which emphasize the internal world and the personality, and place them in the context of the social matrix and mutual subjectivity.

Neither the relational nor the intersubjective psychoanalysts present themselves as spiritually-based. Their theories emerged from the postmodern context in which long-held assumptions about a coherent self, a mind housed in a brain, and cherished scientific and religious beliefs in an orderly universe were being 'deconstructed.' Since the conceptions of self and mind as such became suspect, the notion that our thoughts, feelings, and sense of self are ephemeral 'constructions' resulting from social interaction gained credence. There isn't much room for eternity, ultimate meanings, absolute truths, higher consciousness, or One God in such a formulation – except perhaps as social myths or constructions!

Nevertheless, in the non-theistic sense of spirituality as a richer under-standing of our lives and purpose, a case can be made that the relational and intersubjective perspectives represent progress beyond the solipsistic dualism of an isolated mind housed in a brain, a dualism which implies that each person is totally separate from others and from the universe. If, as relationalism implies, our very self depends on the other human beings who form the past, present, and future matrices of our lives, then there is unques-tionable survival value in attending as much to their subjectivities, their uniqueness, and their well-being as we do to our own. Their 'Thou-ness' is equal to our 'I-ness,' since both are essential to our self-definition. Thus, relationalism and intersubjectivity represent further blows to the centrality of the ego, the great 'I am.' They open the door to ever wider, more inclusive constructions of the self, the psychospiritual self being one which I shall discuss in the next chapter.

So, just as object relations theory – by pointing out how the inner world parallels and influences religious beliefs and the essential spiritual condition of each personality – and self psychology – by emphasizing the integrity of the self as a fundamental 'need' that fulfills the 'spiritual hunger' for wholeness – can contribute to the psychospiritual paradigm, so the relational and intersubjective perspectives provide important avenues for understand-ing and healing the human spirit.

Psychotherapy itself is a case in point. Until the arrival of these perspec-tives, the therapist was thought of as a neutral, objective observer of the patient and his mind (understood as an 'organ' or an inner faculty). The mind as reservoir of thoughts was considered a self-contained, individual 'noosphere' (sphere of knowledge) housed in the brain. The therapist, in effect, modified the self-contained mind, making some adjustments to it by influencing the patient's thoughts and feelings. But, aside from these 'tune-ups,' there was no inherent relationship between therapist and patient. If anything, the only connection between them consisted of the transfer-ence, a wishful fantasy of dependence upon the therapist deriving from the patient's childhood. Patients were thus considered 'social atoms.' As I said earlier, such a view pervaded Western culture as a result of Descartes' mind/body dualism, in which the non-material mind inhabited a small part of the brain, giving it a tiny 'window on the world.' Given such a legacy of a mind housed in a body, the analyst was an objective observer who explored its dynamics with the patient. The real relationship between therapist and patient was only a potential contaminant that played little role in the treatment process.

The relational/intersubjective view shifted the focus from the patient as an object to a perspective in which the therapist and patient are both experiencing 'subjects.' Their interaction becomes real and crucial, for it is what may lead the patient into healthier pathways of living. This perspective challenges the therapist to be fully conscious of his own personhood within the here-and-now context of his relationship with the patient. 'Technique' does not exist independently of the particular therapist.

For example, I treated a patient, Jim, who, several years prior to treatment, was sexually molested and sworn to secrecy. During the initial weeks and months of therapy, Jim, desperately hurting from this traumatic betrayal, needed to re-establish trust by idealizing me as a kindly, concerned 'rescuer' who had only his own interests at heart, omitting the fact that I was also a vulnerable and flawed human being. He soon commenced the important work of recalling the impact of the molestation on his life, and saw how it had generated his persistent psychosomatic symptoms and his difficulties in work and relationships. Then I noticed that Jim was becoming increasingly grumpy, annoyed, and frustrated, and he frequently canceled his appointments. Occasionally, he mustered up the courage to tell me how frustrated he was that I wasn't doing enough for him and that his progress was stymied. The treatment seemed at an impasse.

On one level, I felt that Jim was re-enacting with me his relationship to the perpetrator of sexual abuse, re-experiencing the rage and frustration he felt then, and avoiding me by missing sessions just as he had tried to avoid contact with the abuser. Jim validated this interpretation and verbalized further discomforts with me. However, despite his complaints, he began to attend his appointments more frequently. Yet he continued to express anguish about his incapacity to be emotionally close with others.

In order to sort out why he wasn't making more progress, I decided to look at how my own subjectivity and sense of self contributed to the problem. I realized that – in order to shore up my self-esteem and assuage my feelings of guilt – I was taken in by Jim's idealization of me as an 'expert' and an all-giving rescuer, thereby denying my own vulnerability and anxiety. In order to further protect myself from narcissistic injury, I had perhaps also sworn him to secrecy about confronting my shortcomings and where I had failed him. Furthermore, I realized that I was experiencing vicarious trauma (Pearlman and Saakvitne, 1995) from the traumatic suffering which he brought into my office week after week. I surmised that I had secretly wished Jim would end treatment so that I could avoid my own pain and what may have been his accurate perception of my vulnerability.

I reflected with Jim that I might have appeared at times to be distant and unavailable to him, and that I might have wished he were a 'perfect patient' so that we wouldn't have to experience pain and anger together. I invited him to explore perceptions of me that he could have withheld. He breathed a sigh of relief as he said that he agreed with my reflections and had often wished I had been less of a 'blank screen' and more of an ordinary human being, and that indeed he often became angry and frustrated with me on account of my emotional distancing. Further, he had sometimes wondered whether I could tolerate and help him address the hopelessness, frustration, and anger that was the legacy of his sexual abuse. Bringing my side of the relationship and my subjective experience into the therapy helped Jim to be freer, more at ease, able to express a wider range of emotions. The treatment became less his monologue, and more a dialogue between us, and as a result his loneliness diminished. Further, he began to be more capable of intimacy with family members, co-workers, and friends.

Although it could be argued within a secular framework that what I had done was simply to fulfill my professional responsibility by addressing my countertransference, i.e. the obstacles to treatment within myself, I believe that this clinical experience of mutuality has a larger spiritual significance. My introspection and disclosure of my feelings included relational and soulful elements. First of all, it constituted a type of confessional on my part. By admitting my shortcomings and difficulties to Jim, I acknowledged my dark side to him and implicitly asked for his forgiveness. The admission also served as an act of restitution and reparation, insofar as it acknowledged and helped him to restore part of himself, namely his trust in his own perceptions and his ability to express, explore, and validate them. Further, I indicated my commitment not to defensively perpetuate whatever in myself might interfere with his care. Finally, I placed the therapy in the perspective of a meeting between equals, an I–Thou relationship in which we were both vulnerable, and both capable of growing, changing, and healing, both of us spiritual subjects seeking our common ground.

I hope I will be forgiven a quixotic 'leap of faith' when I say that for a moment, the patient and I saw God together. (Certainly, it would have been grandiose and sentimental for either of us to have viewed it that way at the time – we were just struggling to get somewhere with his treatment!) What I mean is that we formed a connection, a genuine relatedness that was missing or obscured before that juncture. Spirituality, as Buber (1970) suggested, is most fundamentally experienced as relatedness, 'oneness' with an other subject, a 'Thou.' The models of psychotherapy that have been based on duality and separateness of subject and object have great value in allowing us to dissect – and perhaps restore to 'normalcy' – minds that have gone astray, but sacrifice the sense of being inherently and deeply connected to one another in spirit. By viewing therapist and patient as 'subjects in relation' we allow mutuality, and even a sense of mystery, miracle, and awe, to occur. When we do that, I think it is fair to say that a spiritual experience has taken place.

Moving from 'object' to 'subject' in therapeutic discourse is a way towards Buber's 'I–thou' (as opposed to 'I–it') relationships. In such meetings, God is present as holy Other, a presence which hallows the world. Inferences about individual minds and internal objects drop off like autumnal leaves from a tree as our essential humanness is laid bare. Then it is possible for our discourse to have a holy quality, an urgent meaning in the here and now. This is not to negate the importance of an objective consideration of mental structures, which is often crucial in determining the sources of the patient's current dilemmas. But the movement in the course of treatment from detached, objective observation to a relationship between empathically attuned selves seems to me crucial to positive outcomes.

When such movement towards mutuality and relatedness occurs at ever deepening levels, spirituality becomes manifest in two ways. First, there emerges what Ogden (1994) has called the 'analytic third,' the felt presence of an additional subjectivity which incorporates but is beyond that of the patient and the therapist. This psychic presence may be sensed as a fateful movement in the treatment process, an atmosphere in the consulting room, or an uncanny feeling of ghostly presence. Although such experiences of a third are not necessarily identified as God-presence, I believe that they possess a similar structure in consciousness and have the potential to develop in the direction of mystical experience and spiritual awakening. Indeed, Jung held that these presences are archetypal representations of the collective unconscious, and Grotstein (2000) considers them expressions of the ineffable subject. The analytic third also serves as a type of supraordinate guide in the therapeutic journey, and may embody superego taboos and higher ethical values.

A further manifestation of relational spirituality in psychotherapy is an increasing focus upon awareness of the moment with lessened emphasis on historical inferences and reconstructions. Like lovers, therapist and patient eventually want to know what each is thinking and feeling at the moment it occurs. Therapeutic curiosity moves from 'how and why,' to 'who we are in the here and now.' In the long run, the possibility for self-transformation results more from spontaneous interactions between the two parties than from reconstructions of past events, although the latter may be very useful in putting present experience in proper perspective.

Ultimately, the movement in psychotherapy is beyond the relationship as such towards transcendence via the higher self, the 'ineffable subject' (Grotstein, 2000, pp.127–129), the self beyond speech and thought which is yet the source of all life energy and experience. As therapy reaches its apogee, it approaches 'God presence' wherein the 'I' of the patient and the 'Thou' of the therapist awesomely manifest the ineffable subject in each. Simultaneously, the analytic third manifests a holiness and divinity in which God makes Himself manifest at the meeting of two souls. The differentiated, 'objective' constructions that propelled the treatment yield to a relationship that approaches holy union.

Let us now stop for a moment and take stock of the whole. My aim throughout has been to bring together the various strands of modern scientific theories, religious thought, and developments in psychoanalysis and psychotherapy which have the potential to be woven into a psychospiritual understanding of the mental life and the developmental process. My ultimate goal is to accomplish a reversal of perspective from a psychology in which spirituality is icing on the cake, an epiphenomenal add-on to biological and social imperatives, to a view in which spirituality, since it both is inherent within and simultaneously transcends all experience, is the source and mediator of the whole self. The transition from one perspective (the biosocial) to the other (the psychospiritual) is negotiated in part by an in-depth understanding of relationship and subjectivity which has been the focus of object relations theory, self psychology, and the intersubjective and relational perspectives.

In the next chapter, I offer a synthesis of diverse perspectives, a paradigmatic view of human development and structure which is spiritually based. The concept which is at the center of my argument is what I call 'the psychospiritual self,' a self which is connected both to everyday realities and biosocial necessities and also to the much greater, and in many ways uncharted, territory of the unconscious which includes spiritual and religious experience.

CHAPTER EIGHT

The Psychospiritual Self

Up until now, I have been primarily discussing psychoanalytic perspectives which do not explicitly utilize a spiritual frame of reference. With the possible exception of Melanie Klein, I think that the relational theorists would agree that 'Man does not live by bread alone,' that we are driven not entirely by physical needs and instincts, as Freud had said, but seek something meaningful, purposeful, and whole in life. Relationalists would place human beings in the systems context of their relationships with significant others. They would attend to human needs for connectedness, creativity, and self-actualization. But they do not take the step of identifying spirituality itself as a basis for psychological understanding and treatment. I now wish to take that crucial step.

The key that opens this door is not an inspirational litany of man's spiritual achievements, whether moral, mystical, or cultural. However wonderful these accomplishments are, they can all be explained in terms of species survival and as complex self-regulatory mechanisms so that worship in a church or synagogue is a way of forming cohesive groups, and meditation offers a means of curbing desire, lust, and aggression. Further, the reductionist and skeptic can hold that spirituality is merely a cover for man's dark side and primal urges, citing horrific acts of child abuse, genocide, and greedy acquisition which are committed by the same individuals who profess religious beliefs. In such instances religion could with justification be viewed as a group mechanism to sustain the 'splitting' of the psyche, leaving the appearance of altruism and morality in the 'civilized' sector, while the negative half of the split manifests itself in our cutthroat dealings with each other, family dysfunction, antisocial behavior, and malevolent world affairs. These skeptical views are, of course, partly valid, but in my opinion represent not spirituality itself, but man's failure to embrace a deeper, healing spirituality. We have yet to learn how to live our individual and collective lives according to the spiritual principles we profess.

A spiritually-based psychology, to be deserving of the term, would have to show that spirituality is an inherent aspect of self experience, motivation, and behavior and provide an holistic view of the personality, including the dark side of our nature, suggesting ways in which splitting can be tempered and resolved, allowing human beings not only to have spiritual experiences but also to live harmoniously with one another as integrated and whole.

Three important sources of empirical evidence for a spirituality inherent in development are:

- infant research (some of which I previously mentioned) suggesting that a panoply of self capacities are available at the very beginning of extra-uterine life, so that an instinct-driven view of development is now being superseded by a living systems, relational perspective

- expanding research on higher states of consciousness, ranging from dreaming to the slowed brainwaves of meditators, to differentiated left/right brain functions, to the shifts in consciousness that occur with certain drugs and with electrical stimulation of the brain (Austin, 1999)

- studies of the increased capacity for perception, healing, altruism, concentration, intimacy, here-and-now aliveness, and 'God-experience' which are developed through spiritual practices (Levin and Chatters, 1998).

These wide-ranging empirical investigations suggest that there are dimensions of experience which incorporate but go well beyond biological and social necessity. The striking reality is that, until very recently, the systematic study of developmental wholeness, states of consciousness, and psychospiritual modes of healing have not been incorporated into mainstream psychology, whether psychoanalytic, cognitive, or behavioral. An expanding database has been at the disposal of psychologists for several decades, but the theoretical structure for organizing the diverse information is only now beginning to emerge.

Theory is thus a key to unlocking the door of psychospirituality by providing a paradigm and a conceptual framework which includes the spiritual dimension. Within such a rationale, it becomes possible to raise questions, formulate hypotheses, and develop treatment strategies, so that we begin to think of the psychospiritual as a legitimate and systematic area of investigation and practice, rather than a potpourri of personal testimonies, miracle cures, and research that is fascinating but uncoordinated. In what follows, I will give a beginning notion of such a formulation of the self.

To depict the personality from a spiritual standpoint, I sought a central concept rooted in an understanding of the development of the person from infancy onwards. I thought that there must be an inner core of the self which seeks spiritual fulfillment, just as there are aspects of self which seek self-validation and human relationships. Somehow that aspect of ourselves often gets put on the 'back burner,' and spiritual practices such as meditation and prayer help return it to the central place it deserves. I call this aspect of self the 'psychospiritual self'[1] and use this concept as a way of integrating my understanding of spiritual development. I will now try to define and refine that concept, recognizing that all definitions have a fuzzy edge where it is difficult to say what belongs to the definition and what does not. This ambiguity is all the more true in matters spiritual, since that which is of God is ultimately all-inclusive and inexpressible. What I delineate here is a developmental striving of each human being to seek God and/or some form of wholeness and enlightenment. First, however, I must elaborate on what is meant by 'the self' as such.

I am well aware that, especially in Zen Buddhism, enlightenment and transcendence imply the dissolution of and vanishing of the self. This would imply an opposition of self and spirit, which is also implied in Christian concepts of selflessness and of oneness with Christ. As I shall later suggest, experiences of oneness and of apparent dissolution of self are important facets of psychospirituality; but I believe, paradoxically, that a higher, spiritual self is present to experience the loss of the mundane self or ego. Without a self, spirituality would remain unconscious and unrecollected, and furthermore, the individual could not continue to carry out daily functions in mundane reality. I contend that, in spiritual experience, the self expands its circumference to wider circles of being, rather than dissolving.

The self itself

The self is the sum of what a person experiences as aspects of his 'being' and 'doing.' The dichotomy 'self' versus 'not-self' is universally present in development and across cultures. From birth, each of us begins to sort out what is inside himself and his body, what does and does not belong to him, and so on. Furthermore, the self is reflexive, that is, it is in dialogue with itself and knows itself, although some details are hidden from its view. Within such an inner dialogue, the self forms attachments, desires, wishes, values, motivations, and identifications. It incorporates aspects of others into itself. It becomes attached to and identifies with pleasurable and sensory experiences.

Such attachments and identifications fluctuate in the course of a day or a lifetime. I may consider my belief in God to be an integral part of myself, but during a period of doubting, I no longer 'own' that belief and view it as an abstract idea of others. Clinically, a patient with a hysteria may experience a limb in a detached way, believing that she cannot move it, as if it is not part of herself. On the other hand, a patient who has had a limb amputated feels as if it is still present, a 'phantom limb.' Furthermore, we commonly defend against anxiety by disavowing, denying, and projecting parts of self: 'I don't know why I did that – it wasn't like me.' Or else – 'I am not angry! You are!' shrieked loudly. This illustrates how the inner 'map' of the self may fluctuate as a result of our need for security, self-validation, and self-esteem. The boundaries of the self are permeable and in flux, dynamic rather than static.

The self boundary arises early in life with respect to what is inside and outside the body. Usually, 'self' and 'inside my body' are equated, so that if I notice a particular sensation from inside my body, I say that 'I am hungry,' while the chirping of a bird outside my window is 'not me' even though what actually registers in my nervous system is 'inside me' – air pressure on a part of my inner ear and a neurophysiological response to that pressure. Hence that birdcall in some respects resides within myself. It is *my* perception, and *I* make meaning out of it.

Poetry employs the equation of things 'external' with the self in metaphor. For example, T. S. Eliot's poem, 'East Coker' from the *Four Quartets* is about an English village by that name. Eliot writes of the destruction and rebuilding of the village's houses – how they rise and fall, live and die. Describing East Coker within a quickened time frame of generations, Eliot is really talking about our minds, our selves: remembering, forgetting, growing, withering within. The allusion to Ecclesiastes ('A time to live, a time to die…') cannot be missed. Eliot is writing about our spirit within. Ultimately, everything is within ourselves and our spirit.

Therefore, virtually everything we experience is 'self' by virtue of the fact that it is we who experience it. It is just that we attribute some aspects to external reality when our brain and ego compute them to be so. This self/non-self attribution process is very much to the point of spirituality, since God is alternately experienced as a part of oneself ('in our hearts'; 'the still, small voice within'), an external personification or revelation (God speaking to Moses from a cloud), or an 'atmosphere,' ambience, or context (The 'Holy Ghost'; the 'Spirit of my People'; 'God is everywhere, in everything'). While skeptical neuroscientists would conclude that the inability to decipher an object's location is due to the brain's deficiency in tracking the source of stimulation, it can also be viewed as evidence for the brain's extraordinary capacity to see the whole in its parts and parts in the whole. Metaphor and ambiguity constitute the creative ability to find extraordinary attributions within ordinary, mundane existence. Meissner (1986) has suggested that God experience often takes place in this magical, transitional space of illusion, so that God's 'location' may shift within and without the self.

As I mentioned earlier, the malleability of self experience has led some thinkers to consider that 'self' is merely a construction, a social convention, and they have endeavored to 'deconstruct' it, to show that self exists only as a mythical entity perpetuated by political and ideological forces (Rosenau, 1992, pp.42–61). In response, I can only suggest to them that they try to live even one minute of their lives without such a belief. I doubt they could do it. Self-reference is built into our language and our neural networks. I suggest that self is not an invention like television, but a part of us, like our eyes.

As I have suggested, some spiritual texts imply that the 'self' disappears when we experience God or enlightenment. While it is true that the boundaries of the self partially dissolve when one has such an experience, truly enlightened individuals are perfectly capable of recapturing their everyday sense of self at any time. One of my treasured memories is of the time I attended a weekend seminar with the renowned Swami Satchidananda. He spoke about selflessness and exemplified it in many wonderful ways during that weekend, including the tender words he spoke with serenity and grace. Then I laughed when I saw this bearded man in a white robe (Satch himself!) driving a student's sports car gleefully around the grounds! I soon learned that Swami Satchidananda had been an engineer in India, and loved finely tuned automobiles. Satchidananda could have his self and leave it too! He had a very distinct self and a self–other distinction. It was just that he was not attached to it, not overly invested in it. As he himself put it, we should be '*in* the world but not *of* the world.' Wear the garment of self loosely, but wear it.

The self has multiple components, roles, and identifications. I think of myself as a therapist, a writer, a lover, a businessperson, a wage earner who gets up in the morning and shuffles his way to the shower ('Everyman,' so to speak). So the question becomes, where in this mix do we find 'spiritual' selfhood? Is it to be found within our many roles, around, behind, or above them? Does such a spiritual self really exist? Unlike the postmodern deconstructionists, I believe that it does. I am convinced that there is a spiritual center of our being which also penetrates our other self-attributions and evolves throughout the life cycle. It is to this spiritual component of self that I now turn our attention.

The psychospiritual self

I define the psychospiritual self as that aspect of our selfhood which constitutes our enduring essence and reflects what is called the 'spirit,' the ways in which we comprehend and relate to 'the big picture,' that which is outside time and space, is God, or whatever it may be that encompasses us but is larger and more meaningful than us as singular, time-limited beings. The psychospiritual self gives our lives coherence and spontaneity. Although we sometimes seek these qualities in possessions, drugs, and relationships, these efforts often fail us, or else serve as rites of passage on the way to discovering our core spiritual selves. The psychospiritual self is our 'telos,' the background driving force of our lives, through which we are seeking union with a mysterious Other.

In my view, which coincides with Jung's, 'God' is an empty theological concept unless He, She, or It is experienced in relation to this deep part of our own nature. A genuine spiritual awakening opens us up to our core selves as much as it tells us something about God and the cosmos. It has been said that 'Prayer does not change God; it changes the one who prays.' As a change agent, psychotherapy can be thought of as a prayer invoking the spiritual self. Peak experiences upon seeing the mountains or the ocean or a van Gogh painting can also serve as a meditation and a prayer by creating a resonance between our conscious egos and our psychospiritual self.

The central element of the spiritual self, and that which defines our 'being in the world' is our consciousness, the subjective experiencing self, the 'I' that is aware of itself and the flow of experience. The self-as-subject is thus different from the ego and is integral to the Higher Self or spiritual self. When we reflect upon self independently of the objects of perception and experience, we arrive at 'pure consciousness.' The philosopher Edmund Husserl (Smith and Smith, 1995, pp.342–346) called this component the 'pure *I*' or 'transcendent ego.' Buddhism calls it Enlightenment. The Hindus call it bliss. Grotstein (2000, pp.127–129) calls the pure self the 'ineffable subject,' because it cannot be put into words or given definition. It transcends the objects of sensation and cognition. It is that which is unlike anything that exists and yet is responsible for everything that exists.

Parenthetically, but very importantly, I do not wish to imply that the concepts of pure consciousness, transcendental ego, Enlightenment, bliss, and ineffable subject are identical in meaning. A consideration of their similarities and differences would make for a rich dialogue. Rather, I am suggesting that each entails a component in which the conscious, perceiving subject transcends and has a distinctly different status from the objects of his perception. But each specific concept of transcendent subjectivity has connotations related to its specific religious, scientific, or philosophical system of thought.

Awareness of our ultimate subjectivity (independent of the objects of its perception) leads to our ability to perceive and affirm the subjectivity of our fellows. Buber (1970) called the subjective self 'I [in relation to] Thou,' a consciousness in which we see ourselves and others not as things or objects but as hallowed beings. The capacity to empathize with another is an ability of great human import which is acquired in the child's earliest relationships to caregivers (Benjamin, 1990). Autistic children, for example, have difficulty making such a connection, and self-centered, narcissistically disordered individuals do so only reluctantly. This lack profoundly truncates their spiritual and personal growth.

The question of whether pure consciousness, transcendental ego, ineffable subject requires a universal 'otherness' like God is a fascinating one and appears to differentiate various forms of meditation and religious belief. In a remarkable dialogue for our time (DeMartino, 1971), Christian philosopher and theologian Paul Tillich and the Zen master Hisamatsu compared their views on what constitutes an enlightened state. As I understand it, they agreed on all points, except that Tillich held that spiritual consciousness includes an anticipation of God, while Hisamatsu insisted that Enlightenment was immediate awareness without such anticipation. I find intriguing the play on words that Grotstein (2001) uses to bring these views together: 'There is a God; and He is the only one who knows He doesn't exist!' In some of his writings, Jung (Hayman, 1999, p.412) radically implied that when God created the world, He was unconscious! These heretical-sounding statements are attempts, I think, to grapple with what it is that comes before the 'advent' of the sentient subject. Whatever these differences may be – whether God exists, knows He exists, is Subject or Object – contemporary Buddhist and Judao-Christian perspectives are in agreement that there is holiness in the 'subject' as such, as pure non-objectified Being. Whether pure subjective being requires an external 'object' or another 'subject' to realize its holiness, or whether the subject that is empty of otherness is most holy, is the question that was raised in the dialogue between Hisamatsu and Tillich. My stance in this book, a position which admittedly fluctuates in my own thinking about the problem, is that the ineffable subject requires an Other to realize itself. Paradoxically, however, the subject is most capable of such realization when it is emptied of memory, desire, and understanding. That is the paradox of mysticism.

The reader will inevitably wonder about the relationship between the psychospiritual self and the soul. They are related concepts, and while Jung (1933), Bettelheim (1983), and others have set precedents for psychologists referring to the 'soul,' I choose not to use that word simply because, although it is rich and relevant, I wish to avoid some of the connotations of 'soul' in religion, philosophy, and everyday discourse. For example, as I said earlier, I do not think of the spiritual self as incorporeal, i.e. separate from the body and detached from it at death. In my opinion, pure consciousness transcends bodily limitations, but it requires a body to manifest. The spiritual self is in my view profoundly linked to the body, although it has the capacity to differentiate from and transcend the body in some ways. The spiritual self is a 'Siamese twin' of the body, linked to it but different. This confluence of body and soul is reflected in yoga in the idea of a 'subtle body' which includes *prana* (breath) and the chakras (energy centers).

I also wish to avoid the implication that spiritual self is being 'judged' by God, as disembodied souls are in Purgatory. I think that God has unconditional love for each person's spiritual self and He gave it a body for good reasons. After all, if we are to believe Genesis, it is this embodied self which God fashioned to be His or Her mirror image and friend. If God 'judges' anything, it is how we work out our lives and our values, not the essence of our being, which is always His alone.

While I certainly hope and pray that each of us has a soul, for me the usefulness of the concept of the psychospiritual self is that it allows us to study *in vivo* the development of a person's spirituality from birth to death in the context of his embodied existence. While, like the soul, psychospirituality contains a person's unchanging essence, the core spiritual self also evolves and changes over the course of a lifetime. I would like now to explore that developmental process.

The early development of the psychospiritual self

The 'pristine ego'

Although by no means the whole picture, it has often been considered that a baby is born uncontaminated into the world, a 'clean slate,' as the philosopher John Locke put it. Such a view holds that everything we know is the result of learning. Many psychologists now take exception to Locke and believe that the self is born with inherent anxieties (Segal, 1989, pp.122–136), conflicting needs (Sullivan, 1953), distinct temperaments (Kagan, 1994), and 'wired-in' cognitive, linguistic, and cultural schemata (Piaget, 1969; Chomsky, cf. Newsom and Cook, 1995; Levi-Strauss, cf. DeGeorge and DeGeorge, 1972). Nevertheless, there does seem to reside in the newborn a component of self which possesses a purity, wholeness, untarnished innocence, and spontaneity, a 'pristine ego.'

This 'clean, whole, and pure' aspect of self seeks both solitude (Storr, 1989) and human contact, a relationship with 'an other' (usually the mother) with whom to engage in a nonverbal dialogue. We now know, for example, that the newborn baby initiates spontaneous play (Brazelton and Als, 1979). While it was formerly believed that contact and relatedness is initiated by the caregiver and so is learned, we now know that the infant has a 'wired-in' disposition to make contact. The newborn's innate, uncontaminated spontaneity, initiatives, and interactions are, for me, among the first manifestations of the psychospiritual self.

Freud and Klein mistakenly ignored this pristine, contact-seeking aspect of the newborn. So, while their theories are insightful, they are one-sided, reflecting what Ricoeur (1970) called the 'hermeneutics of suspicion,' a tendency to interpret the unconscious with an acute awareness of the discrepancy between what is stated and what it implies. Freudian and Kleinian perspectives presuppose an underlying desire and aggression in all behaviors, an inherent 'sinfulness' underlying all thought and action. While such a viewpoint has heuristic value in uncovering unconscious motivation, it ignores what that every loving parent knows – that an innate part of the infant, both private and 'public,' is innocent, clear, and whole. For me, this pristine ego is the developmental seed of the psychospiritual self.

The self's 'fall from grace'

Tragically, yet central to all spiritual development, this pristine state of being quickly finds itself inundated with conflicts and anxieties. The pristine self soon perceives and identifies with its body, feels pain, discomfort, frustration, abandonment, emptiness, insatiability. In response to such conflict and division within himself, he experiences himself alternately as all-powerful and all-knowing (omnipotent and omniscient), versus helpless and dependent; like Prometheus, powerful, free, and unbounded, then bound and vulnerable. He attempts to work out his inner struggles around pleasure and pain with an 'other' outside himself, usually his mother. He has thus left Eden and entered the paranoid-schizoid position.

These initial struggles are defining moments for the psychospiritual self, which now needs actively to maintain its pristine essence while at the same time surviving and growing in a body in time and space, in the first declension of the flesh (after Dylan Thomas, 1971). The self becomes embroiled in matters of survival and desire. The spiritual self thus begins to work out its existence in the context of the body, desires, envy, aggression, and boundaries, all of which cloud its awareness of its purity, boundlessness, and wholeness. It becomes involved in the process of living, which, however difficult, is also a manifestation of its spirituality.

The stories of Adam and Eve and of Christ reflect this development. The primal couple are ejected from Paradise as a consequence of their serpentine initiation to the awareness of Good and Evil, desire and envy. Thus begins the lineage of the tribes of Israel, tribes that, however troubled and rivalrous, will produce religious precepts, a Messiah, and a diaspora that will take them to many places on the globe and will even survive the greatest curse and violation of all: attempted genocide, the Holocaust. However placid their lives in Eden, Adam and Eve would have remained static and ignorant had they not discovered the 'good/bad' dichotomy and all the sins of which they were capable. The paradox is that sin – despite its potential for harm – is the basis of all spiritual growth because it leads man to conscious self-reflection.

'Redemption' is the reminder that we possess a pure consciousness, a pristine self, to which we must ever return. In Christ, God comes to earth as a human being. He empathizes with humankind, struggles with His demons in the desert, proclaims His godliness, suffers persecution, and is crucified. But in his brief sojourn among suffering humanity, Jesus conveys the message that our inherent spirituality is pure, uncontaminated, undying, and eternal. He tells us in so many ways that we, as collective humanity, have forgotten this aspect of ourselves – we have, in psychoanalytic language, repressed its memory. We become quickly caught up in externals and forget who and what we are in our origins. Yet, paradoxically, this forgetting initiates our development, and ultimately, resurrection.

The 'salvation' provided by 'good enough mothering'

Importantly, 'good enough mothering' (Winnicott, 1960a) can and should mitigate the child's loss of pristine innocence and 'fall from grace,' providing a buffer that allows the child space in which to grow both in the world and in spirit. In this context, Winnicott described the functions of mother's 'holding.'

According to Winnicott, mother provides a 'holding environment' through which the infant can survive disruption, acquire a sense of 'going on being' (1960a, p.47), and experience his continuity in time. Erikson (1950) spoke of 'basic trust' and Eigen (1985) talked about 'faith' as outgrowths of these earliest experiences of holding and safety. The infant acquires a trust that the environment will provide for its needs in a dependable way. He has faith that mother is potentially available to him even when she is not directly present. These experiences of being held generate the precursors of a faith in a God who is not of the senses, whose availability is immanent even when He appears to be absent, and who provides for our 'daily bread,' even when rewards seem sparse.

An evolving faith in someone or something 'invisible' to the senses is what allows the core spiritual self to proceed on its journey. This is one of the remarkable puzzles and paradoxes of the soul, that it seeks both a visible and invisible world, that it loves the experiences of the senses, but at the same time has a relationship to the unseen, the mysterious, the 'wholly other,' 'pure thought,' essences. For the infant, this mystical connection is a 'weak force' which is easily derailed, but the need for it runs deep and emerges early in development. Without an emotional connection to an unseen essence, a human being cannot grow and, if anything, will become a mere image, vestige, and imitation of himself, a 'false self' (Winnicott, 1960b). An acquired faith in an invisible maternal essence is what allows the infant's self to 'go on being' in the expectable absences of visible, palpable nurturance.

The transitional space and object

In the context of 'going on being,' a rudimentary 'space' develops in which the infant utilizes parts of his own body and external objects for soothing and comfort in mother's absence. First the infant sucks his thumb in place of the breast. Then he clings to a soft terry cloth. Eventually, he hugs and drags around a doll or teddy bear. The infant makes of this 'transitional object' (transitional between self and mother, self and world, one developmental stage and another – cf. Winnicott, 1951) whatever he wants and needs: one minute to hug, the next to drag, tear, and pummel! The parents respect this object and the space in which it exists as if it is 'sacred,' meaning that it is the infant's sanctuary, its domain, its 'first not-me possession.' They intuitively recognize the transitional object to be an important part of the infant's developing self. Winnicott held that the transitional object links the early experiences with mother to his subsequent attachments to the larger world of culture and society, with its collective norms, symbols, and meanings. He does so because it is an external object which the child can invest with his own personal significance.

The transitional space and object are, according to Meissner (1986), the developmental basis of the sacred space and objects of the religious sanctuary and rituals. The transitional space provides an emotionally secure environment in which to fantasize, create, destroy, and imagine the seashores of endless worlds (after Tagore). Similarly, in the sacred religious space, a person can be free of the demands of the world long enough to make God his own in communion. Not only is the space of the sanctuary made available for such purposes, but also the sacred objects, liturgy, rituals, and atmosphere of the religious service serve as transitional objects for stimulating and channeling inward communion and meditation.

The significance of the transitional space and object for development is poignantly seen when they are disrupted. For example, a young man, Phil, came to treatment following a suicide attempt. He remembered that, in childhood, his chronically depressed mother had deprived him of all his toys. Years later, Phil sought to destroy himself because the inner space in which he could exist and grow was already decimated. In his own words, he felt 'empty, helpless, and inadequate to fulfill myself and become a person.' He lacked the transitional space and objects by which to develop his true self and his potential.

The emotional significance of the transitional space is one reason why – by extension – we need to respect a person's religious beliefs, whatever they may be, and however they differ from our own. At its best, religion allows for a transitional space where the self can 'go on being.' It provides cognitive schemata that negotiate between the requirements of daily life and the psychospiritual self. However, individuals sometimes utilize religious convictions in a desperate way, clinging to them rather than remaining open to new experience. Therapists know that at times they must clarify and rectify this defensive use of spirituality, yet must not challenge the patient's belief system prematurely. Likewise, a spiritual teacher has a sense of when and when not to guide the aspirant into the 'briar patches' of darkness and uncertainty which are an essential part of the spiritual journey. A teacher who leads his student prematurely into these realms without a transitional 'teddy bear' may induce a state of spiritual emergency. Such states of psychosis and trauma have become a growing concern of religious seekers and mental-health workers today (Grof and Grof, 1989).

Winnicott's true and false self

Returning to the subject of child development, if the processes of maternal holding, going on being, the development of trust and faith, and the evolution of a transitional space and object go well, the child becomes able to negotiate between the Scylla of direct confrontation with his spiritual core and the Charybdis of the demands of real-life interactions with others that constitute his evolving functionality, competence, narrative, and autobiography. He does not need to retreat into himself and erect a 'false self' (Winnicott, 1960b) to shield him from feared catastrophes with others, but can, relatively speaking, 'be himself,' his true self, genuine and authentic both in solitude and in interactions with others. Then, and only then, can the self have access to a wide range of feelings and desires to propel spontaneity, creativity, and living structure. By contrast, the false self is fragile and regresses to early dependencies, or else acts out destructively. We see this vulnerability manifested in addictions and compulsions, where the person turns to a substance for temporary relief and stimulation, while simultaneously seeking and avoiding feared contact with the true self. Drugs and alcohol, for example, may provide a euphoria and altered state of consciousness akin to religious ecstasy. However, the experience is never integrated with the necessities of daily functioning in the world. The person may become increasingly dependent on the substance for relief and less able to cope with the demands of reality.

In psychological trauma, the false self may initially be the only protection remaining to the wounded true self, so that traumatized patients often dissociate and withdraw emotionally to cope with the overwhelming event. The 'assumptive world' (Janoff-Bulman, 1992) which contains the person's core beliefs is damaged, dissociated, and sequestered as a result of such violations of boundaries and security. The person acts 'as if' he is functioning normally, when in fact his true self, inner world, and meaning context have been shattered by the trauma, a condition that Shengold (1989) calls 'soul murder.' There is evidence that spirituality and practices of transcendence can help restore the assumptive world and the true self that have been damaged by psychological trauma (Pearlman, 2001, pp.219–220).

In my view, Winnicott's (1960b) 'true self' is closely related to, but not identical with, what I mean by the psychospiritual self. These self systems do, however, overlap and ideally should have a mutually facilitating relationship. The true self interfaces with the world and strives for genuineness and authenticity in the face of difficult social realities and conformity pressures. It is an interpersonal system. The psychospiritual self seeks to preserve essences in the face of disruptions, sensory stimulation, and desire. It is a transpersonal system. In order to be genuine and authentic, one needs to know one's essence, and, conversely, in order to access and preserve essence, one needs to exist interpersonally in an authentic way. The person who is genuine and authentic can negotiate relationships with a high degree of access to his evolving spiritual essence. He can 'own' his self-developed meanings, beliefs, doubts, feelings, and fantasies while maintaining closeness with others. The true self is thus a self-regulating aspect of our being which allows for spiritual survival and growth in transactions with others and with the world. It allows the spiritual self to experience its descent into the flesh while retaining its pristine connection to the invisible, ineffable subject. By way of illustration, 'To be or not to be' is the dilemma faced by Hamlet's psychospiritual self. Polonius' advice, 'To thine own self be true' is encouragement to Hamlet, a disenchanted prince, to maintain his authenticity (true self) in order to sustain his spirituality under duress. In Shakespeare's drama, Hamlet's spirituality is challenged by the evil that surrounds him and is sustained by the meaning context of fidelity to his father, the murdered king, and the moral order of the kingdom.

The importance of the true self in negotiating life's vicissitudes is shown by the fact that patients often come to treatment with difficulties in integrating their spiritual essence with 'real world' needs and concerns. Whether stressed from their careers, in conflict with their families, or confused about relationships, they often articulate painful dilemmas in reconciling their deepest convictions and sense of self with life situations and their interactions with others. They feel 'frustrated' with their life trajectory and thwarted in realizing their destiny. As Eigen (1998, pp.95–116) suggests, they can be plagued by such dilemmas even when they are highly evolved in other areas of spirituality, for example, in the practice of meditation. Meditation strengthens one transpersonally, but psychotherapy is often needed to enahance the true self's ability to regulate the balance between spiritual needs, relationships, ambitions, and daily life.

Spirituality, desire, and reality

The need for essence and authenticity are as crucial for emotional development as the need for food and security, and this is true even for a child. The traditional account of children's 'frustration' is misleading in this respect, holding that the child is a 'beast of desire and greed' who becomes upset, frustrated, tearful, and rageful because his wishes and demands for gratification are not immediately fulfilled. 'His majesty the baby' (a phrase used by Freud) wants what he wants when he wants it. He must learn, his caregivers say, to tolerate delay of gratification and to live with moderate provisions.

It is true that some of the child's frustrations are material, but many of them are interpersonal and spiritual. Freud and Dann's (1951) study of children during the London Blitz showed that children coped better with the daily disruptions of bombardment within their home and family than when taken to safety in the countryside, away from their parents. The point is that some frustrations are related not to survival and satiation (the Freudian 'id') but to the deeper needs of the true self and the spiritual self.

Children's spirituality consists of access to the 'numinous,' the mysterious, ineffable, and magical. The mysterious and the magical are not just about fantasy and illusion – they are also an avenue to essences within the self. When children are frustrated and 'whiny,' they are sometimes calling for a 'refueling' of numinosity which restores their sense of self. Sharing a quiet time reading a fairytale, taking a walk in the woods, having a mutual appreciation of the mystery of it all, and good-natured laughter, can be soothing and healing to children. It allows them to return to their often confusing daily lives feeling understood and true to themselves. They have recontacted their spiritual essences.

What are the 'real world' requirements of the adult's psychospiritual self? The conventional religious answer is: 'Nothing!' After all, say the preachers, our spiritual hunger is gratified by God. Of this 'daily bread,' some believe they are completely nourished by virtue of their religious convictions. They may berate others for having impulses and desires. In psychotherapy, we sometimes find that such individuals, despite their bland exterior, are bitter and envious or contend that they have been betrayed by someone significant in their past. The truth is that, because we are human, our spiritual needs and hungers require renewal and replenishing in the context of significant others. Even infants and young children can become spiritually deprived and needy. Psychospirituality, far from representing total self-sufficiency, seeks realization in life itself. Here, in fact, is where the present paradigm differs from that of Jung. It is our lives as lived that constitute our spirituality. Archetypal images and myths are simply templates for realizing our spirituality in our lives. The ultimate determinant of the quality of our spirituality is how we incorporate such archetypes and our spiritual essences in our lives as lived, in our journey, in our emotional and interpersonal reality.

The 'Trinity' of spirituality: union, infinity, and the mysterious other

We see that the psychospiritual self has inner needs that seek realization in our life's journey. Through the vehicle of the true self, it tries to realize its numinosity in its journey, its narrative, its interactions with others. Strivings for possessions, sex, and power incorporate spirituality as the self seeks to meet its deeper, soulful needs.

The special needs of the core spiritual self are for *oneness* (union, communion), *infinitude* (oceanic feelings and expansiveness), and access to the *mysterious*, invisible essence of its own divine Source and Lifespring. Psychospirituality strives for *purity, innocence*, and *wholeness*.

The core spiritual self feels restricted by boundaries, rules, and limitations. It wants to attain an original oneness with all things, great and small. It is the part of ourselves which longs to dissolve the boundaries with a lover, become fully absorbed in creative work, and/or be united with a 'Higher Power.' It seeks a relationship with the mysterious and the dimly known, unseen Other. Union, infinity, and the mysterious Other form a 'Trinity' of spirituality.

It is striking that these three needs and experiences have been either omitted in traditional psychology or regarded as by-products of motives which are based on our separateness and isolation: pleasure and the need to relieve pain. I know of no mainstream psychology where strivings for union, infinity, and mystery are considered fundamental to human existence. In truth, spiritual selfhood requires experiential nutriments to keep it from wasting away or perpetually longing for another existence. In a very real sense, 'Spirituality is destiny.' Whatever personal goals a person pursues in life, his spiritual nature will eventually make itself known, whether in its re-alization or in the price paid for ignoring it.

Oneness, union, and communion

Contemporary culture places so much emphasis on technology, acquiring in-formation, making calculations, and achieving concrete goals and objectives that our wish for union and communion is ordinarily attenuated. For instance, most of us appreciate the ecstatic feeling of being one with a lover, whether in embrace, sexual ecstasy, or sharing a moment of joy together. And most of us enjoy being carried away by a sports event, music, a work of art, or a scene in nature, relishing the temporary dissolving of the boundaries between ourselves and the world around us. We can recognize the Darwinian 'survival' value of such experiences of union and communion, since they enhance our lives within the group, foster our interest in the world, and provide a creative 'muse' to inspire us in our ambitions and purposes. Such inspirational and motivating experiences can thus be attrib-uted to our survival needs, our social existence, and our need to explore new possibilities. Experiences of oneness have also been shown to reduce stress (Benson and Proctor, 1985), which is valuable for our physical and mental health. In daily life, these experiences of union come and go, but, sadly, may succumb to practical pressures. Under such circumstances, we feel a lack in our lives.

Although our conscious, adaptive ego seeks union for survival reasons, oneness is not a contingent process but essential to the sustenance and growth of the self. There is a developmental explanation for the fact that oneness is a primary need. Prior to birth our spiritual core is properly sheltered from, and has never known, separation as such. In the womb, existence depends on connectedness and continuity with the amniotic fluid and mother's bloodstream. Soon after birth, the infant manifests anxiety when separated from mother. Later in life, when we encounter a major loss, there follows disbelief, as if separation from the loved one doesn't belong to our universe and can't be understood. Our spiritual selves cannot easily grasp separation, which induces what could be called 'spiritual suffering.'

Until the self has undergone the painful 'dying of the soul', the spiritual self feels traumatized each time it makes contact with the reality of separation and loss. Once it has 'died,' it eternally experiences oneness. We must die in order to be reborn in a state of union. Chronic unfaced fear of death perpetuates a very limited existence. There is a continual trade-off between life and death of self. Our earthly existence itself militates against union: what defines us also separates us. So, in order to 'be' spiritually, we must die in the self, and in order to define ourselves humanly, we must yield some of our primal unity. But this unity is a universal component of our spiritual nature, a longing which never leaves us.

The ego-psychological explanation of our desire for oneness is that it derives from the infantile period of 'blissful symbiosis' with the mother (Mahler, Pine, and Bergman, 1975). In Mahler's theory the infant is born emotionally separated and isolated from the environment. The pleasure principle and the need for a caregiver precede and stimulate the experience of oneness and establish its desirability. When the child discovers a 'need-satisfying object,' he wants to be 'one' with this object, and experiences a 'blissful symbiosis.' While I do not discount the importance of need gratification in stimulating such an attachment, I also view 'oneness' as a primary state of being within the self. An important premise of the psychospiritual paradigm is that we all possess an inborn 'template' in which it is oneness that is natural and separation that is unfamiliar and problematical. I believe that, as a result, we all intuit, remember, and desire union. Further, *all* desire is ultimately for oneness. Fairbairn (1952, p.33) said that 'Pleasure is the signpost to the object,' meaning that relationship is the primary motivator, not instinct. The psychospiritual paradigm goes even further and holds that relationship and attachments are signposts to union. We relate to others out of a primary striving to re-create our original oneness.

For well over a century, mainstream psychology and psychotherapy have been dominated by the notion that oneness is a manifestation of mental illness. Within such a framework, differentiation is the goal of development, and those who lack the self–other distinction are 'insane.' For instance, psychiatrists note that the psychotic individual fails to differentiate between self and object, has merged with the outside world, and as a result cannot distinguish reality from fantasy. The schizophrenic, for example, thinks that what he has imagined is real, and vice versa. Clinical experience, however, tells us that this premise is only a half-truth, for psychotic patients are profoundly isolated, and have difficulty establishing contact with others. Their inordinate need to merge with others is, in my opinion, a way of coping with their isolation. Their fusion of self and other is in many cases a desperate attempt to obtain an illusory contact, when internally they feel like a particle of self in a voided world. Psychosis is primarily a disease of emptiness, fragmentation, and betrayal, not of oneness and union.

Significantly, spiritual union is not so much a loss of distinctiveness as it is a joyful interplay of self and other. It is an exchange process and dialogue, rather than a state of confusion and loss of distinction. It is an emotion, attitude, or sentiment of 'semi-permeability' that does not obliterate distinction but transcends it. I can be one with a lover, with God, or the cosmos and yet fully aware of my surroundings and able to relate to my fellow human beings as distinct and separate persons. Union and communion of the spirit is a resilient and adaptive state of mind that allows a person more, not fewer, options for responsiveness to significant others and the demands of life.

Western psychology has become estranged from healthy experiences of union. The current spectrum of 'scientific, evidence-based' psychotherapies, whether cognitive, behavioral, solution-oriented, or psychoanalytic, aim at disillusioning patients from such sentiments, correcting their cognitive distortions, and seeking behavioral changes so that they may follow the laws of logic and necessity. When a person is in a state of union, binary (true/false) logic is replaced by 'divergent thinking' – the ability to see possibilities – and logical 'necessity' becomes secondary. But anyone who has experienced such union knows how meaningful and personally relevant it is! We would gladly give up many needs and gratifications in order to sustain the exhalted state that we are in!

The prejudice of traditional psychology against states of oneness and union is not entirely without foundation. 'Oneness' can indeed become a problematical state. We need our boundaries and separations. The origins of difficulties between oneness and separateness start with the self's awareness of its skin (Bick, 1968). In living systems terms, the skin is a semipermeable membrane which both sustains contact with the outside world through its pores and sense of touch, and establishes a boundary which keeps out toxic substances. When you touch someone, you simultaneously feel the boundary (separation) and the contact (oneness). Yet the core spiritual self does not initially have a skin! It lived in a warm fluid for nine months as a fetus, where distinctions between self and other were almost non-existent. It will need considerable reassuring contact with mother's skin in order to feel 'safe' again.

There are patients who compulsively cut their skin. Most people think it must be painful to do so and wonder why anyone would do that to themselves. But these patients will tell you that they feel better when they cut themselves, even that it is pleasurable. This is not merely masochism. They are trying to break a skin barrier that has proved so confounding to them. They have a special difficulty restoring the sense of oneness that we all take so much for granted that we don't even notice we are bathed in it as we go about our more differentiated activities. When they puncture the skin barrier, these patients feel a temporary contact with a world from which they ordinarily feel cut off.

Drive theories give primacy to primal urges and instincts. Object relations theories such as those of Fairbairn and Winnicott give primacy to interpersonal systems. Attachment theories such as Bowlby's (1969) hold that bonding is itself a basic instinct, thus implying a distinct line of development of attachments. Psychospiritual theories of self go beyond all of these perspectives and hold that oneness and union as such are built into the very molecules that are the building blocks of life, and are reflected in more complex personality and mental systems. Oneness is a fundamental living systems principle, and the root biological instincts and bonding processes of mammalian life are reflections or by-products of the connectedness and oneness that all living systems require for survival. Once a biological system is cut off from its surrounding sources, it dies.

Biosystemic, interpersonal, and psychospiritual union differ from each other more in their scope than in their essence. Spiritual union involves the union of the whole self with an Other who is all-encompassing and all-enveloping. Interpersonal oneness involves limited aspects of the self and the other. Satisfying a hunger or thirst is still more limited and momentary. For example, a sensation of oneness can be gotten from eating and 'merging with' a delicious icecream sundae (or, more dangerously, a drug), but the experience is only partial and brief. A feeling of merger with another person on the basis of physical desire is more emotionally encompassing, but it is short-lived and only gives us a 'sensation' of the ecstatic and the divine.

By contrast, a genuine spiritual awakening has a lasting impact on many levels of the personality. The individual is changed and transformed. In fact, one of the adaptive features of the psychospiritual self is that experiences which filter through it have an impact throughout the psyche. It constitutes a powerful reorganizing force in development. It is holistic rather than specific. It is integrative rather than splitting, fragmenting, and divisive of aspects of self. It is, in a word, infinite, another concept which traditional psychology finds difficult to assimilate.

'The void and formless infinite'

In *Paradise Lost*, the poet John Milton wrote:

> The rising world of waters dark and deep,
> Won from the void and formless infinite.
>
> ...
>
> So much the rather thou, celestial Light,
> Shine inward, and the mind through all her powers
> Irradiate, there plant eyes, all mist from thence
> Purge and disperse, that I may see and tell
> Of things invisible to mortal sight.

(Milton, 1667)

The human need for infinite, boundaryless, and even 'chaotic' experience, evident in John Milton's poem, which was written during the 17th-century Restoration period, later provided a motivating force for the Romantic and Modernist movements in literature and the arts. Yet, to the logically minded positivist, such a universal need seems a wanton and unreasonable assumption, and the logically minded have dominated psychology and psychoanalysis since their inception. It could be cogently argued that the repression of infinitude has done as much or more damage than the repression of sexual desire which was a root cause of emotional distress during the Victorian era. Now that sex is *au courant*, amounting to a marketable commodity and a multi-billion-dollar global industry, and now that we have sophisticated ways of 'improving' human relationships, from designer perfumes to couples workshops, we often ask ourselves why, in this 'best of all possible worlds,' we are so unable to stay rooted and know who and what we are. One reason is that we have systematically undone our need for infinitude. We are obsessed with quantifying, demarcating, capturing, naming, and truncating every aspect of our experience.

Infinity is both a mathematical concept and an emotional state. Mathematically, infinity means very simply that you can never stop the process of counting. You can't limit the number. Yet infinity does have mathematical meaning: there are numerous mathematical studies devoted to infinity. There are orders or magnitudes of infinity. It has proved possible to think about the infinite even though it can't be given a specific number. Indeed, our brains seem inherently to know about infinity. The brain is comparable to a personal computer that has access to the internet and cyberspace. Its 'hard disk' (memory and cognitive schemata, the brain's 'software') has a massive but finite amount of memory 'gigabytes,' but cyberspace, for all practical purposes, contains infinite gigabytes of information. The brain that is open to itself and its environment acquires infinite dimensions. Under those conditions, the mind expands and opens to new realms. As Grotstein (1978) says, the mind is capable of not just four dimensions (three-dimensional space plus time) but an infinite number of them. A metaphor, for instance, has infinite dimensionality; and so do certain passages in music. There is no limit to what these metaphors and musical experiences can connote. Our mind seems to go to all these infinite places at once. We realize there is a 'cutting edge' to such experiences, that possibilities mean as much as probabilities. For example, Blake's metaphor of the 'Tyger, tyger, burning bright' with its 'fearful symmetry,' and the last movement of Beethoven's Ninth Symphony invoke such infinite possibilities. The scope of these works seems to have no bounds in our consciousness. The tiger's 'fearful symmetry' has unimaginable power. The joy of human friendship and freedom expressed in Schiller's poem 'Ode to Joy' and Beethoven's symphony leads to heavenly ascendance.

The spiritual self seeks and requires experiences of the infinite. The emotions of such moments are ecstasy and awe. Even children crave the infinite: the magic lands of fairytales and the boundless enthusiasm children show towards new discoveries and skills reveal to what an extent the infinite is part of their consciousness. We are born with this capacity for infinitude. The mother's breast sometimes must feel like an infinite provider to the hungry infant. The core spiritual self needs this infinite breast as much as our physical hunger and thirst need milk. It is a way out of the claustrophobic sensation of being enclosed within the womb, the birth canal, the skin. The infinite is a way of opening the door to genuine intimacy, to our dreams, fantasies, imagination, and God.

The mysterious and invisible essence

We live in an age where the entire universe appears to be calculable and knowable. As I mentioned earlier, the Enlightenment philosophy of the 18th and 19th centuries (for example, the work of Bacon, Descartes, Locke, and Hume) implied that the universe is analagous to a large clock and that every piece of machinery in it could eventually be described and predicted. Current positivist thinking similarly holds that all meaningful entities are describable logically and in terms of sense data (Sarkar, 1996). Some scientists are busy looking for a set of equations that would account for the totality of the universe since the beginning of cosmological time (Hawking, 2001). By contrast, a few philosophers, like Immanuel Kant (Allison, 1983), claimed that there were areas of 'unknowability,' that what we do know leads inevitably to the awareness of what we do not know, and that knowing that this is true is the gateway to still deeper truths. The most important things in life are mysterious and unknowable – this much we can surely know.

Spirituality itself is one of those mysterious and unknowable essences. No matter how much we are in contact with this aspect of our experience, aspects of it remain inaccessible and mysterious, like the enigmatic smile of the Mona Lisa. This 'ineffability' is what gives us the feeling of a disembodied 'soul' lurking somewhere deep inside. We can't speak about it, see it, describe it, but we know it is a part of us. Our mysterious soulfulness is, as Grotstein (2000) says, a 'psychic presence.'

Like attracts like. The core spiritual self qua mystic seeks a relationship with the mysterious, ineffable, hidden, unknown part of life. It has an affinity with the night sky, the cloud, the foggy landscape, the depths of the ocean, the hidden emotions of the mysterious stranger. Ultimately, it seeks contact with the most unknowable, mysterious, ineffable Being of all: God. The 16th-century Cabalist mystic of Safed, Isaac Luria (quoted in Bion, 1970, p.114), said about his mystical states: 'I can hardly open my mouth to speak without feeling as though the sea burst its dams and overflowed. How then shall I express what my soul has received, and how can I put it down in a book?'

The English Romantic poet, John Keats, said that one of the traits required for writing poetry is 'negative capability, that is when a man is capable of being in uncertainties, mysteries, doubts, without any irritable reaching after fact and reason.' Keats (1817) here described the ability to *not* know, which in turn enables us to see, through the application of the creative imagination, what does not yet exist, but is possible, which for Keats was beauty.

Even a newborn infant requires a degree of negative capability in order to fathom his experience. Bion pointed out that the infant's ability to experience and tolerate absence (the 'no-breast') provides a 'gap' which allows the baby to think his first thoughts (Symington and Symington, 1996, pp.82–84). The unknown and mysterious have important functions in discovery and creativity. We know only by virtue of not knowing, of being in a 'cloud of unknowing.'

The psychospiritual self is that aspect of our selfhood which is rooted in the unknown and mysterious essences. It has an affinity for that which is silent, elusive, ungraspable in words and concepts. Perhaps our psycho-spirituality harks back to our animal nature, when we drifted among waters, woods, and mountains, without words and concepts, and with the barest of perceptions necessary for survival. Yet at the same time, it is the source and expression of the divine, the numinous within. It derives from our 'lower' nature, our darkness, our instincts, yet it seeks divinity, the ethereal, the essence that lurks behind all Being, the immanent moment of truth that is never quite present but eternally 'to be.'

Purity, innocence, and wholeness

The spiritual self is born pristine, pure, innocent, and whole. Like a clear lake on a windless, cloudless day, it is silent and still, a perfect mirror for experience. However, the vicissitudes of life, of pleasure and pain, impingement and deprivation, cause ripples, waves, and vortices on the lake's surface and disrupt its serenity and clarity. The spiritual self is always seeking to restore its pristine state. Each time it is even partially successful in doing so, the psyche becomes capable of increased growth, resilience, and compassion. Whenever pristine selfhood is restored, even if for a moment, a degree of self-transformation, however small or unnoticed, takes place.

Modern life, religion, and psychology have given a cynical cast to purity, innocence, and wholeness. They pit survival and acquisition against such traits, and make it appear as if they are qualities that need to be outgrown, or at best luxuries for a few monastics and wise persons, emergency measures useful during periods of turmoil and danger, or else 'add-ons' in later life, when one has acquired or used up one's supplies and is awaiting death. Freudian psychology reduces such qualities to a state of drowsy quiescence when the drives have been satiated. Lacan (1977, pp.292–325), the father of the 'back to Freud' movement in French psychoanalysis, believed that fragmentation was man's destiny and that wholeness was an illusion.

While I agree that we cannot grow and learn without some sacrifice of purity, innocence, and wholeness (this is the essence of our tragic nature), I believe that the disruption and reintegration of our pristine self is a cyclical process in which these qualities become, not destroyed, but tempered by experience into a resilient, adaptive structure for living, like a piece of wood that is cut, aged, and sanded to perfection and useful purpose. When these qualities are severely damaged, as they may be by trauma, insatiable greed, and ruthless dissection, the personality becomes warped and driven to extremes in a desperate attempt to regain them.

Purity, innocence, and wholeness of self are a microcosm of the unified, infinite, and mysterious Other which our spirituality seeks. They also constitute the state of self in which it can mirror, reflect, and contemplate this Other. When ripples and waves disrupt the clear lake, it is impossible for us to 'see' and know the Other. Physiologically, the clear lake represents the brain's quietude and integrative capacity, in which it forms a telescopic 'neuro-lens' capable of perceiving the Other in and beyond the ripples of sense perceptions and the waves of impulse and desire.

Emotions are the guideposts of perception, motivation, and action. Spiritual states have emotional correlates. The pure, innocent, and whole spiritual self which seeks union, the infinite, and the mysterious Other experiences and evokes a variety of feelings. Spiritual emotions are global and all-encompassing. Unlike the discrete ripples and eddies of anger, hurt, and fear that we feel in the course of a day, spiritual emotions well up within us as 'auras' that surround experience, so-called 'apperceptions.' Spiritual emotions can be calming, stilling the self, or else intense and overwhelming. They signify the attainment of purity, innocence, and wholeness, as well as the turbulence that threatens these attributes.

It is an understatement to say that the psychospiritual emotions have been neglected in modern psychology. Indeed, they have been virtually ignored, or else truncated to lower-intensity emotions: desire instead of unconditional love, anxiety instead of terror, and so on. Hence there is a need to study the powerful feeling states that are evoked in the context of spirituality.

The psychospiritual emotions

Theories about emotions have a checkered history, sometimes shedding more confusion than light on the subject. Emotions are difficult to grasp conceptually because they are not as sharply delineated as are specific perceptions and memories, and they are simultaneously internal (mental) and external (behavioral), subjective and objective. Furthermore, there are marked cultural differences in emotionality. For example, individuals from Northern European cultures show more muted emotional expressions than those from Mediterranean countries. Envy is more predominant in cultures where possessions are emphasized, and so on. Freud added that emotions can be repressed or denied. So we sometimes don't even know what we are feeling – until someone says, 'You look upset' or 'You sound angry.' Despite such complexity, several theories of emotions have been proposed that have held particular interest for psychologists.

William James, the 19th-century 'father of American psychology,' held – paradoxically – that emotions are the sensations resulting from bodily reactions (James, 1992). In the so-called James–Lange theory, the behavior 'causes' the emotion rather than vice versa. The internal feedback from these reactions – such as tightening muscles or a lifting of the corners of the lips in a smirk or smile – provides the clusters of sensations that we call feelings. Thus, for example, we don't run because we are afraid, but rather we are afraid because we run. That is, according to James, the emotion of fear is nothing more than our sensations of a fast-beating heart, muscle tension, and so on. A panic episode, for example, can often be alleviated by slow, deep breathing. Altering the bodily process causes changes in emotionality.

The James–Lange theory was modified by Canon and Bard to say that the inner feeling and outer behavior of an emotional state emanate from a common source in the brain. We react behaviorally to an emotion at the same time as we experience it within. The Canon–Bard theory (Thompson, 1988) holds, for example, that when a predator (or other fearful stimulus) appears in our field of vision, the perceptual, memory, and cognitive processing components of our brain identify it as a serious threat, then send signals to our body to 'get moving' and to our mind to both maintain a high state of alertness specific to that particular danger and develop strategies to cope with the threat. The emotion of fear that we feel is a combination of our inner state of arousal, thought processes, and the behavioral changes of muscle tension, increased heart rate, and rapid breathing. The Canon–Bard theory is consistent with the fact that emotions are regulated in the limbic system of the brain, which simultaneously can affect the arousal, sensori-motor, and cortical systems.

Schachter and Singer (1962) much later added to the James–Lange theory that the perceived situation or context contributes to the particular emotion that is experienced. For example, tears can mean both grief or joy, depending on whether we are on the winning or losing side.

An alternative point of view to both James–Lange and Canon–Bard was expressed by Tomkins (1995), who noticed that the infant's emotions were often responses to face-to-face contact with a significant other. He thus understood emotions not as 'visceral' biological responses but as innate patterns of neural firing in the context of interpersonal signals. A prime example is the emotion of shame, which results automatically from a lack of response or negative reaction from others well before the child understands what they mean. Recent studies of shame (Nathanson, 1987) resulted from Tomkins' theorizing and also formed the basis for new understandings of the psychotherapy process (Basch, 1988; Lewis, 1971).

Each of these theories of emotions addresses only a part of the picture: James and Canon–Bard focus on adaptation, and Tomkins emphasizes neural firing and face-to-face interaction. Taken together, they suggest that emotions serve as motivators which guide thoughts and actions in particular directions and give certain reactions a particular significance in a given situation.

In keeping with my view that spirituality possesses its own inherent motivations, functions, and structures in the psyche, I believe that there are kinds and degrees of emotions which have neither interpersonal nor adaptive purposes as such, but emanate from the core spiritual self. These feelings and sentiments have their counterparts in everyday feelings of affection, attachment, anger, fear, and joy, but they are more intense, global, and sustained, potentially leading to fundamental transformations in our personality. Spiritually based emotions put us in touch with and highlight experiences of life-changing critical events as well as those which can alter our overall picture of the world. One could say that, like their 'everyday' counterparts, they have adaptive value, but in the broader, multidimensional sense of total adjustment to life as an ongoing process. The psychospiritual emotions are 'markers' of alterations in states of consciousness, alerting us to transformational experiences. Eventually, on account of their global nature and their basis in deep layers of the psyche, the study of psychospiritual emotions may lead to a new theory in which emotions are related to states of consciousness and whole-brain function.

It is common to think of spiritual feelings as loving and inspirational, but they may also involve fear, anger, and other disturbing affects. While emotions reflective of deep, abiding love and inner peace are readily acknowledged to have spiritual sources, feelings of rage, terror, and grief appear to reflect our darker, 'lower' nature. Yet such disturbing and distressing emotions are frequently depicted in the Bible, as well as in Hindu texts, for example. God leads Abraham, Moses, and Jonah along spiritual paths by instilling fear and rage in them. Kali, the Hindu goddess of destruction, plays a significant role in growth and change. Spiritually distressing emotions are responses either to the immensity of spiritual experience, or else to a threat to one's spiritual fabric and meaning context. For example, when the World Trade Center was attacked on 11 September 2001, I was safely far away from that location. Yet I felt rage and terror at the news. My rage was my response to the fact that everything I believed and held sacred was deliberately violated. My terror stemmed not only from physical danger but from a feeling that chaos, evil, and fear was loose in the world. These were spiritual feelings of ultimate concern. Of course, I also experienced 'ordinary' fear and anger, which made me want to protect myself and my loved ones, and to retaliate. But far beyond these self-centered anxieties, there was another level that had to do with the meaning context of my spirituality, my wish for a world in which peace, love, and respect for life prevail. Where on earth could God be at a moment like this?

In summary, I would tentatively classify the psychospiritual emotions into two general categories: positive (embracing, accepting) and negative (threat to the spiritual core). The positive emotions include unconditional love, serenity, ecstasy, and awe. The negative emotions include terror, rage, despair, and grief.

The positive spiritual emotions

Love, serenity, ecstasy, and awe are the positive emotions associated with the spiritual life. Spiritual love, *agapé*, is an open rather than exclusionary form of loving. While 'desire' wants the object for oneself, spiritual love wants the object not only for oneself, but for others, and, importantly, for *it*self, for its own sake. It is an expansive, all-encompassing love, taking in past, present, and future and including God and the entire cosmos in its embrace. It seeks and manifests purity and innocence, excluding awareness of the 'baser' and more immediate desires. It implies a profound ethic of preservation of the good as an absolute. Spiritual emotions are informed with a higher knowledge, suggesting that their inner, neurological source in the brain involves the gray matter of the cerebral cortex, and also that the brain functions in a unitary way, rather than in parts. When one loves spiritually, it is as if the wisdom of the ages is awakened, and all the different parts of the self – drives, memories, 'right-brain' images, 'left-brain' cognitions, and action – are highly consistent and coordinated.

Serenity is an emotion associated with the acceptance of life as it is given to us: 'God grant me the serenity to accept the things I cannot change.' It is different from 'calm,' which can easily be disrupted and sometimes carries with it a feeling of foreboding, as in 'the calm before the storm.' Christians refer to serenity as 'the peace which passeth all understanding.' Eastern 'bliss' refers to a similar emotional state. Serenity usually results from persistent spiritual discipline, whether meditation, asceticism, a careful, thorough series of contemplations, or a way of life such as that of Confucius and perhaps the Hellenic Greeks, which emphasizes balance and the care of all things, great and small. Serenity is not the same as stoicism, which implies toughness of disposition in the face of adversity. Rather, serenity and peace appear to represent a comfort that comes from relinquishing control, and letting life flow.

Ecstasy consists of almost painfully extreme and sustained pleasure and joy. Much of the time we experience a compromised version of ecstasy through intense sensory pleasure. Sexual orgasm and some drug-induced states sometimes approach spiritual ecstasy, but are not quite 'it.' Ecstasy transcends pleasure in two respects: in ecstasy, ego boundaries dissolve; and ecstasy reinforces and sustains hope, faith, and meaning, whereas momentary pleasures merely lead to the search for more pleasure. Boundary dissolution is the primary accompaniment of ecstasy, just as sexual orgasm involves not only heightened pleasure, but also a sensation of the self dissolving into the other. In spiritual ecstasy, boundlessness includes a quality of All being in One and One being in All. A recognition – i.e. a shift of attention and awareness – rather than a stimulation has occurred. The extraordinary intensity of ecstasy stems from compound psychobiological release in several systems all at once: sexual, neuromuscular, emotional, and cognitive. But the ecstasy itself is the heightened awareness of oneness with 'no strings attached.' Ecstasy implies spiritual freedom, 'as if I had wings.' It is to be distinguished from the emotions of love and serenity because it is more immediately intense. Yet, spiritual ecstasy has a lasting and benevolent impact. One's destiny has changed. Recently, I saw a radical feminist bumper sticker that said, 'Life's a witch, and then you fly!' Ecstasy signifies that you are going to soar.

Awe is an emotional response of wonder and mystery in which we feel small and insignificant in relation to that which is large, infinite, and all-encompassing. As an adolescent, I spent my first summer in the country at my uncle's cottage in Maine. On some days, I would pack a lunch and hike around the hills and seaside. Having grown up in the heart of a noisy, claustrophobic city, it was the first time I had seen vistas of nature: mountains, seascapes, and the night sky filled with stars. I felt my heart pound, music pulse through my veins and arteries, and a sense of the vastness and mystery of it all. This experience was repeated the first time I made love, flew in an airplane, listened to a great symphony, read a grand novel, discovered an earth-shattering idea. I found that I could feel small and insignificant by comparison to the worlds that opened before me, yet retain, even enhance, my sense of self. I was driven to seek out further awesome experiences, all of which seemed intimately linked to my sense of purpose, meaning, and destiny.

Many reports of spiritual awakenings and the awareness of God are filled with awe. Moses was awestruck at God's voice speaking to him. The magi experienced wonder and awe at seeing the Christchild in the manger. St Paul was struck off his horse by a lightning bolt when he discovered God and his own mission. Bill Wilson, a founder of Alcoholics Anonymous, was awestruck by a vision of God while in a hospital withdrawing from alcohol. He never drank after that and was led to assist hundreds of alcoholics in recovery. The felt presence of God, 'through a glass darkly, then face to face,' is perhaps the most awesome experience a human being can have, and leads to permanent change in the personality and one's purpose in life.

The negative spiritual emotions

My work with victims of psychological trauma suggests to me that there is a spectrum of negative, distressing emotions that are indicative of spiritual awareness, of dangers to the psychospiritual self. Rage, terror, despair, and grief are intense, almost overwhelming, emotions that accompany trauma and loss. When a person expresses such extreme feelings, he and others may think that he has lost control or is falling apart. Yet who in America did not feel rage, terror, despair, and grief when the World Trade Center was demolished by a malevolent act with the loss of so many lives? These emotions can, properly understood and assimilated, provide the beginning of healing because they are expressions of violation of our psychospiritual selves. They are clarion calls that signal a spiritual danger or urgency and the need to respond with profound inner change.

Unfortunately, there is a trend in contemporary psychiatry to discount 'negative' emotions like anxiety and depression as illnesses which can be alleviated with medication and cognitive therapy (Solomon, 2002). Although I do think that these treatment modalities can be helpful when we identify clusters of symptoms and episodes which persistently and seriously interfere with daily functioning, I am concerned that there is emerging a wave of enthusiasm for happiness and optimism as the only reasonable and 'rational' state of affairs. Some cognitive therapists and psychopharmacologists are contending that when logic and reason prevail in a person's psyche, depression decreases and is replaced by 'positive emotions.' The pharmacologists believe that when the neurotransmitters are in proper balance, extremes of

emotions are reduced or eliminated. While there are indeed emotional insta-
bilities, such as bipolar disorder, that require medication, it is dangerous to
generalize from specific diagnoses to the human personality as such. The
millennium of contentment that modern psychopharmacology and
cognitive therapy promise seems to me strangely reminiscent of Huxley's
Brave New World, where happiness and ecstasy are cognitively, behaviorally,
and chemically engineered.

A spiritually-based understanding of our emotional life runs counter to
this psychiatric enthusiasm. Extreme emotions occupy a profound place in
our search for depth, meaning, and a spiritual center for living. The history
of religion, philosophy, literature, and the arts contains countless examples
where mystical and creative insights occurred during or after states of
profound depression, terrifying loneliness, and panic-ridden disorientation.
I am not saying that such emotions are inherently spiritual or creative, but
rather that, in some individuals, under certain circumstances, they play a significant transformative role. Psychiatry needs to differentiate between
growth-producing states of anxiety and depression and those that are inhib-
iting or debilitating, a distinction that is sometimes not readily made.

The 'negative' spiritual emotion that is most misunderstood is that of
rage. Rage is an acute mixture of anger, helplessness, and grief in response to
the occurrence of the totally unacceptable. Clearly, not all rage is spiritual.
The tantrum of a child when refused a piece of candy, the rage of a lunatic,
the unmitigated wish for revenge, are not spiritual, but indications of low
frustration tolerance, unresolved conflicts, and chemical deficits. Such rage is
maladaptive. Spiritual rage is rather an appropriately profound reaction to
serious violations of the self, accompanied by a sense of loss and the helplessness to combat these violations. When Dylan Thomas (1971) wrote,
'Rage, rage against the dying of the light,' he was talking about spiritual
protest against the inevitability of death. When a woman is raped, or
witnesses the murder of her child in an 'ethnic cleansing,' and cries out in the
night, that is spiritual rage. Were she not to rage at seeing the very essence of
what is meaningful and spiritual destroyed, she would be less than human.
When a patient experiences spiritual rage in a therapy session, I consider it
light in the darkness. It is completely different from vain protest or helpless
anger. It feels to me, as a witness, to be the very expression of life itself. In
such situations, I support and empathize with the patient in feeling the rage.
Without such rage, there is no hope of moving through the stages of grief
and loss to a new beginning in life.

Terror is to fear as rage is to anger, an extreme of a commonly occurring emotion. The two basic responses to danger or threat are 'fight and flight.' These responses evolved early in evolution, and a substantial part of the neurochemistry and structure of the nervous system are aspects of flight–fight mechanisms. To think of terror as a spiritual emotion seems sacrilegious to the modern humanistic temperament. Humanists will point out how preachers have misused terrifying visions of hell to frighten parishioners into righteous behavior. James Joyce, in *A Portrait of the Artist as a Young Man*, described how such 'hellfire and brimstone' preaching drove the young Stephen Dedalus away from the Church and left him with deep, irreparable anxieties. If God is Love, then how can terror be of God?

Yet, there are rare moments of terror that have a deeply healing potential. In such moments we are driven to the very wall of our inner being and must redefine ourselves. Melville's *Moby Dick* and Conrad's *Heart of Darkness* profoundly articulate how the soul is stirred to terror and led to greater awareness of the darker side of self and the unconscious. I have worked with patients who have had horrific and terrifying memories of sexual and physical abuse emerge in sessions. Facing and surviving the terror led to new insights and inner strength.

I once attended a lecture by a prominent American Buddhist. He described the terror he felt during an extended period of isolated meditation in icy blizzard midwinter weather in the Himalayas, with minimal food and shelter, lack of human contact, and the ever-present danger of starvation, frostbite, and death. Eventually, however, the meditation gave him the inner resources to survive and grow through this nightmarish experience, enabling the detachment he needed for the more difficult and treacherous times in life.

Despair represents the lowest point on the scale of depression. It is a state of hopelessness and emptiness, when one perceives no light, no resolution to one's suffering. Suicide is often chosen as a solution to despair. How, then, can despair be regarded as spiritual when in fact it represents the absence of faith, belief, meaning, and hope?

A yoga teacher, Lilias Folen, once said to me, 'You have to be lost in order to be found.' Many spiritual awakenings occur at points of despair. Jesus on the Cross cried out, 'My God, why hast thou forsaken me?' The philosopher Soren Kierkegaard (1983) emphasized the importance of despair in achieving a vision of God. While one certainly does not invite despair, if it comes our way it may be better to submit rather than avoid it. Despair may be the 'cloud of unknowing' which precedes mystical vision. Only when one has given up one's precious illusions and anchor points in life can clarity of vision occur. Despair is the point where we may stop grasping at straws, empty our minds of past beliefs, and – if we can see a glimpse of truth – become open to real solutions.

I once treated a young woman who thought of herself as a complete outcast. In her mind, she was totally unloved and rejected by her family. When her boyfriend, her chief emotional connection to others, left her, she began planning her suicide without telling anyone. She had arranged everything, but at the last minute called me and asked for help. At my recommendation, she hospitalized herself. When she returned to outpatient treatment, she was able for the first time to begin to see that her despair had originated in a process of victimization she had endured in her childhood and for which she had blamed herself rather than be a vocal witness to her parents' misdeeds. Her despair, although it stemmed from an horrific real-life family nightmare, allowed her to reach a point where she could accept a new, forgiving perspective on her guilt and self-hate.

Grief, the response to profound loss, is like homeopathic medicine: it is an illness that cures another illness. The symptoms of grief resemble those of clinical depression and include despondency, insomnia, crying spells, loss of appetite, feelings of worthlessness, difficulty carrying out daily tasks, and hopelessness. The illness that is being treated is a disruption of attachment. The fabric of the self has been ruptured by a break in continuity, safety, love, and the illusion of immortality. As grief does its healing, the bereaved person gradually restores his connection with his fellows and with life. When grief is repressed, prolonged, or complicated by conflict, it can lead to prolonged depression and also compromise the immune system, leading to physical illness (Cox, Bendiksen, and Stevenson, 2001). So grief is nature's uncommonly painful cure for loss.

One of the most interesting statements in our spiritual heritage is Jesus' beatitude: 'Blessed are they that mourn, for they shall be comforted.' How can one who mourns be blessed, when he is in such a state of pain and suffering? The answer is fourfold. First and foremost, mourners perform a sacred rite of looking after the dead. Whether we think of that role in terms of the afterlife or of memory and respect for the deceased, mourners are carrying out a vital social and religious function of assuring continuity and eternity. Second, mourners are bereft, emptied, and therefore humbled. When you grieve, you feel that you are nothing and – for that time – are stripped of your earthly possessions, even if you are among the wealthy and famous. Grief takes away everything. Third, mourning contains the potential for self-healing. If you mourn, you will eventually find new joy in life. If you deny your grief, it will only prolong your resentment and isolation. Fourth, I believe that Jesus was saying that God has compassion for those who suffer out of love.

The emotions of rage, terror, despair, and grief are 'rock-bottom' emotional responses to violations of self and the loss of safety, identity, continuity, and dignity. They are spiritual because they cannot be resolved without a significant transformation of self. While no sane human being would ask for such experiences, they are inevitable, and when they do come, our best chance for healing is to utilize the pain to learn lessons about ourselves and life. This openness to difficult and painful experience is often the basis of what is called 'God's grace.' At that point, we may receive unexpected gifts of insight, compassion, love, and hope.

Having depicted the concept of the psychospiritual self in terms of its early development, its role in the personality, its needs, and its emotions, I now would like to consider its evolution over time through the successive stages of the life cycle.

Endnote

1   I use the terms 'psychospiritual self,' 'spiritual self,' 'core self,' and 'Higher Self' interchangeably throughout.

CHAPTER NINE

Spiritual Development throughout the Life Cycle

Psychospirituality seeks unchanging essence, but paradoxically is always in a state of dynamic, ever-changing flux. The interaction of spiritual essence with the dynamic tensions of the personality propel spiritual development throughout the life cycle.

Thus far, I have described dynamics which emerge in the first two to four years of life and continue throughout life, i.e. the paranoid-schizoid position and the depressive position as they occur within the mother–child relationship. As the father and siblings increasingly enter the picture, the child moves into the stage which Freud considered most critical for development: the Oedipal phase. In this chapter, I would like to consider some aspects of development beginning there, and go on through the life cycle, from adolescence to adulthood, to old age. My intention is to elucidate how the dynamics of the evolving personality consist of psychospirituality in a state of evolution. Think of development as a spiritual journey in which forward movement depends upon reconciling worldly experience with the needs of the spirit, and you will understand the telos which propels human growth and development.

Oedipus and spirit

I will begin with what Freud considered the major milestone of child development: the Oedipus complex. Here, the child's struggles with parental authority, sexuality, and emergence into societal life were portrayed by Freud in relation to the basic drives of sex and aggression, but I believe that this rite of passage has great spiritual significance as well.

For Freud, the Oedipus complex represents the culmination of child development and the structuring of the personality. Indeed, he held that, as a result of the resolution of this complex, the psyche is well-consolidated by ages 5–6. Unlike Freud's 'closed system' account of the psyche, an open systems, relational view would argue that there are opportunities throughout life for significant personality change. While I believe that the Oedipal phase is singular and significant, I have always objected to Freud's reductionist view of the self as a fixated, pre-determined set of patterns. (See Mullahy, 1948, for alternative interpretations of the Oedipus complex.)

In his discussions of the Oedipus complex, Freud emphasized infantile sexuality, although he also pointed out its significance for social development. The child, whether male or female,[1] at that time 'falls in love' with the parent of the opposite sex (in some instances, with the same-sexed parent, a 'reverse Oedipus complex'). He subconsciously wishes to 'murder' the rival parent, usually of his own sex, whom he perceives to be a powerful competitor for the love object. Oedipus, of course, is the protagonist in Sophocles' drama, who unknowingly kills his father and sleeps with his mother. His ignorance of his heinous deeds corresponds psychologically to the 'repression' or forgetting of the Oedipus complex of childhood.

Several alternative, neo-Freudian (Mullahy, 1948), self psychological (Kohut, 1977), and object relational (Steiner, 1989) interpretations of the Oedipus complex have been offered. This is not the place to review this important literature. However, in order to place the Oedipus complex within the psychospiritual paradigm, I want to point to the spiritual component of the Oedipal dilemma. My position does not contradict Freud's theory of psychosexual and ego/superego development but merely suggests a broader perspective. I fully agree that children do indeed have sexual and aggressive feelings towards their parents, but would add that these emotions are significant developmentally because they bear upon the child's need to understand his world and to discover and validate his own essence.

The dilemma for the child in the Oedipal phase is twofold: he must leave the maternal orbit and incorporate parental authority into his repertoire of interpersonal relations, and thereby accept a more limited role in family life; and he must find ways to incorporate gender difference and sexual desire into his perception of self and world. These issues create a spiritual dilemma for the child insofar as they imply an increased awareness of earthly desire, inevitable and profound differences between self and other, and a further dethronement of his 'godlike' status as the 'center of the universe.' Resolving these dilemmas leads to changes in the child's numinosity (his spiritual core and imagination), his place within the kinship system (Levi-Strauss, 2000), and his grasp of the moral order (Wuthnow, 1989). In effect, his numinosity becomes increasingly embedded within a cultural matrix which includes a set of rules, precepts, and prohibitions emanating from a socio-cultural source outside of himself. At the same time, the child hopefully retains his own 'space' for imagination and numinosity.

The Oedipus complex highlights two psychospiritual elements in the evolving personality: *sacrifice* and *mystery*. The need for sacrifice comes about in several ways. First, the child must renounce the fulfillment of his wish for exclusive access to the love object. By extension, he no longer has exclusive access to 'God' (i.e. the source of protection and power in his life), who must now be shared with others. God must help many humans, and, tragically, one person may be sacrificed for the others. Like Isaac, the child now discovers ironically that the 'sacrificial lamb' could be himself. Further, he is faced with the dilemma of choice: whether to obey the 'God' represented by parental injunctions, or his own sense of self. Is God a part of himself or is He manifest in the parent who is now seen to have great power and potency?

Oedipus, upon discovering to his horror that Iocasta, his wife, is also his mother, blinds himself in the shame of incest. The child does not literally blind himself, but instead represses his impulses. In addition, he reluctantly 'accepts' his symbolic wound in the form of reduced status with respect to the parents, paralleling Oedipus' self-blinding, dethronement, and exile.

Lacan (Sarup, 1992, pp.120–123) holds that the Oedipus complex is built into the signified–signifier relationship of language structure, in the so-called 'phallic symbol' and the 'castration complex.' The child finds that the phallus (which for Lacan is not the biological penis but a cultural and lin-guistic representation) is possessed by the father. The child must now accept the 'law of the father,' the societal rules and prohibitions symbolized by the powerful phallus. He sacrifices and renounces his own wishes in order to conform to social structure. In effect, he thus sacrifices parts of himself to a patriarchal God. (The Old Testament is a chronicle of such sacrifice. The equivalent of sacrifice in the Oedipus myth is that Oedipus yields his throne and departs from Thebes.)

Chuck, a young adult male came to treatment complaining that he was continually frustrated in his relationships. He was frightened to pursue them and felt easily hurt, anxious, and rejected by women. He had experienced frequent conflicts with his father, and like David facing Goliath, he felt as if the odds were against him in facing up to his father's strictness and anger. He and his mother adored each other, but his mother's love did not bolster his self-esteem vis-à-vis the women he dated and idealized.

In psychotherapy, Chuck once again fought his battle with his father on the playing field of the transference relationship to the therapist. Finding that the therapist neither rejected Chuck nor passively accepted his 'sling-shot' victories over him, he gradually learned that battling with his father was not the answer to his need to feel grown-up and masculine. Further, he learned from subsequent exchanges with women that his age-appropriate role was neither to have power over them, nor to overidealize and be adored by them, but to experience genuine intimacy and partnership. By accepting his rightful place in the society of his peers, he was eventually able to spend time with women on a dating basis and experience empathy and compassion for them rather than seeking sexual conquest. His angry feelings towards his father also lessened as he became able to sort out his father's arbitrarily harsh strictures from the necessary rules and boundaries that allow men and women to negotiate with each other in fairness, and to accept frustration and limitations. He was no longer fighting an angry, patriarchal God, and could then internalize his mother's love along with an appropriate social structure for relationships.

In this way, the healthy resolution of the Oedipus complex leads to an internalization of God as firm, but compassionate and loving, combining masculine and feminine qualities, in contrast to the harsh vision of a punitive and arbitrary (paranoid-schizoid) God, which derives both from persecutory internal objects and from the all-too-real failings of parents who over-control, punish, and abandon their children emotionally.

An often overlooked aspect of the Oedipus complex is that it changes the child's relationship to the mysterious and numinous within himself, which constitutes a change in the relationship between the spiritual self, the true self, and the ego. In Sophocles' drama, self-blinded and bereft Oedipus, with the compassionate assistance of his sister, Antigone, travels to Colonus, where he is given sanctuary by King Creon, lives a humble life, and dies an honorable death. His life has shifted from a life of conquest and power to a life of the spirit. His sensory blindness has given him the inner vision to see himself as he really is and acquire a sense of the eternal mysteries.

For Freud, the three 'mysteries' of childhood are sex and gender differences, how babies are made, and the events in the parental bedroom – what he called the 'primal scene' (cf. Knafo and Feiner, 1996). Sex and gender differences involve such discoveries. Interestingly, a child initially believes himself to be bisexual, both male and female. When he observes that some people have penises and others vaginas, this difference is mysterious to him. Furthermore, the child initially believes in 'autochthonous' birth. That is, he believes that the baby is self-generated by either himself or the mother. A religious derivative of this idea is, of course, the 'immaculate conception.' Creation myths of many cultures – which are 'autochthonous' in that they do not involve a co-creating 'couple' – are possibly related to early naturalistic explanations of birth. We can see that Genesis and the birth of Christ are biblical representations of authochthonous birth. God is Father of both the universe and of His Son. The Son is God's re-affirmation of His creation of the universe and humankind.

For the child, the parental habitat is a prototype of a numinous space, a mysterious 'other place', 'far away' where something unknown but of great importance takes place. The child, early on, simply sees the parents 'disappear into the void' and then may hear intriguing sounds emanating from there. This quickens his curiosity and imagination.

With the Oedipus complex, this mysterious realm of gender, sex, and birth undergoes a profound change. First of all, the awareness of sex difference is consolidated – the child realizes that biological difference is inevitable. This can lead to painful dilemmas about gender and sexual orientation. For everyone, it presents a problem of how to incorporate the 'shadow' (anima and animus) qualities of the opposite sex into one's sense of self. Second, the mystery of sex and gender is partially 'solved' – gender and intercourse become facts that can be explained, puzzles to be assimilated into the child's cognitive schema, rather than inchoate imaginative fantasies. Furthermore, the child must gradually become disillusioned with himself and his beliefs, as he finds that he can no longer be both sexes and hence self-creating, and that he is excluded from the parents' bedroom and their 'secret' life together. In general, numinosity becomes challenged by 'facticity,' rationality, and objectivity.

The spiritual problem for the child is how to retain his childlike innocence, his creativity and spontaneity, and his sense of the mysterious, when the Oedipal phase makes it clear to him that there exists a moral order, a procreative couple from which he is essentially barred, and a gender protocol which renders him incomplete, less whole, and a creation of others.

Kohut (1977, pp.220–248) correctly inferred that during this period, parental empathy and mirroring help the child to sustain a cohesive self in the face of such disenchantment. Empathic reflection and enjoyment of the child's strivings helps preserve the spontaneity and creativity of the true self by preserving the 'transitional space' of imagination and play. Attuned parents not only empathize; they are capable of 'regression in service of ego,' allowing the 'child' part of themselves to become manifest. This 'sacrament' permits the child to feel loved, graced, and free. In such a state, he can safely continue to pursue the mysterious 'within' of his own psyche. A 'sanctuary of the mind,' a sacred space, is preserved under the aegis of the true self which allows the child to maintain spiritual selfhood with access to the numinous during a time of sacrifice, loss of illusion, and acceptance of a moral order.

I once treated an adolescent boy who suffered from anxiety triggered by the presence in his home of his mother's new boyfriend. Even though the latter was a kindly father surrogate, the young man accurately sensed that his special relationship to his mother was threatened. Although I could easily have analyzed and interpreted his feelings, something inside myself prompted me to 'do nothing at all' with him. I decided to trust this inner voice, and when he told me he enjoyed sports, we discussed that topic for several weeks, and studiously avoided even the semblance of therapy! I merely let him ventilate his feelings, and enjoyed his presence. His symptoms quickly vanished, and he became more at ease with his mother and her boyfriend. I think the reason for the success of his 'non-therapy' was simple: he was able to detach from his conflict, become less anxious, play again, find himself mirrored by a male adult, and re-establish his inner space as a context for growth.

The successful resolution of the Oedipus complex places the child's spirituality on an entirely new plane. In one respect, it is one of the greatest accomplishments in the lifelong challenge of reconciling the pristine ego and the life of the spirit with disillusioning reality, human failings, and inner 'demons.' The child finds that there is a moral standard, a 'tribal' role, and a sex and gender reality that has some possibility of reconciling the tarnished world with the will of a Creator as accessed inwardly by the psychospiritual self. He will struggle with this dialectic throughout his life, because the vital moral structure that is created is often violated by himself and others, and because parts of himself do not neatly fit such a mold. For instance, if he discovers that he is gay, he will have to find a way to maintain a moral order that is consistent with his alternative sexual orientation, and this path will be different from the gender norms of his society and conventional religious teaching. Or when he has a strong creative impulse he will have to go against what appears to be 'the law of the father' in order to actualize his art. Meeting such challenges strengthens the sense of self and its spiritual connection. Avoiding or failing such hurdles leaves the self at sea. The confusion, however, can be a further source of growth.

The dialectic between the numinous versus 'the law,' i.e. the rational and formulaic side of man, is what allows us to leave the protective cocoon of our childhood and stand a chance of flying like a butterfly in a difficult world. The rational side provides the mechanism of the wings that are necessary to fly. The numinous provides the freedom of flight and identifies the flowers we choose to light upon. Rites of sacrifice provide the suffering we must endure to continue to acquire faith and sense of meaning in a world where spiritual values are ephemeral and elusive.

Spirituality in 'latency,' adolescent, and adult stages of the life cycle

It would take an additional volume to fully explore the life cycle from a psychospiritual vantage point. Each stage of life has its specific spiritual qualities, challenges, tasks, and rites of passage, and they are all related to one another, generatively and causally with respect to the earlier phases, and teleologically in terms of evolving towards the later ones. What I can do here is provide some impressions of the spiritual issues and concerns that arise during adolescent and adult phases of development.

Latency

The stage of *latency* follows the Oedipal phase of development and consists of the school years prior to puberty. The child's focus is now on forming relationships outside the home with his peer group, and he engages in an extended process of acquiring culturally determined knowledge and skills (Sarnoff, 1976). Freud (1908) called this phase 'latency' because he believed that the psychosexual impulses are repressed and sublimated in social and educational activity. Spiritually, the child evolves from preoccupation with self and family to a beginning sense of community, civility, and achievement. He struggles to resolve conflicts with other children, channeling his competitive striving in directions consistent with ideals and morality, and acquiring socially appropriate behaviors.

The spirituality of latency thus plays out in the difficult arena of social relations. The sensitivities of this period have the potential to evolve into the philosophy of non-violence, preservation of the environment, and other societal 'visions' incorporating spiritual understanding. On the other hand, stereotyping, aggression, and a warrior-like mentality can result from the tensions of this stage. In my own latency period, in the years 1947–1953, I

recall fights in the schoolyard, a fascination with war stories and paraphernalia from the Second World War, learning fair play in sports, and an
interest in how other ethnic groups in the neighborhood lived their lives. I
also recall the kindness of my gentle friends and how that differed from the
gang mentality of neighborhood bullies – formative experiences that gave
me a lifelong interest in the dynamics of war and peace. It was as if both my
'warrior' and peace-seeking numinosity were projected into the life of the
societal complex. My spiritual self was striving to reconcile its need for
oneness and peace with the risks and threats that existed within my
community.

Adolescence

Blos (1979), Erikson (1950, 1959), and others have written extensively
about adolescent developmental phases, during which there is an upsurge of
energy combined with a search for activity and identity through which this
energy can be structured and channeled. On account of this energetic
expansiveness, the teenage years have the potential to be an extraordinarily
generative phase of spiritual growth. Adolescence has unfortunately been
exploited and corrupted by our market economy, which both dissipates the
juices of adolescent sexuality and creativity into the banality of mass culture
and downplays the *Sturm und Drang* of adolescence to create a false ideal that
appeals to the adult world's wish to remain perennially young.

When we are able to see beyond these myths and distortions, however,
we find that in adolescent vitality and 'super-growth' there is to be found an
upsurge of energy and excitement that is simultaneously sexual and spiritual.
Perhaps such vitality is related to the *kundalini* energy at the base of the spine,
of which the yogis speak, which starts as physical and sexual energy, but is
capable of rising to spiritual heights. The spiritual challenge and quest of
adolescence is to channel this spiritual energy into realizable sexuality,
ambitions, ideals, and relationships, in a radical reconsolidation of the
psyche. Thus there occurs an upsurge of experimentation, whether with
drugs, sexualized displays, body modifications such as tattoos and rings, and
personal and collective 'projects' ranging from musical groups to
world-changing demonstrations and protests. These experiments are
attempts to reconcile the dark, libidinal, and aggressive side of the self with
the 'unbearable lightness of being,' personal and spiritual freedom, and the
'light' of idealistic principles and beliefs.

I have occasionally treated teenaged members of the so-called 'punk rock' culture. My impression is that many of them are caught up in a world of hostility, violence, deviance, and control. In their attitudes and appearance, they project a defiance of conventional culture and a disregard of self-care. Yet at least some of them appear to be seeking ideals and a genuine relatedness to others and often have a 'soft' and creative side to their personalities. They seem to be covering up a severe sense of rejection and narcissistic injury which they re-enact in their lives in a victim–victimizer pattern. Their psychotherapeutic treatment, if it is to have any chance of success, needs to be sensitive to their vulnerable side.

For example, I treated Deirdre, an adolescent girl who was brought to me by her mother after she threatened a female friend. Deirdre was creatively gifted on many levels. Her poems, stories, and art work, however, were filled with despair and images of death. She had become sexually attracted to her girlfriend and deeply attached to her. The latter did not perceive the depth and desperation of Deirdre's attachment and instead understood her advances and seductions as hostility. The patient felt rejected and humiliated, and threatened the friend as an expression of her narcissistic rage. After a careful assessment of risk, I concluded that Deirdre had no intention of carrying out the threat, although we know all too well that some adolescents act out their warnings, so that there was reason for concern.

Therapy with this girl consisted of gently setting limits on her verbal expressions of wrath and explaining why appropriate communication was necessary for her well-being and that of others. I also welcomed her disturbing creative productions and tried to help her account for her obsessive images of despair and death by understanding their sources in her own life history. We both gradually recognized how severely she was abandoned and traumatized in her childhood despite her parents' good intentions. With such empathy and insight, the benign parts of herself could then be integrated into her personality. Deirdre's self-esteem improved markedly, and she was able to channel her 'dark side' into adaptive achievement and relatedness to others. I hoped that, as she grew into adulthood, her wounds and her 'shadow' would be safely integrated into her ambitions and ideals.

Early adulthood

In early adulthood, the spiritual focus shifts from efforts to channel psychospiritual energies, into a goal-directed search for purpose and meaning. Erikson (1968, 1969) formulated this stage in terms of the consolidation of identity, and his prime example was Mahatma Gandhi, who found his life work challenging colonial subjugation in India through non-violent action. In so doing, he lived his spiritual truth with saintly dedication. The spiritual challenge of early adulthood is to sustain and develop the spiritual self during a time when achievement and the need for an enduring structure for one's life create priorities which pressure the person to relinquish or at least delay many complex and spiritually-based aspects of himself. Life can become so reality-oriented and goal-directed that one forgets 'who one is,' the nature of one's deeper purposes and destiny, and even that one has a body that needs nurturing and care, as the stress-filled lives of so many career-oriented individuals attest.

Early adulthood, precisely because it is so channeled into structure-building and economic priorities, is, despite its enormous possibilities for constructive goals and action, possibly the most one-sided phase of development in our work-oriented culture. We have too much become a 'celebrity culture' and a world of 'winners' and 'losers.' Externals have become more important than the inner life. We lose sight of principles, innovation, nonconformity, and creativity. The fact that most of the major scientific discoveries, exceptional business ventures, and serious creative productions are propelled by young adults bypasses most of the young workforce, who are dissipating their spiritual energies trying to adjust and achieve conventional goals.

The despair and anomie of early adulthood is like no other. The *Sturm und Drang* of adolescence, the 'mid-life crisis,' and the involutional depression of senescence pale in comparison to a young man's or woman's shame, self-loathing, and suicidal confrontations with life, often at the very entrance to or achievement of material and social success. I think this is because these young people feel that they are untrue to themselves at the core, that an enormous gulf is developing between the self they are presenting to the world and their inner essence.

Carol, a twenty-three-year-old woman, came to me for treatment with depression and suicidal ideation at a time when she was 'set for life' with a career and was beginning to date interesting and caring men after an adolescence of relative social isolation. Her mother had treated her as a virtual extension of herself throughout her childhood. As a result, she felt she could not be 'real' (emotionally alive and authentic), and she was unable to relate lovingly and assertively to her peers. Her eyes were vacant, her appearance austere, and she treated her therapist and significant others with cold detachment and objectivity.

Her therapy consisted of helping her to find and access her true self with its emotions, spontaneity, and capacity for concern. In group therapy, she began by cruelly dissecting and attacking the other members. Gradually, as the group offered her concerned feedback, she began to be more aware of their subjectivity and emotional needs. She discovered for the first time that there was a part of herself which required nurturing and empathy.

A curative role in Carol's treatment was played by her dog. She valued her canine friend, who gave her unconditional nurturance and regard and brought out the physical and playful side of her. When her dog died during her tenure in group, she experienced genuine grief for the first time. She expressed her grief to the group, and they appreciated her sense of loss and vulnerability. After that experience of mutual understanding, she became more capable of genuine intimacy in one-to-one relationships, and she made a career change to a field more consistent with her self-needs. She no longer submerged her true self because she found its validation through others.

Mid-life I

This is a period with two sub-phases. The first involves the potential for actualizing one's life goals. Wealth, security, fame, and success can be at their apex (of course, many do not have such good fortune). Ideally one's acquisitions and achievements coordinate with one's inner sense of accomplishment. It can be the time of the 'magnum opus,' the ideal job, the position of power, the kids going off to college, the great enduring work of art, the grand professorial project. In addition to further sustaining and nurturing the true self, the spiritual dilemma of the 'successful' mid-life career-person is how to come to terms with corruption, greed, and desire in both self and other. The ineffable subject, the pristine ego, is crying out for recognition and reparation regarding the personal and ethical compromises the person has made in the course of his adult life.

Mark, a successful professional, came to treatment with depression stemming from mid-life feelings of compromise and failure. He was deeply disappointed that, as he put it, he had 'missed the boat' to reaching the apex of his field, thwarted in becoming one of the great and true masters. He envied the few who had achieved this goal. Moreover, he felt frustrated that the more self-aggrandizing, materialistic, and cold-blooded of his peers had acquired positions of power in his company. Although he had a loving wife and family, and all the financial security he could want, he felt like a 'born loser.'

Initially, we explored what prevented Mark from fulfilling his ambitions. Throughout his career, he had manifested a passivity, receptivity, and introversion that society labels as 'feminine' and 'nonconformist,' and which created a 'glass ceiling' for him in his profession. He had a difficult time joining and being accepted among the high achievers and the 'good old-boy network' of his firm. Mark had always preferred art and music in his leisure time to the usual round of golf, the cocktail party, or after-work conversation at the tavern. We contracted behaviorally for him to become more assertive, take appropriate business risks, and network with the high achievers, but he was unable to pursue these objectives.

Eventually, since urging him towards greater assertiveness was not effective, I focused on what it was that made it difficult for him to accept himself as he 'really was,' sensitive, artistic, loving – all of which could be seen as personal strengths. He acknowledged that he was always comparing himself to others 'better than himself,' as he had with his father. Drawn to family life, religious and philosophical pursuits, and creative interests outside his career, he hated himself for those endeavors because his introverted personality had negative business consequences for him. Rather than seeing his difficulty with business competitiveness in light of his refined ethical sensitivity, he perceived it as a failure to achieve 'alpha-male' assertiveness which could win him victories in his career.

Gradually, trusting his introverted side, Mark began to introduce his night dreams and daydreams into therapy sessions, and became fascinated by the archetypes he found in them. In daily life, he paid more attention to his children. He renewed his religious practices and interests. His intimacy with his wife increased as he became less preoccupied with his job and 'image.' From a spiritual standpoint, he was able to make the mid-life transition from career ambitions to the inner life and ethical values and purposes.

According to Buber (1950, pp.16–17), the Hasidic Rabbi Zusya said, a short while before his death, 'In the world to come I shall not be asked: "Why were you not Moses?" I shall be asked: "Why were you not Zusya?"'

Why wasn't I more myself? More true to my values? More focused on the eternals and the simplicities of everyday life? These are the questions that must be asked at the height of mid-life success, or conversely, during the acute awareness of one's external 'failures.'

Mid-life II

The second sub-phase of mid-life arrives with the slow but rude awakening to the decline of one's powers and the sense that the two epicenters of adult life – family and career – are waning. Men in our culture often mourn their loss of power, pride, and virility. Women fear becoming less beautiful and desirable. For both sexes, there is an emptiness, a void, being devalued, a fear of the unknown, dread about 'what's next.'

The great writer and observer of the contemporary scene, Tom Wolfe, tells a humorous story of how he was driving on a New York City thorough-fare with his wife. Their mid-life status was obvious from the outdated station wagon he drove. His anachronistic condition was further given away by driving slowly in Manhattan, where most drive at breakneck pace. Just behind him, a chic young woman, obviously a 'yuppie' and a status seeker, frantically drove a state-of-the-art BMW sports car. She became frustrated with Wolfe's sluggish driving and tendency to drift across the traffic lanes, and wildly honked her horn. At the next red light, she pulled up beside him, opened her window and shouted, 'Disintegrate, you senile old bastard!' Wolfe lightly reflected that the worst part of the insult was that she thought he was 'old.' 'Old' in our culture means outdated, out of synch, out of energy.

The deeper problem, and the spiritual challenge of 'mid-life II' is less one's tarnished career or role in life, and more how to 'fill the void,' whether generated by the imminent closure of life projects as the children leave the fold and one downsizes the career, or by the awareness of an emptiness and lack of genuine intimacy, masked throughout one's adulthood, or by the ending of an epoch of power, sexual 'steaminess,' and procreativity.

Spiritually, the 'void' we feel under such circumstances is the chasm between 'fullness' of being and of God, and the Buddhist notion of 'empti-ness,' which is also spiritual, because it is paradoxically 'filled' with the present moment, and is unattached to demands. The void, as opposed to non-attached emptiness or no-mind, is a state of spiritual neediness that comes in the wake of strong investments in achievements and desires. The 'container' that craves to be filled then reveals itself to be a massive, leaky juggernaut, and the objects it is supposed to hold prove perennially unsatis-fying and in danger of dwindling. The failure of the container then leads to disillusionment each time that 'supplies' are less available. In late mid-life, the container/boat we have built is going to sink, no matter what we do. We're going to have to learn how to get out of the sinking boat and swim to shore. Even if we build up secure pensions, a home in the country, and plans for fun in retirement, it is going to become apparent that none of these 'containers' are sufficient to make us fulfilled and secure.

The conventional solution to this problem is to reorganize one's practical priorities. The 'empty nest syndrome' and the waning of the career are 'resolved,' for example, by more vacations with the spouse, a love affair, divorce, in some cases starting a new family, a new career, and increased pursuit of hobbies. All these – except for the extramarital affair, which often ends in disaster – are effective to some degree. That is because they have a spiritual component of new areas for self-actualization. However, the most durable solution to the problem of the void is in the increasing spiritualizing of one's life. This is the challenge we face in old age and the pressing awareness of mortality.

Old age

Ageing is a difficult, painful process, and all of the anti-wrinkle creams, medical procedures, and 'fountains of youth' can't change that reality. A few years ago, I was fortunate to hear Maggie Kuhn, the founder of the Gray Panthers, reflect about her experience as her body became fragile and her functional capacities declined. She described what it was like to awaken in the morning barely able to move, to see friends die one after the other, to wonder if she herself was going to survive through the day. Yet she stood at the podium with rare grace and beauty and spoke with clarity and dignity. She was cheerful, spontaneous, and caring. She was unpreoccupied with herself and gave her full attention to each person who spoke with her. Her spiritual self appeared remarkably unaffected by the physical agony of growing old. I think it was her acceptance of the inevitability of ageing, and her role as an advocate of the elderly, that gave her such serenity, so that she saw herself as a member of a group rather than an isolate, and found grace in a human process that others regard as a curse. Unlike those who relentlessly seek 'fountains of youth' as they get older, Kuhn experienced and confronted her fear, pain, physical decline, and closeness to death, accepted them, and transcended them.

The quality of 'transcendence' – rising above the fray and seeing the eternal values with pristine clarity – is a fine quality to have throughout the life cycle, and an increasing number of people attend religious services, meditation retreats, rebirthing classes, sweat lodges, and a host of other spiritual experiences, seeking such a state. But transcendence is imperative in old age if one is to experience it with grace. In order to cultivate transcendence, it is necessary to go both inward and outward: inwards towards one's spiritual center, and outwards towards I–thou relations with others.

The inward journey of ageing can be accomplished in various ways. My father, in his eighties, loved to sit at outdoor cafés in Greenwich Village, enjoy an espresso, and watch the passers-by. Often, when walking back to his apartment, he gave a small amount of money to one particular destitute man in Washington Square, whom he called his 'ward,' to remind himself, he told me, of the importance of altruism. He often lightened our conversations with a gentle sense of humor. My father was a social reformer and far removed from religious practices, but he knew intuitively that, in old age, material things are insignificant in comparison with human love and concern and the 'quiet times' contemplating the 'river of life' going by. He often told me that he had 'made his peace,' and that he had no regrets. I always suspected that somewhere quietly within himself he had worked on this process throughout his life, trying to find a way of peace.

Reaching out towards others in an I–thou relationship is also critical for the elderly in order for them both to affirm their lives and reconcile themselves to death. Some will wait to reach out on their death beds, telling a family member for the first time how much they love them, forgiving someone from whom they felt alienated for many years. In my opinion, this process should begin earlier than that. The elderly should openly discuss their issues and concerns with receptive friends and family members. They should actively work on changing their priorities from material concerns to expressing their feelings towards loved ones and affirming the generativity of life beyond their own.

One of the reasons the elderly often have difficulty transcending is that, in our culture, they are subtly and not-so-subtly denigrated and shamed by those around them, whether acquaintances, family members, or caregivers. They are treated like 'children,' that is, as if they are overdependent and losing their faculties. Their money and possessions are eagerly awaited, and their closeness to death is regarded with fear and pity. Everyone's spirituality, at every age, can be enhanced by perceiving and affirming the holiness of the elderly, seeing beyond their physical bodies to their spirit. My grandmother's grief when she lost her husband, her kindness to all those around her, and her deep warmth in the hospital as she told me she was going to die, were holy I–thou meetings that blessed everyone who came in contact with her. In part, these intimate exchanges emanated from her unsullied, innocent nature, and in part they were facilitated by her family, since her adult children gave her full credit and love for who she was and made sure that her old age could be lived out with dignity, among her neighbors, friends, and community. They did not destroy her spirit by robbing her of human closeness and contact.

Table 9.1 summarizes the stages of spiritual development as I have portrayed them. The chronological ages are, of course, very rough approximations, the description is incomplete, and it is important to realize that each stage is emergent, a new beginning that never stops changing and developing in itself. With new challenges to spiritual growth, new issues come to the forefront. This chart is by no means the 'last word'. However, I hope that this phase-specific model of spirituality will give the reader a sense of how psychospirituality evolves throughout the life cycle in coordination with other aspects of development, biological, emotional, and social – and is neither a static process nor simply a matter of 'finding God.' Rather, spiritual growth constitutes a life-long struggle to meet difficult challenges, a struggle that involves many components of the personality. The theme that unites the stages, the 'river that runs through it,' is reconciliation of the purity, innocence, and wholeness of the spiritual self with the vicissitudes of living in a tarnished world circumscribed by time and space.

Table 9.1 The stages of spiritual development

Age	Spiritual phase	Issues and dynamics
Birth to 6 weeks	The pristine ego: the pure spirit	• being here, now, in the world • establishing first contacts with others • establishing a self boundary
6 weeks to 6 months	Persecutory anxiety and the 'descent into the flesh'	• entering the domain of time, space, desire, and pain • dynamics of the paranoid-schizoid position
6 months to 3 years	The capacity for concern	• awareness of the needs and subjectivity of others • evolving numinous narratives • empathy and altruism • awareness of potential for harm, guilt, and reparation

3–6 years	Oedipal conflict, desire, and sacrifice	• sustaining the numinous in the face of 'reality' and external power and authority • entering the moral order • enduring sacrifice
6–12	'Latency': a peer group community	• developing a beginning sense of community, civility, and achievement
12–18	Puberty and adolescence: the upsurge of spiritual energy	• channeling spiritual energies • integrating the 'dark side'
18–40	Early adulthood: finding spiritual purpose	• finding meaning and purpose in ambitions and tasks
40–55	Mid-life I: actualizing the self	• finding meaning and purpose in long-term goals and achievements • exploring new aspects of self
55–70	Mid-life II: filling the void	• rediscovering and confronting corruptability • overcoming spiritual void and meaninglessness
75–	Old age: transcendence	• achieving transcendence • achieving I–thou relatedness • completing unfinished business • expressing forgiveness and love

Endnote

1   The girl's version of the Oedipus Complex is sometimes called the Elektra Complex. As with the rest of this book, I have used the generic 'he' in this context. For the purposes of my particular argument here, there is no inherent difference as a function of the child's gender. However, an in-depth study of male and female development during this phase might elucidate differences in religious sentiments and archetypes between men and women and between patriarchal and feminist theologies.

CHAPTER TEN

The Circles of Being
Towards a 'Psychospiritual Map'

An important project for a paradigm of psychospiritual selfhood is to articulate the relationship of spirituality to the scope and structure of the mental life. Freud (1923) proposed a 'structural' theory of the mind which consisted of three organizational units or systems in interaction: id, ego, and superego. For Freud, the ego, in its role of adjustment to reality, mediates between id impulses and superego prohibitions, while the self occupies a niche within the ego as a reservoir of self-images and self-perceptions. Thus, in Freud's view, the self is a small and relatively powerless part of a psychic apparatus dominated by unconscious urges and societal taboos. Kohut (1977) added to this model what he called a 'supraordinate self,' the experiencing subject who integrates these structures into a cohesive state of being. In Kohut's perspective, the self has the power and potential to weave all the elements of the psyche into an integrated whole.

Spiritual experience tells us that even with these self psychological additions, Freud's structural model is too limited to encompass the vast array of human experiences and 'awakenings' at multiple levels, and the transcendence of which the spiritual self is capable. Therefore, I offer in Figure 10.1 an expanded model which incorporates id, ego, superego, and the supraordinate self but expands outwards beyond them. I call the radiating, expanding, and dimensionalizing aspects of psychospirituality – from the adaptive ego to the mysterious Other, the awesome God – the 'circles of being.'

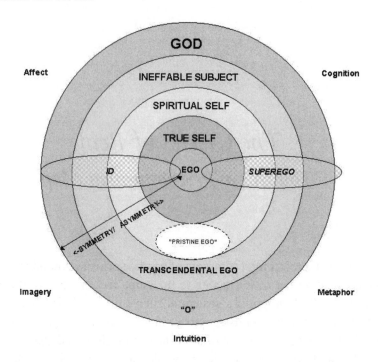

Figure 10.1. The circles of being

It is important to note that such a 'map' is bound to have many uncharted regions, areas of the psyche which have yet to be systematically delineated by explorers of the farther reaches of mind and being. What we call 'psychospiritual' is in part a global term for those aspects of psychic functioning that we have yet to depict in a systematic way, even though we have had numerous glimpses and revelations of these regions, and we can suppose that much territory remains undiscovered, some of it forever beyond our reach. In these regions, there may or may not be the possibility of paranormal phenomena such as 'past lives,' extrasensory perception, and clairvoyance. For me, this is a question for which science has yet to supply a firm answer.

I call this map of the psychospiritual realm 'the circles of being' because it is not just about cognition, emotion, and behavior but implies aspects of the person which are 'un-thought' yet can lead to self-transformation. That is, the realms of psyche, soma, and spirit are expansive and interconnected in ways we don't yet fully understand, and any conceptualization of 'mind' must take into account spheres of influence not explainable in terms of conscious experience. Psychospiritual studies include states of 'being' as well as 'doing,' sequestered knowledge (that which is repressed and 'sealed off' from awareness), and potential (as yet unborn), as well as actual experience.

Because the full dimensionality of such a map cannot be represented in a two-dimensional diagram, a few points are worth making by way of clarification and qualification. Like a map of the earth, the 'real' dimensions and coordinates of the map cannot be visualized on a flat plane. In principle, the map's rings expand beyond the page to infinity as the circles widen. In addition, the layered spheres overlap and interpenetrate one another as 'living systems.' One way to think of these multi-dimensional systems of experience and mind is in terms of complexity and integration. As the psyche expands beyond the ego, it encompasses more and more aspects of experience and integrates them more fully. In addition, the concentric circles fail to represent the interpenetration of the various structures. For example, God is present in the ego in 'traces' such as acts of kindness and various images and symbols of Him. Aspects of the superego (ideals, prohibitions, taboos) derive, as Freud suggested, from the id (impulses, needs, desires), and also include 'traces of God.' (Of course, I strongly agree with Jungians that, while Freud viewed the 'idea' of God as a personified aspect of the superego, the full and complex understanding of God and Higher Self encompasses far more than superego prohibition and morality.)

Within the circles of selfhood, I distinguish between the 'true self' and the 'spiritual self.' I suspect that both Grotstein (2000) and Eigen (1998) would take exception to this partitioning. My reading of Eigen suggests that he, like Winnicott, regards the 'true self' as the vital core of the psyche. For me the true self is the expression of vitality, but not its source. I differentiate the true self from the spiritual self (the individual's source, soul, or spirit) because I view the true self as the vehicle whereby the soul can actualize itself in living. The true self exists in space, time, physical body, and interpersonal relations as a spontaneous manifestation of the spiritual self, which, in keeping with Einsteinian physics, is timeless and 'poly-spatial,' yet, through the true self, is expressible in actions, symbols, meanings, emotions, physical contact, prayer, and so on.

In the circles of being, God is also closely related to, but differentiated from, the 'ineffable subject.' Modernist religious thought, such as that of Buber, and to some extent Merton and Tillich, appears to equate God with the ineffable subject in a genuine attempt to demythologize God and emphasize the fully human experience of I–Thou being and love as God manifest in self and community. I see this theological development as a crucial advance in our understanding of God because it makes Him, as our own ineffable subject, a part of us in our collective lives, and answers the need for an understanding of God which is compatible with both modern science and humanism. However, I agree with Bion (1970, pp.87–91) that the very nature of thought requires the assumption of something 'wholly other,' the 'thing-in-itself' from which all thought flows. The ineffable subject, which is our highest state of selfhood, must itself be generated by forces outside of self, whether we think of such forces naturalistically as neurochemical events or spiritually as Otherness. That is, the theory of the unconscious mind presupposes a God beyond our subjectivity as the Other which mysteriously creates and influences that subjectivity. Bion (1970, p.26) labeled this Otherness 'O,' in order to keep it an open region of exploration rather than superimposing conventional ideas about God upon it. Jung, in his early writings, spoke of the 'pleroma,' a reservoir of archetypes beyond the senses, 'the sum total of God's powers and emanations' (Hayman, 1999, p.201). Interestingly, both Jung and Bion utilized Kantian philosophy to posit 'thoughts without a thinker' which pre-exist beyond awareness yet contribute to that awareness. 'God' is the 'O,' the archetypal Other, from which the ineffable subject draws its creative power.

Grotstein (2000, pp.59–81) implies that the ineffable subject is the ultimate source of all our experience and the closest we can ever come to knowing God, while I contend that the ineffable subject is seeking God and inspired by God. This is in keeping with both Kant and with Tillich in that the subject, however transcendent, requires an 'O,' a 'thing-in-itself' which is beyond all subjectivity. I should add that this is my own reading of these profound thinkers, with which they might differ. Engaging these differences is far more important for establishing the paradigm than resolving them.

The ego, the decision-making executor of cognition and action in ordinary time and space, constitutes the subject-matter of modern secular psychology and psychoanalytic 'ego psychology.' Winnicott's addition of the 'true self' to Freud's structural model represented a genuine breakthrough in bringing authenticity, spontaneity, and creativity into focus as important elements of the psyche, moving in the direction of Maslow's 'self-actualization' model.

As one flies outwards towards and through the ever-widening circles of the psyche, the mind becomes more complex and paradoxical to our experiencing egos, whose thoughts are formulated in a cognitive mode that Matte-Blanco (1975) has called 'bi-logic' or 'asymmetrical logic' – that is, reasoning that obeys the laws of contradiction and the 'excluded middle,' so that a statement and its opposite cannot both be true. A wider bandwidth of self-experience (such as dreams, images, and metaphors), incorporates symmetrical logic or 'bi-logic.' In that realm, as Freud (1900, pp.361–363) early suggested, both a statement and its opposite can be true, along with the gradients between the opposites.

As we ascend from the center of the circle to its infinite circumference, thought becomes increasingly symmetrical and holistic. That is, the apparent contradictions within our experience are encompassed within one whole, which transcends both three-dimensional space and any particular system of thought. Simply put, we, within our limited 'ego space' must intuit and creatively comprehend these levels, developing theories and metaphors which point to them but can never fully encompass them (Schermer, 1999). Quantum theory, living systems, and chaos/complexity theories include multi-dimensional symmetrical logic, and so too do the intuitions, narratives, and images of literature, the arts, cultural rituals, and archetypal myths. Yet, they never quite capture the 'thing-in-itself.' Indeed, such theories and representations include recognition of their own limitations.

Since we know that the brain/mind grasps experience through multiple vehicles such as imagery, affect, cognition, metaphor, and intuition, I have indicated these mental functions on the map (Figure 10.2). God has been *approached* and expressed imagistically in works of art, as well as through intense feelings such as ecstasy and awe, through theological and philosophical cognitions, metaphors such as the 'Rock of Ages,' and intuitive sources such as mystical revelations. These represent the capacities of the ego to comprehend that which is complex, inchoate, and dimly understood, within the confines of our descriptive abilities.

I am concerned that the circles of being may imply incorrectly that the ego is at the center of the psyche, which is not my intention. Indeed, the ego is at the center of our mundane waking life and allows us to negotiate the world around us. It is 'the place where we live,' from where we start any journey of the spirit. But, as Freud pointed out, the ego is a small, superficial region of mental function, which provides at best a 'window on the world' and the self, and at worst is the source of the greatest illusion of all, that 'what we see is who we are' (rather than that we have an unconscious and a spirit), a mechanistic myth from which Western scientific culture has suffered perhaps since Aristotle, and at least since the Enlightenment and the advent of the Cartesian body–mind dualism. I chose the 'concentric circles' way of mapping the psyche only because it is near to day-to-day experience, since we see ourselves most of the time as the center of our universe, and because it correctly implies that the larger circles are more encompassing and multi-dimensional than the smaller, and include the smaller within them.

The diagram makes clear my position that the Freudian id and superego are only a small part of the unconscious. When Freud superimposed the structural theory on his earlier 'topographical model' of conscious, preconscious, and unconscious thought (Freud, 1915), he inadvertently narrowed the range of what his earlier point of view included and emphasized, namely the realms of 'primary process,' the 'uncanny,' and the infinite combinations and disseminations of metaphors and images of which we have glimpses in our dreams. These regions of symmetry and bi-logic intercalate far more than our biological instincts (id) and social learning (superego) imply. Deep transformational components of the self, and 'God's energy,' are parts of the unconscious that do not fit into the category of drives or instincts. And the harsh superego which Freud thought of as arbitrary and primitive is only a minute reflection of the moral capabilities of man and their source in a God or holy Otherness that are stored in our collective unconscious.

I see God as 'unthought' Being beyond the ineffable subject, although manifest within the latter. The ineffable subject not only reaches down into the true self and the ego, but also looks outward, upward, and inward towards the mysterious Other, which it experiences as its primal source. This Other consists both of aspects of which we may intuitively be aware, and of components which are in some way barred from our comprehension, just as we see subjective colors, but not the light rays impinging on the retina (which are known only through scientific experiment and inference). Similarly, subjective experiences of God must be distinguished from the awesome and mysterious 'cause' of our universe and our destinies, which we infer from such experiences.

There are several ways to describe the existence of God: as a sense perception (for example, visions of God), a 'real,' provable entity, a faith or belief, and the subject of subjects (the experiencing self itself). As an experience, God is like the color green – private, unprovable, but each of us can know God if we 'see' Him in a vision or hear his voice, or, less spectacularly, sense His presence in a person, a flower, or a poem. As a concrete object, God is a verifiable entity or process like an electron or a magnetic field. We confirm His existence through observation, measurement, and experimentation.[1] As a faith or belief, we posit God's existence as a way of explaining and giving meaning to our lives. As subject of subjects, God exists as pure consciousness itself ('I Am that I Am').

In the circles of being, 'God' is a variegated matrix of phenomena (observable events) and noumena (truths, abstractions, things-in-themselves). The experience of God as One, as a profound unity which is our Creator, reflects the Judao-Christian belief that there is a single, unified Source. Polytheistic religions such as that of the ancient Greeks and of Hinduism may actually possess a deeper grasp of the complexity of forces than does monotheism. Monotheistic religion is an 'advance' over polytheism only as it transcends specific images and 'idols' and brings us into a central dialogue with something above and beyond us. It does this with a potential loss of complexity which we must be ever vigilant to retain.

The ultimate goal of a psychospiritual paradigm would be to detail and elaborate a map of the entire mind/body/spirit/God complex – circles of being which go well beyond our current conceptions. The diagram suggests that there are many as yet uncharted regions looking for 'space travelers' to visit them and cartographers to chart them. This disciplined journey of exploration – heretofore relegated to a few 'divine hallucinators and storytellers' – will require the cooperation of psychologists, neuroscientists, philosophers, mystics, and theologians. That journey has indeed begun, starting with Freud and Jung, and continuing on to this day in a remarkable mix of studies and speculations that need to be coordinated and synthesized into a new view of human experience.

Despite the fact that there are large gaps in our knowledge of the circles of being, my position in this book is that the little we do know is well worth applying to psychotherapeutic and psychoanalytic treatment. I am not referring only to the holistic healers and spiritualists who offer their intuitions, inspirations, and transformations, but also to those of us who practice mainstream psychotherapies. The spiritualist as psychotherapist will doubtless feel that he has already gone well beyond the rather cautious generalizations that I have made within a more conservative mode of theory and treatment. What I do offer in Part II of this volume are some ideas that may stimulate an expansion of naturalistic and social science-based approaches to include a measure of spirituality within their purview. Gradually, the region of the circles of being encompassed within psychotherapy and psychoanalysis may expand to new frontiers. Hopefully, over time, a consistent data-based psychospiritual perspective will emerge about how psychotherapy works and how to make it a still better instrument of psychological healing.

Therefore, in Part II, I discuss selected aspects of psychospiritual treatment. I begin by reconsidering the traditional psychotherapy contractual arrangement from a psychospiritual perspective. Then I take up the narratives and myths that mark the spiritual journey of psychotherapy. This is followed by a discussion of the therapist's listening process in terms of mystical experience. Our journey together ends with a brief consideration and summation of the rich potential of psychospirituality as well as its difficulties and hazards. As an addendum, and something of an anomaly in the present context, I utilize the Twelve Steps of Alcoholics Anonymous as an instance of an approach to healing which incorporates spiritual principles. I suggest areas of both overlap and difference between AA's comprehensive restructuring of the personality along spiritual lines, and conventional psychodynamic and cognitive-behavioral therapies.

Endnote

1   Some 'spiritualists' such as Edgar Cayce and his followers, and even, in a certain sense, Jung, believe that the existence of God is scientifically provable. Just as we can infer and verify the existence of God by experimenting with prayer, spiritual healing etc., so God is an object of scientific study.

Part II

Spirituality and Psychological Healing

CHAPTER ELEVEN

Spirituality in Psychotherapy

Depth psychotherapy is an interpersonal experience in which at least one party, the 'identified patient,'[1] has the potential to undergo a self-transformation which alleviates his symptoms and enhances his quality of life. A spiritually-based psychology offers the psychotherapist avenues for exploration and ways of introspecting, understanding, illuminating, and communicating that include but go beyond those available in traditional psychotherapies. What would be added to psychotherapy by including a conscious psychospiritual intent, theory, and praxis, and what would such a treatment process look like?

The schema for the personality and its growth and development that I have articulated in the preceding chapters suggests that the bare minimum of a psychospiritual treatment process would consist of 'consciousness-raising' at the most basic levels for psychotherapists, allowing them to work with a widened scope of processes and narratives in the consulting room, without necessarily altering the specific techniques they use. While it is true that some therapists today pray and meditate with patients, others who are spiritually oriented continue to practice their traditional brand of treatment in a way that could be called 'spiritually informed.' For example, at a panel discussion on spirituality in psychotherapy (Gottlieb, 2001), family therapist Molly Layton presented an instance of an intervention with a young girl which helped her 'individuate a self' (Bowen, 1978) by making an especially empathic and well-timed intervention acknowledging the child's painful enmeshment and entrapment by her mother's confusing messages. Layton, who incorporates Buddhist principles into her practice, however, saw her effectiveness stemming not so much from her comments as from her own striving for emptiness and detachment during therapy sessions. Her mindset, or if you will, 'no-mindset' enabled Layton to directly intuit the child's 'true self' and, in a heightened state of non-attachment, she timed and phrased her intervention in a way that resonated compassionately with the child's own strivings. Furthermore, it is possible that the child was able to internalize Layton's 'no-mind' state in a way which allowed her to detach from the double bind in which she felt placed by her mother.

So, one can 'do' psychotherapy using any workable approach, such as Bowen's (1978) model of family therapy, but with heightened spiritual awareness. Since the therapist's own being can be as effective in treatment as any specific method, we can hypothesize that the therapist's own spiritual awareness may positively impact upon treatment outcomes, regardless of technique. If not a guru, the psychotherapist can certainly embody and convey new ways of thinking, feeling, and being to the patient.

In addition, spiritual concepts and practices allow us to view psychotherapy in a new light, at a more evolved plane, in which the implicit background understanding of what occurs is richer and more meaningful and more likely to effect significant change. By holding the process in the 'light,' we may be better able to perceive and encourage the emergence and development of the spiritual self in our patients, and also have a framework whereby therapists and treatment outcome researchers can begin to 'compare notes' and establish testable hypotheses. If this were to be done in a consistent way, psychotherapy might evolve new forms quite different from those we presently know. At present, however, the more traditional psychodynamic, contextual, and cognitive-behavioral approaches can be made serviceable in a spiritually informed way.

In this chapter, I would like to discuss some of the ways in which this evolution can be fostered. I will be speaking mostly from a psychodynamic perspective, but the same ideas and principles could be utilized within other approaches. For me, the critical ingredients of a psychospiritual approach are:

1. the context, the contract, and the therapist's commitment as 'sacred'

2. working with spiritually informed myths, narratives, and metaphors

3. therapy as 'state changes' and transformations

4. spiritual practices as analogs and scripts for psychotherapy.

The context, the contract, and the therapist's commitment

One of Freud's greatest accomplishments (cf. Rieff, 1979) was to remove psychotherapy from its institutional and medical contexts and place it on the basis of a freely entered contract for a 'talking cure' between the patient and analyst. This revised contract facilitated a 'parity' (Cohen and Schermer, 2001) between analyst and analysand which reduced the societal pressure implicit in the idea of the therapist as an authority figure possessing institutionalized power. The patient became a 'free agent' in a 'co-authored' process that involved 'free association,' i.e. the privilege of uncensored speech. Further, he could choose when to begin and end treatment and formulate his own goals and objectives. He could engage in independent thinking and articulate ideas and images which were socially 'taboo.' In this respect, Freud, although he was a naturalist and a reductionist in his theorizing, granted the patient his own mental essence or 'soul' (Bettelheim, 1983) which was to be respected and nurtured. This acknowledgement of the person's inner core constituted a significant advance over authority-based therapy interventions like hypnosis, practiced in institutional settings such as a psychiatric ward, where the patient was under considerable pressure to change and was far from being a free agent.

In Freud's famous case of 'Dora' (1905), an adolescent girl with hysterical symptoms entered treatment under considerable pressure from a man to conceal sexualized contacts between them. Courageously, Freud helped Dora to express her every thought, memory, dream, and fantasy, thus maintaining her parity and freedom. At the same time, a careful reading of the case shows that he struggled with his own tendency to exercise physicianly authority, repeatedly insisting to Dora that the events she alluded to were childhood fantasies rather than current realities, and pressing for further early memories rather than addressing her present needs and concerns. Freud's self-honesty, however, was such that in a 'Postscript' to the case, he acknowledged that Dora's premature termination was partly the result of his countertransference, his own unresolved conflicts. Such self-introspection was, so far as I know, almost unheard of among either the clergy practicing 'confessional' or physicians prior to Freud, and constituted a major step forward in helping to release the mentally ill from the grip of authoritarian attempts to control their words and behavior.

Freud respected the patient's 'soul' even further by shifting the focus of treatment from the direct cure of symptoms to a process of self-exploration in the presence of an 'other' who provided a commentary – a process, by the way, not unlike a rabbinical commentary on a text. Psychoanalysis thus took on quasi-religious and quasi-philosophical functions of self-knowledge, the search for meanings, and an investigation of the forces for good and ill that existed in each person. A connection was thus inititiated between psychotherapeutic treatment and the wider scope of civilization, namely, literature, art, the social sciences, theology, and philosophical investigation. Indeed, the modern psychological 'care of the soul,' of the whole person in his many levels of existence, was almost single-handedly initiated by Freud. Although his own perspective remained limited in that he omitted from his theory and practice approaches like body work, analysis of current vulnerabilities and needs, and religious practices, he opened the door to treatment of the whole self, a door which was opened wider still by the subsequent interpersonal, existential, and humanistic psychotherapy movements. In sum, the psychoanalytic contract and 'frame' (Langs, 1976) was from its inception deeply embedded in healing and religious traditions and not merely a strategy for curing the patient of his mental illness.

The problem with Freud's pioneering view of the 'talking cure' was not in his deep and moral understanding of the process, but in the fact that, to paraphrase one of his own remarks about object relations, the shadow of his theories fell upon the patient and, without Freud intending to do so, significantly limited the patient–therapist discourse and unintentionally imposed an external belief system on the patient. (It is likely that every therapist does the same in his own way, as an inevitable part of human interaction. He must periodically detach from and become aware of his own biases insofar as that is possible.) Thus, because Freud's theoretical orientation was reductionistic and naturalistic, the very fact that the therapy contract itself is spiritually based was clouded and obscured. A spiritual understanding can, in my opinion, expand and deepen what is involved in the type of relationship and commitment that is involved in psychotherapy.

Freud implied, but did not state, that the therapy contract is hallowed in the sense that it embodies and honors certain high values and ethics, and also in the quality of the special relationship that develops between therapist and patient, who often feel an inviolable bond between them. The sacredness of the contract itself is seen in the meticulous introspective study and rectification of deviations from the analytic 'frame' (Langs, 1976), the latter representing a contract that includes confidentiality of disclosure, regular hours (comparable to the hours of a church mass, and the observance of the Sabbath), acknowledgement and correction of the therapist's errors (which can serve as a form of amends and reparation which establishes trust and assures that the patient does not have to distort his expressions to suit the therapist), and the sustained attention of the therapist (akin to spiritual practices of single-minded concentration and meditation). The frame thus provides a sanctuary for the mind, a place where the honest expression of thoughts and the deep understanding of them is regarded as 'holy,' even if it means the deconstruction of ideas held sacred in other contexts. When the mind is given sanctuary, it is capable of creatively constructing and deconstructing its own world view, which may emerge as different from that of the society at large. In object relations theory and self psychology, the sacredness and sanctuary of the mind is further manifest in the maternal functions of holding, containment, and empathy whereby thoughts and emotions are apprehended in a way which validates them and gives them form.

The commitment of the therapist, from a spiritual perspective, is thus to ensure the freedom of mind and spirit of the patient within the sacred time and space of the therapy hour. At the same time, he engages the patient in a dialogue which tests and challenges the patient's assumptions, beliefs, and behaviors. It is this dialectal dance between the 'freedom to be' and the setting of a series of hurdles, challenges, and differences, which can result in emotional and spiritual growth. Since the two poles of this dialectic are contradictory, one implying non-interference and the other propelling change, therapy at its best becomes a moral and interpersonal process where risk and opportunity converge. The meltdown of either of these poles for any length of time can distort or truncate the treatment process.

A patient, Maggie, came to me with the painful dilemma that her husband, whom she loved greatly, was having an affair. She felt betrayed and at the same time loved him and did not want to leave him. As treatment proceeded, Maggie gained insight into herself and her own feelings, realizing, for example, that she herself had long felt frustrated in the marriage and had more than once fantasized about having a love affair. In treatment, she made significant progress in untangling her own conflicts, but her husband continued to be involved with the other woman. He told his wife that he still loved her, but had also fallen in love with the other woman. He himself was in a quandary about what to do. At this point, Maggie seriously considered starting an affair with a man at work whom she found alluring.

It appeared likely that if the patient did not take some concerted action to preserve the marriage, it would dissolve. Therefore, I encountered a moral dilemma about whether the patient's freedom to go on seeking insight in the therapy hour was more or less important than the sacredness of the marriage vow. I tried to preserve both sides of the equation by prioritizing the marriage for a period of time in the treatment, while continuing to trace the deeper roots of her own love fantasies. I further suggested that she and her husband pursue couples counseling. At the same time, I allowed the patient to continue the narrative of her own fantasies and connected them to the marital relationship. Eventually, after much difficulty, the husband ended his affair, and the marriage was re-affirmed. The patient continued to gain insight into herself within the context of her own narrative and self-exploration. Throughout this process, I frequently wrestled with my dual commitments to facilitate emotional and spiritual freedom in the session (and freedom of choice in life) and to challenge the patient to act and change in a way consistent with her marriage vows.

So, therapy is not merely a means of treating illnesses and symptoms, it is an endeavor where deep moral and spiritual concerns are focused. Every competent therapist knows that these moral concerns form the context of all treatment. A spiritually-based approach highlights and invigorates our awareness that therapy offers a sanctuary for the mind and soul, and that the moral/spiritual dimension is not simply a background for the treatment, but rather is the essence of what cures, the motor that makes the process happen, and the very heart of the therapy relationship. This emphasis constitutes the recovery of the 'lost Atlantis' of the talking cure, the part of the process that derives from theological, religious, and philosophical teachings that a modernist empirical approach had diminished.

Patient narratives and metaphors from a spiritual perspective

The central element of psychotherapy is the patient's 'story,' which affords the therapist an opportunity to initiate insight and change. In this telling of the tale, the asymmetry (Cohen and Schermer, 2001) between therapist and patient is apparent. The therapist remains opaque, telling very little of his story, and then only to empathize with and/or enlighten the patient. He becomes the oracle, the Greek chorus, the commentator, vis-à-vis the patient as the protagonist in the drama. In telling his story, the patient, even as he states 'facts,' actually constructs a narrative, part memory and part imagination, which may consist of a re-constructed history of his life and emotional development. In the process, he creates a myth about himself, a persona. For example, the narcissistic patient presents himself as grand, self-sufficient, and universally approved; a depressive patient presents as burdened, failed, and tragic; an anxiety-ridden patient portrays himself as trapped, helpless, and imprisoned in a world of imminent, nameless dread. In addition, the patient may create a 'novella,' for example, a tale of fractured relationships with suspenseful outcomes. Or he may describe the different parts of himself as if they were characters in a play, each having their own subpersonalities and interacting in such a way as to create a denouement which the patient perceives as his destiny. An internal struggle between good and evil, intimacy and aloneness, compulsion and freedom, honesty and deception emerges, and the patient may find himself engulfed, beached, abandoned, tempted, adrift.

The therapist, in his turn, relates as a second subject to the patient's narrative, identifying with it, or else correcting the story, questioning its consistency and its distortions, suggesting alternative narratives and ways to play them out behaviorally, and empathizing humanly with the cast of characters. All the while, the therapist is aiming to elevate the patient's narrative to a higher level of discourse which is more appropriate to the current situation, more resilient and nuanced, more informed with an awareness of the human condition.

The spiritually attuned psychotherapist will perceive that within the patient's narrative can be heard the core spiritual self and the journey it is taking. For instance, the depressed patient's spiritual journey often reflects his frustrated search for good in the world and in himself. The narcissist's journey conveys a sense of having been arrested at the point of trying to bridge the gap between self and other, so that he can only include the other as an extension and mirror of himself. The anxiety disordered patient seems 'lost in the wilderness,' desperately wanting to flee, but unable to move. Jung considered the core spiritual self in terms of archetypes, primal images and situations of universal consciousness. Spiritually, these archetypes are complex representations of fundamental dilemmas of meaning and relatedness which each person experiences in his or her life. Understanding the patient in terms of basic meanings and relatedness constitutes a bridge between the psychodynamic/relational perspective and Jung's archetypes. At the limit, they intersect in the numinous within the patient's narrative, where his being-in-the-world meets his Being with God.

A spiritually-based psychotherapy reaches for the ultimate spiritual journey that is contained in the patient's story. This process evolves over time, highlighted by moments in which therapist and patient are profoundly connected and the narrative reaches an emotional peak. A severely depressed patient told me that, as an altruistic gesture, he had recently clipped some of the hedges on the avenue where he lived. He thought that drivers couldn't see the turnoff ahead and might get into an accident. At that moment, I knew that he was warding off a catastrophic danger to his being, that his journey needed to be clearer, and that, as his therapist, I needed to be more available and transparent to him. I interpreted this to him, and it led us to be more open with each other, and to mutual efforts to trim and clear his thoughts about himself.

The 'circumcision' ritual of trimming the hedges could also be seen as an obsessive-compulsive action to cope with an overwhelming impulse to 'make a mess' that could cause an accident. While such a Freudian 'anal' interpretation is, for me, incomplete, omitting the patient's deeper struggle for being and connectedness, it strikingly points to the fact that, from a spiritual perspective, it is important to recognize and work with the rites and rituals that interweave with the patient's narrative.

The therapist invokes his own rites as well. On a personal note, I recall that, for several years, my own therapist greeted me at each session in a kindly but standardized way. He opened the consulting room door, stood partially hidden behind it, and then walked with me to our respective chairs, separated by his desk, placed his fingers limply on the desk, and stood silently until I sat down. This, I believe, was his ritual of transforming himself into a wise, knowledgeable, and authoritative physician. At the same time, he seemed to be telling me that the space of therapy was now given to me, that the door was open to my thoughts, but that the 'law of the desk' would ultimately prevail – I must put all thoughts into words. At the same time, as the 'second subject,' he seemed to be reassuring himself that some untoward aggressive or intimate event would not occur between us! For several years, his 'sacred greeting' and the desk-as-altar offered me a reassuring boundary that also created a distance and objectification which I found frankly disturbing, never certain whether it was he or I who had created the difficulty!

I worked with a woman patient, Rachel, who engaged in necessary and recurrent grieving about various hurts and losses over a period of months and years. When she completed her treatment, Rachel articulated that she had used me as a container for all her 'garbage.' I immediately felt 'used,' but the patient laughed gently, and I laughed with her. I saw that therapeutic containment symbolized for her an arduous spiritual journey in which she was a child born late in her mother's life, which created a deep but troubled bond between the two of them. She was grieving for their mutual love and mutual exile. Only gradually did the emotional rift between the patient and her mother begin to heal. Rachel's spiritual journey was based on a powerful striving to reconcile with her mother by experiencing and grieving their common fate. She encountered me on that journey as a kindly stranger on the road and successfully transformed me into the healer and 'obstetrician of the soul' that she needed. She knew that, through therapy, she had given birth to herself once more.

The patient's narrative simultaneously obscures, explores, reveals, and alters his state of consciousness. Ordinary waking experience is only one of several states of mind. In the course of a day, we make the transition from sleep (which itself includes deep sleep and REM or dream sleep) through hypnagogic (falling asleep) and hynopompic (waking up) states to wakeful states which vary in alertness and fluctuate between left-brain and right-brain activity, i.e. cogitative versus imagistic, emotion-laden states which Freud called secondary and primary process respectively. Furthermore, in meditation, our brainwaves slow down, and our vital bodily functions attenuate and decelerate, while at the same time peaceful feelings emerge, spiritual experiences occur, and lasting benefits are noted, from physical well-being to improved concentration and mental functioning. It is in the interplay of altered and alternating states of consciousness that transformation of the self can occur.

Psychotherapy is therefore a place where narrative, human interaction, and altered states of consciousness come together. However, with the exceptions of hypnotherapy (Phillips and Frederick, 1995), neurolinguistic programming (Dilts, 1983), and work on dissociative states in traumatized patients (Bromberg, 1998), altered states of consciousness are rarely addressed in contemporary clinical work. Yet they are important, perhaps crucial, signposts and transformative elements of treatment.

Therapy as 'state changes' and transformations

Many years ago, I attended a lecture by a prominent psychopharmacologist, Wolfgang Vogel, who possessed a delightful sense of humor. His talk was delivered in the beautiful, spacious chapel of a hospital facility in a rural setting. Gleefully, in a guttural German accent, Vogel began his discourse on hallucinogens by saying, 'Welcome to this chapel! We are all taking an LSD trip! The brain has natural hallucinogens which produce an altered state of consciousness, and they are released in this place of worship.' Vogel was pointing out that alterations in consciousness occur naturally and frequently without drugs and are triggered by context. Just as they occur in a place of worship, so they must take place during psychotherapy. The question is, what is their significance in the treatment context?

A spiritual perspective on psychotherapy as invoking a sacred time, space, and mission implies that the consciousness of both patient and therapist will shift towards spiritual states in the course of treatment. For example, in the classical psychoanalytic method, the patient lies on the couch, which induces a dream-like state where 'primary process' images, emotions, and memories predominate over cognitive rationalizing processes. Freud viewed such regression to primary process thinking as a replay of what he believed were childlike and primitive experiences. These, he held, in turn facilitate the transference of childhood relationships, wishes, and fantasies onto the therapist, where they can be analyzed and revised. In so doing, Freud downplayed the fact that such a relaxation of cognitive processes can be therapeutic in itself, facilitating imagination, mystery, play, a sense of oneness, and other functions that are manifestations of the spiritual self – what Jung (Hayman, 1999, pp.191–193) called 'active imagination.' In the psychospiritual paradigm, the so-called 'primary process' imagery and emotionalities are not necessarily primitive, but have a potential for mind expansion, transcendence, and personal growth. Consciousness is altered in such a way as to evoke dimensions of experience not accessible to linear, rational thinking.

Prior to Freud, Janet (1886) had viewed hysterical symptoms in terms of dissociated states of consciousness, meaning that the patient's symptoms formed a complex of thoughts and feelings that were sequestered and kept apart from the ordinary flow of mental associations. Freud in effect rotated Janet's dissociation theory ninety degrees, contending that such clusters of ideas and emotions derived from memories of early childhood that were later repressed, i.e. forgotten and thus hidden from view. That is, for Freud, the sequestering was 'vertical,' in time, rather than 'horizontal,' in a dissociated state of consciousness. Emphasizing the historical dimension, Freud became the first detective of the mind, striving like an archaeologist to unearth these buried traces of the past, becoming a modern Tiresias, a truth seeker of the deeper layers of the soul.

In that role, however, Freud abandoned Janet's interesting implication that unconsciousness is itself a state of consciousness or even an alter ego or sub-personality. From that standpoint, the patient enters the unconscious realm for periods of time and avails himself of its 'symmetrical logic' (Matte-Blanco, 1975) of imagery, paradoxes, and ambiguity of meaning. Then, in the process of acquiring insight, and partly through the analyst's interpretations, the patient re-enters the light of waking consciousness, and in moments of awareness that constitute genuine epiphanies, leaps briefly into a transcendent state of higher spiritual awareness. The patient's state of consciousness, then, is frequently shifting throughout the session. And the state of the therapist's consciousness must flow in ways that facilitate growth and change in the patient.

Dreams, of course, represent an altered state of consciousness, and so provide a vehicle for transcendence and transformations of the psychospiritual self. For example, one patient reported a dream about finding her authentic self in a moment of intense anxiety during a dream. The anxiety was triggered by images of a near-death experience in which she survived drowning in a lake. She recalled seeing her own face very clearly in the dream and was surprised to see that it was her face as a child. She simultaneously had a sensation within the dream that she could 'get up off her feet' after the traumatic event of the dream and walk away from it unscathed. The dream represented a milestone in her treatment, since it was the first time she perceived anxiety as a source of growth rather than just a painful symptom from which she sought relief. Recalling the dream, she felt excited and 'reborn.' When she told me about it, I noticed that I myself felt lighter, more centered, and aware of an aura, a presence in the consulting room. I felt surprisingly refreshed and at peace at the end of the session. The patient's therapy and our subsequent interactions became more energized and purposeful.

Woollcott and Desai (1990) cite evidence from neurophysiological studies suggesting that meditation leads not only to mystical awareness but also to improved integration of left- and right-brain activity as well as limbic and cortical functions, so that cognitive, intuitive, and emotional processes may be more fully integrated and effective. My contention, which is an important basis for the psychospiritual paradigm, is that optimal psychotherapy evokes states of consciousness similar to meditation, through the ebb and flow of primary and secondary process, attuned interpretations, and work with dream material, childhood memories, and fantasies in the context of an intersubjective search for understanding.

The therapist's ability to detect changes in his own consciousness and their connection to those of the patient can be useful in treatment. For an extreme example, I once worked with a patient who literally put me to sleep in sessions! Of course, he was surprised and upset by my somnolence, as indeed was I. But, by exploring how my narcoleptic 'tuning out' related to his monotonous narrative of self-denigration and shame, as well as his tendency to deceive and manipulate, we were able to resolve some of his chronic problems with self-esteem, denial, and manipulation. His affect improved markedly, and the therapeutic alliance was greatly enhanced.

On another occasion, I conducted an initial interview with an apparently 'normal' patient who, surprisingly, put me in a paralyzing trance where I could not think or move! Recovering my bearings, I soon discovered that, despite his apparently normal conversation, he was in a psychotic state of hallucination and delusion.

When patients achieve emotional insight, they are in a different state of consciousness than when they are reporting dreams, images, and memories in a freely associative way. Going back and forth between these states allows the patient to integrate left-brain and right-brain experience, which in itself can be therapeutic because such a dialogue within the self is part of the problem-solving process in daily life. We generate images, experience emotions, and process them cognitively to resolve conflicts and see new possibilities for responsiveness and action.

Specifically transcendent states of consciousness are not ordinarily achieved for any length of time in conventional psychotherapies. I think, however, that they are probably occurring intersubjectively when the therapist's intuition is highly 'in synch' with the patient. For example, an African-American patient was very depressed. She bowed her head low. A song by Billie Holiday, 'Good morning, heartache,' went through my mind. I shared my thought with her, and said, 'You know, Billie had a very sad life, but she gave so much to us. I'll bet it's the same with you.' I was surprised when she told me she was an avid Billie Holiday fan. It was as if at that moment, without direct communication, the patient lifted me up and out of my usual preoccupations, giving me a moment of dwelling on some beautiful but tragic music that networked with her own psyche. She also gave me a glimpse of her soul. Most therapists have had moments with patients where it is as if they are improvising music together. A prominent jazz saxophonist, David Liebman, has told me that when a jazz group is really 'swinging,' they are in an altered spiritual state. I couldn't agree with him more, and I think that applies to psychotherapy as well.

Bion (Symington and Symington, 1996, pp.168–169) referred to a dream-like state of 'reverie' which characterizes the mother's interaction with the infant. The mother is at those times finely tuned to the infant's needs, and therefore can contain and respond to them appropriately. Therapists can attain a similar receptive attunement to their patients. In such states, mutually held transitional spaces and objects become sources of nonverbal communication. In one therapy session, gazing intently upon a patient's beautiful antique necklace and locket brought back to me a series of warm memories about my grandmother. In turn, the recollections facilitated my bonding with the patient, and she herself began to elaborate her family's intergenerational history. The 'transitional object' of the locket altered my state of consciousness, and I experienced both reverie and reminiscence. Such a transformation induced by the locket enhanced my closeness to the patient.

Religious liturgy, rite, and ritual, like psychotherapy, produce altered states of consciousness and the potential for transformation. While I have reservations about conducting religious practices in sessions, I do feel that if we can regard the therapy process from a psychospiritual standpoint, it may heighten our sensitivity to spiritual states as they occur spontaneously. I will now try to exemplify the confluence of psychotherapy with spiritual ritual and practice.

Spiritual practices and concepts as analogs to psychotherapy

One way to approach a psychospiritual understanding and methodology for psychotherapy is to examine actual spiritual practices for analogs and metaphors to naturally occurring events and processes in treatment. The structural differences between a house of worship and a therapy office, or between various liturgical and therapeutic 'texts,' obscure deep similarities that stem from the fact that psychotherapy and religion have many convergent sources in history and human need. How can a Jew reciting the Torah, a Muslim bowing to Mecca, a Christian taking the Eucharist, or a Buddhist sitting in zazen – all forms of devotion – be compared to a therapist in an urban office building, with no obvious object or task of devotion, and with a minimum of ceremony? Yet, if we examine the deeper structure of such practices, parallels become apparent. Prayer, spiritual poverty and simplicity, affirmations of faith, and birth, confirmation, and death rites, for example, all occur spontaneously within psychotherapy.

Prayer

Michael Eigen has said, 'Psychotherapy is a prayer.' At first, that statement puzzled me. After all, in prayer, an individual bypasses other persons and appeals directly to God. He makes a request of God, expresses adoration to God, and so on. (Prayer is *trans*personal.) In therapy, the patient is communing with another person, not God. (Therapy is *inter*personal.) Furthermore, if the patient makes a request of the therapist, the latter is as likely as not to refuse it and ask the patient to continue talking or to introspect on what the request might represent emotionally. Patients frequently complain that their therapists answer precious few of their prayers! But when I continued to meditate on Eigen's statement, I thought of a number of ways in which therapy is indeed like a prayer and also bears a resemblance to other spiritual practices.

A prayer is a request made to an Other for help and solace. Since psychotherapy is a personal and interpersonal process, it is not self-evident that a higher being is ever evoked for aid, although I doubt that there has ever been a therapist-in-training who has not at one time or other prayed for his supervisor to intervene! Of course, one could pray for a patient in distress, or therapist and patient could pray together. But there is a subtler sense in which therapy is prayer.

As I previously mentioned, at all times in life, and specifically in intensive psychotherapy, there is a felt presence of an Other that pervades all experience, whether this be considered our unconscious, our 'double,' or God. We invoke and reach out to this Other in many of our thoughts and actions, and we wait, patiently or impatiently, for an answer. We wait for an idea or memory to come to our consciousness, the solution of a personal dilemma, a wish to be fulfilled, and so on. The act of waiting reflects a certain faith that an answer will come to our request, and, in effect, constitutes an unspoken prayer.

Psychotherapy itself is an 'action prayer' that a suffering individual will receive help and sustenance. It in no way resembles an immediate medical intervention like an intravenous injection, where a chemical will produce a predictable effect within a short time. Both therapist and patient approach the task with a hope and faith that the process will yield a good outcome. They reach out to each other, to what they know and do not know, to spontaneous ideas and images, to an Otherness beyond them, for signs and clues about how to proceed. They know that there is an intangible Otherness that must come into play if therapy is to succeed.

There are two kinds of prayer: devout prayer and 'foxhole prayer.' The latter is a desperate plea to be rescued. It is replicated by the patient who feels helpless and wants the therapist to 'do something' to save him. Devout prayer is a deeper and more disciplined process of surrender to God's will. It changes the one who prays more than it changes God. It is literally a way of being in the world rather than a cause–effect relationship. Devout prayer consists of living in the presence of God, ever mindful of one's need for God, being known to Him and 'naked in his presence,' invoking Him in every thought and action. It is a state of awareness that, no matter what one's strength and power, one is always dependent upon and needful of an Other who is central to one's being and destiny. Such mindfulness is holy.

Therapy, then, is a devout prayer to the extent that the participants meet in an 'I–Thou' relationship in the presence of an Other, with a sense that this Other constitutes the ultimate source, the 'final cause,' the knowledge, and the outcome. The aura in which the self-knowledge that is being pursued reveals only a small fraction of the self that is known to the Other lends a humility to its participants that is a catalyst for surrender and change. (One sign that this humility is at risk occurs when patient and therapist lock horns and their own egos take over.) The awe and reverence given to this Higher Being allows for the holiness of subjectivities to be sustained, facilitating spontaneity and transformation by waiting for new and unexpected possibilities to emerge from that Otherness.

Reston, an obsessive-compulsive patient, whose cognitive style was to insist upon unerringly rational explanations for events, came to me with an existential dilemma which appeared unresolvable to him, namely, that despite his many successes and achievements, he felt an inexplicable shame and self-loathing. We worked on the problem for over a year and examined every angle in minute detail. But he continued to experience himself as unworthy. Both of us began to doubt whether any resolution could take place. Then, one day, for no apparent reason, his self-hate lifted and he experienced a newfound happiness and contentment. 'I can't figure out how this happened,' he said. 'I'm totally surprised. It's so wonderful, and I didn't do anything to bring it about.'

My first, narcissistic thought was, 'Doesn't he realize how good a therapist I am?' and my second, altruistic musing was, 'Why can't he see that it is the result of all the effort he put into exploring his psyche?' Then I paused, realizing that the answer really did emerge from sources beyond our conscious egos. Events beyond our control conspired to bring about a solution when the patient was ready to receive it. His logicality had to break down before he could accept the answer that therapy had brought to him. I reflected to him that his astonishment constituted a new awareness on his part – he had learned that his conscious deliberations were only a small fraction of his own mind and of the cosmos. He smiled in wonder, and I was startled at the free flow of images, thoughts, and emotions which then occurred, in stark contrast to his usual cogitations and confusion. It was as if he had begun to access his own Otherness, his own holiness.

With all our combined brainpower, all the patient and I had really done in our time together was to 'pray' and wait for an answer. Our mutual pursuit of logic and memory was like a conversation on a train going to a particular destination. It played little role in getting us there! Our therapeutic 'head games' were in large measure disguised prayers for the patient's self-transformation.

Spiritual poverty and simplicity

Therapy offices that are well adorned and richly appointed do not impress me. In my opinion, a therapy space should be warm and inviting, a comfortable place where two people can meet and talk. Such was Freud's office in Vienna. Ascending a flight of stairs at 19 Bergasse, one found a pleasantly appointed doctor's waiting room. In the private consulting room there were a chair, a divan covered with a rug and some pillows, a desk, and a collection of archaeological objects which Freud had collected during his travels. Freud, despite his international fame, always lived the reserved life of a family man and maintained a simplicity of demeanor with his patients and his many guests. There is a very real sense in which a therapist takes a vow of spiritual poverty and simplicity, and asks the patient to join him.

In psychoanalysis, the most important manifestation of this 'vow of poverty' is the analyst's anonymity, opaqueness, and non-disclosure. The technical reason for this stance is that it permits the patient to project and transfer his mental life onto the person of the analyst, making it available for observation, learning, and modification. Yet, properly used, not as a hiding place for the analyst but as an opportunity for the patient to learn and grow, the therapist's willingness to stay in the shadows conveys a sacrifice he is making to the process. He is placing his inner space and energy at the disposal of the patient. He must yield a great deal of his narcissism and self-centeredness for the duration of the hour, although some of those impulses can be channeled to help the patient. He must set aside his daily preoccupations and personal difficulties. At the same time, he needs to open himself to be sensitive and vulnerable in order to empathize with the patient's feelings. And when he is attacked, challenged, or seduced by the patient's verbalizations, manipulations, and attitudes, he must 'turn the other cheek' and use his feelings to help the patient, rather than respond in kind. All of these sacrifices and self-disciplines are clearly akin to spiritual renunciation and selflessness. While these practices are an aspect of any socially responsible role, whether parent, physician, team leader, soldier, or artist, they are more central to psychoanalysis than in almost any other context because the patient is making himself vulnerable at the deepest levels of his soulfulness. The therapist, therefore, is tending the most precious garden of all. If the therapist temporarily deviates – which we all do – his errors are usually not irrevocable, but will often be responded to by the patient at the deepest level. In this respect, therapist and patient represent two different aspects of God – the transcendent, idealized Father, and the imminent, suffering Son. The sacredness of therapy transactions thus stems from the special vulnerability of the patient when, in a state of pain, shame, guilt, and conflict, he trusts the therapist to understand and respond appropriately. This 'covenant' makes the necessity for simplicity and self-sacrifice in the interactive matrix crucial to the outcome of treatment. Grotstein (2000, p.221–4) considers the analyst's readiness to suffer humbly and silently for the patient to be analagous to Mary's holding of the body of her son, Jesus, after the Crucifixion, as represented in Michaelangelo's Pietà.

Affirmations of faith

In religious services, faith is expressed in gestures and rituals which assert and reinforce belief in the premises of the religious system. These rites and gestures are, at their best, simple, tender, and intimate. The Christian eats a small wafer and washes it down with a sip of wine. The Jew touches the Torah with the humble threads of his prayer shawl and then kisses the threads. The Muslim bows in the direction of Mecca, his spiritual home. The Hindu says 'Om Namaha Shavaya': 'I greet the Divine in you.' For me, these simple gestures are more meaningful than the lengthier statements of faith that occur within liturgy itself, because, like a handshake or a hug, they are closer to our primary relationships with significant others. Whenever I touch the Torah, I remember the gentle way my grandmother would touch me on the shoulder, light a holiday candle, or offer me a macaroon.

Psychotherapists, unlike ministers of the cloth, don't expect their patients to actively affirm their belief in the therapy process or their particular approach. Yet there is a variety of ways in which therapists and patients indicate their faith. For example, my own treatment with a Sullivanian analyst, who emphasized interpersonal engagement, was marked by many moments when he would pause, lean forward, and speak in a sensitive, compassionate voice. His language embodied a matter-of-factness and friendly informality which conveyed that we two were vulnerable creatures seeking an understanding. These expressive qualities reflected Sullivan's emphasis on mutuality in the treatment process. My subsequent Freudian analyst, on the other hand, was staid, reflective, quiet. He reminded me at times of the mysterious rocks on Easter Island that were placed there by a prehistoric civilization. He was thereby conveying his faith in the stoical process of unearthing the remains of the past amid present struggles and conflicts. Looking back, they were both very helpful to me, although in different ways. I affirmed my faith in each of them by producing dreams which fit with their respective schemata, a well-known occurrence in psychotherapy. Moreover, my attire and body language often conformed to theirs, as it might to a rabbi or priest. With the Sullivanian, I wore casual clothing and slouched laconically into the chair. My speech reflected awkwardness and embarrassment. With the Freudian, I 'religiously' wore business clothes, even on weekends. I spoke introspectively and authoritatively. I watched and waited for my inevitable slip of the tongue or fleeting thought which would give away my true motives and conflicts. With each of them, I soon became a true believer, the Bar Mitzvah boy dutifully studying the therapeutic 'Torah.' Neither was in any way dogmatic about his beliefs. Rather, it was out of appreciation and deference to them, not to mention my fear of hurt and rejection, that I took their 'vows.'

Such affirmations of faith in the 'true religion' are both a blessing and a curse in psychotherapy. The blessing is that, without a shared system of beliefs, therapy would become chaotic. An important healing factor in psychotherapy is the patient's willingness, motivated by his suffering and his openness to new experience, to adopt a way of thinking and being from the therapist which is hopefully better than the maladaptive patterns that brought him to treatment in the first place. The curse is that the patient loses some of his individuality and uniqueness. We all know of and cringe from therapy patients who are 'reformed neurotics' and preach therapy truisms in clichés and psychobabble. Much more seriously, training analysts and institutes may manifestly or subtly enforce their beliefs and values on students, who then become inflexible and dogmatic in their work. Ultimately, patient and therapist must discover their own individuality.

Yet psychotherapy has elements of faith which are not doctrinaire and are essential to good results. The faith in the patient's own resources, the belief that he can get well, that human beings are inherently resilient and well-motivated, that a degree of vulnerability and trust is necessary for psychological well-being, that there are consensually validated norms and realities against which the patient's responses can be compared, and that life is inherently worth living are necessary for therapy to proceed. As the patient internalizes these articles of faith, windows of opportunity for growth and change open up to him, and a revitalized basis for living emerges. With all the strategies and techniques at our disposal, it is likely that this faith, these values and beliefs, are the most important sources of psychological healing.

Finally, and especially in long-term, open-ended treatment, there must be a faith in the value of watchful waiting. Like devout prayer, psychotherapy does not expect immediate answers. In this respect, the therapist's silence is a rite affirming a trust in God, the cosmos, the process, the life instinct. The best silences lend a sanctity to the consulting room. The therapist watches and listens to see if the seeds he has planted will grow. Winnicott once compared therapy to planting a seed and watching it germinate. Some therapists try to force the seed to grow, push it up from the ground, make it sprout branches, leaves, and blossoms. Such impatience and pressure is of no avail. A faith in growing and being and patience to wait for change is necessary for healing. Each patient has his own 'telos' or direction. The therapist is merely a catalyst.

Birth, confirmation, and death rites

Most religions grant three major rites of passage to their followers. Each is an affirmation of the person's faith and membership in the group, combined with an imprimatur of salvation and a good life in the present and the hereafter. These rites occur at birth, the transition to adulthood, and death. The Judaic and Christian birth rituals are instructive about their meaning and purpose.

A male baby born into a Jewish family is circumcised. He is thus forever 'marked' as a Jew, and his family is made aware of the sacredness of his gender, his vulnerability, and his initiation into a life which has the potential for power, joy, and procreation but at the same time can be diminished or 'cut short' by pain, injury, deficits, and death. The once-prevalent notion that the foreskin can be a source of infection suggests also that the infant is cleansed and protected by his faith.

The Christian ritual of baptism consists of dipping the baby in holy water – which represents purity and wholeness, and is also transitional between the fluid-filled womb and life outside it. In form, at least, it is perhaps not unlike the Hindu ritual of bathing in the Ganges River as a way of renewing faith. Baptism appears to be a bit less harsh and more comforting to the baby than circumcision, and it is accessible to male and female babies alike. But it contains its own symbolic risk and sacrifice in drowning (in tears, symbolizing Christ's suffering?) as opposed to injury.

In psychotherapy, birthing rituals are, of course, muted and implicit in the process. In psychoanalysis, the supine position on the couch is in a sense an 'obstetrical' initiation rite. Very rarely, one sees a patient who tries to take over the therapist's chair, and the feeling is that he is challenging the entire process and the therapist's authority. He does not wish to be born/borne into this faith which may make him 'well' (baptized and so chosen or saved).

'Little births' or re-births occur frequently within the treatment process. Interpretations and insights themselves contain a small dose of the therapist's faith. Pauses occur which are reminiscent of the 'caesura' of the infant in the birth canal. Some interpretations are like circumcision, 'snippets' of disillusionment of the patient's prideful sense of self. Empathic interpretations are sometimes experienced as 'cleansing, purifying waters' that allow the patient to experience his essential goodness and belonging.

For many, psychotherapy can be a contemporary vehicle for initiation into full adulthood, a confirmation rite. Taking on the task of self-insight represents a challenge that helps the person separate and individuate from his family of origin and achieve full-fledged adult status. The psychotherapist serves as a tribal mentor and priest. The patient begins to experience his power, his sexuality, his identity, and his role in society in an integrated way, and his life gains momentum.

A young man, Joe, came to me complaining of obsessive worry, acute shame, and feelings of inadequacy in the presence of attractive women. He felt like 'a loser' and wished he could be more assertive and heroic in his life. On one occasion, he expressed shame that he was too frightened to come to the aid of a woman who was being harassed on the street. He wished he could be stronger and more commanding in everyday transactions with co-workers and friends.

In treatment, he realized that his father's passivity and lack of availability as a role model had contributed to his shame-based perception of himself as weak and inadequate. He eventually summed up the courage to take a series of new and healthy risks, initiating relationships, intelligently questioning the therapist's approach, interviewing for a better job, traveling, and so on. His greatest challenge, however, was to terminate therapy and overcome his dependency on the therapist. He avoided dealing with this eventuality for several months after I raised it with him. Finally, in his last session, he expressed apprehension about 'going out into the wilderness,' but was excited about the opportunity to test himself out.

Psychoanalytic interpretations are one of the 'secret rites' which provide small *in vivo* initiations into the society of the 'well-analyzed.' To some degree, the patient initially experiences even the most accurate interpretation as a foreign element and is puzzled and disturbed. Finally, he 'eats' the interpretation (somewhat reminiscent of the Holy Eucharist and the breaking of bread), recites the expected catechism of agreement, and, as a result of numerous such experiences, is initiated into the pantheon of those who have achieved analytic insight. His resistance to accepting the interpretation is as important in his initiation as his acceptance, because it suggests that he has learned how to question and explore, chew and digest the interpretation rather than swallow it whole. Resistances also serve as the 'fodder' which propels the analysis. A notorious hazard of psychoanalysis is its potential for doctrinaire imposition of incorrect or premature interpretations on the analysand. The analyst's awareness of his countertransference and use of the intersubjective perspective place well-deserved limits on this pitfall in which the analyst acts as an intercessor of the unconscious.

It is easier to perceive elements of psychological birth and initiation in psychotherapy than to see the specter of death in the consulting room. After all, therapy is first and foremost an affirmation of life and healing, not an acceptance of or confrontation with death. Yet all of life entails encounters with death. The Talmud says that 'As soon as a man is born, he begins to die.' Therapists are often called upon to administer 'extreme unction' to patients who are in the midst of life and nowhere near approaching their physical demise. But something has to die in them in order for them to go forward.

I treated a high-achieving businessman who also craved women and sex. He obtained the same 'high' from a seduction as he did from a business victory. Unfortunately, his sexual escapades were destroying his business and his marriage. The patient's sexual compulsivity was so uncontrollable and unyielding, that I began to think he was incurable. During the extended course of his therapy, I painfully saw this otherwise decent and brilliant individual stripped of virtually everything he valued and possessed, as he experienced the personal consequences of his risky sexual behavior and deceptions. He became suicidally depressed after each dispossession, as his wife rejected him, his career was demolished, his friendships were derailed by others' discoveries of his secret erotic life and violation of responsibility. Each time he came up for air, he was determined to get well and devoted himself tirelessly to treatment. Then he would engage in another escapade, and when discovered, he would suffer another exposure, humiliation, and loss. He became numb from the loss of parts of himself and his spirit. Eventually, however, he was able to give up his sexual acting out and start a new life on a firm, spiritually-based foundation. I think that he had to be 'pronounced dead' a few times before he could live again. He needed to experience repeated deaths of self in order to restore his potential to grow and change. Each time he lost something and died in himself, he gained some inner spiritual resource which eventually enabled him to start a new life.

Many patients go through 'little deaths' in the course of treatment. As they give up a cherished defensive posture, detach from an unhealthy relationship, or retrieve a memory from the archaeological site of their repressed unconscious, they encounter their mortality. The therapist at these times serves with his compassionate impassivity as a witness to these deaths of parts of the self. Bion (1977) compared therapy to the legend of the burial at Ur, in which the royalty of a more advanced culture plundered the jewels from the mass gravesite of an earlier society where royalty became intoxicated and had themselves buried alive. We all enviously snatch jewels of life from the jaws of death. It is only by experiencing the many deaths that have occurred in our 'previous lives' – our stages of development – that we acquire an appreciation of life and the capacity to go on living. Therapy is a process of plundering our own graves, leaving the bones there, and pillaging some of the riches we find.

The story of the burial at Ur is an example of a narrative which is a meaningful metaphor for the therapy process (Schermer, 1999). It illustrates the role of dissociation (intoxication), repression (buried alive), the ego (royalty), curiosity (excavation), and greed (plundering) in human life, not to mention the process of uncovering the past in psychoanalysis.

Both religion and psychotherapy are cultural structures and processes, and all of culture is expressed in myth, story, rite, and ritual. The patient's story and ongoing narrative are so central to psychotherapy that they assume a life of their own. They can be understood as an expression of the patient's spiritual journey, his travels during his search for spiritual growth and meaning. I would now like to explore that narrative and journey in greater detail.

Endnote

1   I utilize this term from family therapy because it implies that the 'patient' is not necessarily the only person in the room who is sick, vulnerable, or in need. He is merely identified as such.

CHAPTER TWELVE

The Spiritual Journey
Story, Rite, and Ritual as Metaphors for Psychotherapy and Healing

I have alluded to therapy narratives and rituals as elements that can be understood in terms of evolving psychospirituality. Since the patient's 'story' is the hub of psychotherapy, around which everything else revolves, I now wish to take up that matter in greater detail, suggesting how it reflects the patient's spiritual journey.

According to the anthropologist Levi-Strauss (2000), there are two forms of expression universal to all cultures: 'diachronic' and 'synchronic.' The former is linear, set out in real time, and logical. When we discuss objects, facts, and abstractions, diachronic discourse allows us to develop our ideas in logical, temporal order. But when we speak about ourselves, our lives, and our feelings, our discourse becomes multilayered, with many levels of connotation and implication. The multiple layers, like the harmony and counterpoint of symphonic music, overlap and synchronize in time, and are 'synchronic.' A poem, a story, a musical melody are all set out in diachronic time, but their beauty and their meaning are 'synchronic,' deriving from the multiple layers of experience they contain and evoke within us. The root and guiding force of these multiple synchronic layers is ultimately mysterious and spiritual. Lacan (Sarup, 1992, pp.46–49) held that meanings 'slide' underneath their 'signifier,' the words and sentences that describe them. That is, psychological meanings are elusive, related to the totality of language structure, and give an impression of coming from an unknown source, which Freud called the unconscious. Our spiritual essences reside somewhere in the deeper layers of the signifier/signified complex of language, text, and symbol.

One of the main things that therapists and patients explore together are the multiple layers of the patient's experience contained in his narrative. For example, a female patient, Lorraine, told me that her boyfriend's frequent absences made her depressed, hurt, and angry. The first layer that we examined was transactional, i.e. the interaction between them, and we found that she perceived her partner as a little boy whom she had to control. In fact, he sometimes behaved like a self-centered child in that his 'disappearances' were for him a way to avoid intimacy with her. Thus, she became 'parent' to his 'child,' and her own 'inner child' felt neglected. To resolve this difficulty, this couple needed to find a way to explore their interactions with each other and contract for changes.

Probing below the surface, it became clear that, for Lorraine, the next deepest layer of this 'unhappy couple' saga was her need to remain in control and obsessively arrange her life and relationships so that she could feel secure. Her narrative shifted from 'I feel abandoned by my boyfriend when he's gone,' to panic: 'I feel as if my life is out of control, and I will break down!' Her chronic anxiety was connected to her mother's 'getting out of control' with drug abuse and her father's shame and guilt in response to it. Finally, we saw that her mother failed to hold, contain, and support Lorraine sufficiently throughout her infancy and childhood, so that as an adult, she continued to feel helpless and abandoned in many interpersonal situations. These synchronic layers of narrative appeared recurrently during the course of her therapy, and working them out at multiple levels of meaning allowed her to construct a new narrative in which she felt competent, strong, and self-sufficient and could distinguish her neurotic wishes from her real needs in relationships.

Lorraine's narrative also contained archetypal myths and stories of a universal significance which Jung called the 'collective unconscious.' She sometimes compared herself to Cinderella and Little Red Ridinghood, pointing out her 'servant' role and her naive tendency to be manipulated and seduced. She talked of her father as if he were a knight in shining armor whose goodwill and comforting way of speaking rescued her from her mother's harm. She saw her mother as a queen who always insisted on having her way. She found that such universal myths and stories helped her to access her childhood feelings, feel less isolated, see herself as belonging to a community of assertive women, able to find elements of hope in the good outcomes of some of these stories.

The psychospiritual thread that wove its way through these multiple layers was Lorraine's struggle to become a spontaneous, alive, and assertive

person. She envied her boyfriend because he, at least, could play in a spontaneous way, while she, on the other hand, was constrained and inhibited in
her friendships and at social events. She experienced social anxiety in these
situations, with persecutory expectations of being rejected and envious
feelings that others possessed all the stores of pleasure and success. I began
to feel that, in a way, she had not been fully born into the world, which she
experienced as a strange and threatening place. Parts of herself were
projected into others, so that she could not access and integrate them into
her personality. Her 'spirit' was in a state of suspended animation, seeking
release.

The therapeutic benefit she received came not so much from my interpretations as from the fact that she could repeatedly come to sessions with a
feeling of 'falling apart' and re-establish trust, holding, and support through
which she could restore her sense of self and negotiate the passage to
becoming an individual in her own right. Through a series of hurdles and
crises, her spiritual core gradually discovered that it could maintain its
innocence and coherence while navigating a troubling 'real world' of interpersonal difficulties. She was then able to fulfill herself creatively and began
to socialize freely and spontaneously.

It is through such exploration of the multiple synchronic layers of
meaning in the patient's narrative that self change becomes possible and the
spiritual journey can be resumed on a new basis. The problem faced by the
therapist who wishes to promote in-depth rather than superficial changes is
how to work with the multiple layers to access within them the core spiritual
self, and engage it in dialogue rather than merely reinforce the patient's
painful monologue, which is an expression of the ego's separation from the
core self and from God, resulting in spiritual loneliness. The process reminds
me of the ending of the childhood story, 'Peter and the Wolf.' The wolf has
swallowed a duck. The hunter kills the wolf, and the story ends with Peter
being saved, and told that, 'If you listen carefully, you can still hear the duck
quacking in the wolf's belly.' The duck is still alive – the spirit survives even
though 'swallowed up' by life's conflicts – but you have to listen very
carefully for its muted sound.

Multiple manifestations of the spiritual self are contained in the patient's
narrative. One must listen for the emergence of that which is *universal, early,
emotional*, and *insistent*. Jung emphasized universality, seeking to connect the
patient's personal unconscious with the archetypal collective unconscious,
the storehouse of images and myths which express the deepest human
motivations as they have evolved over eons. Freud and Klein emphasized the

early infantile precursors of the patient's experience according to the equation 'early means deep.' The earliest experience is most primal, generalizable, anxiety-provoking, and critical to development. Freudians and Kleinians believe that working at that level brings about more pervasive and lasting personality change than simply working with current materials. Self psychologists attune to conscious emotions in the here and now, especially those which express shame and vulnerability. Finally, when particular themes, dilemmas, and impasses become insistent and recur ever more forcefully as therapy progresses, we know that they are more central to the spirit than the ones which come and go or are easily resolved. Relational psychologists, in particular, look for these insistent themes and try to work with them within the intersubjective matrix of the patient–therapist relationship.

Jung early and profoundly recognized the connection between mythology and the numinous nature of the unconscious. Universal myths, narratives, rituals, and images are likely to carry a strong spiritual message. Many of them are incorporated within religious systems. Archetypes embody ultimate meanings and implications within a particular cultural context. For example, creation myths (like Genesis and the marvelous Scandinavian 'Kalevala' (Pentikainen and Poom, 1999) give form to the wonder of origins and birth; individuation myths such as the 'birth of the hero' address the need of human beings to survive challenges, endure suffering, establish a personal 'frontier,' and differentiate from the masses and the enveloping mother; warrior myths (for example, the search for the Holy Grail) are about traits necessary for conquering both inner self and external enemies; and polytheistic myths such as those of Greek antiquity address the universal aspects of fate and destiny, social relations and roles, and the inner dialogue among subselves.

On the addictions unit where I served as a staff therapist, I sometimes used dramatic improvisation with the inpatient community. As many as seventy of us sat in a large circle, and I asked the patients to select and play the various roles in an archetypal story, and to improvise around it. On account of their sorry state, the group preferred tales of woe, and the one they most strongly identified with was that of Job. The patient who played Job would readily come up with many instances where he felt God had abandoned him. Those who played God were stone-faced and impassive in the face of Job's complaints. The group identified strongly with Job's struggles and worries. On the one hand, they viewed his tribulations as 'self-pity,' avoiding responsibility for his fate and destiny. On the other, they identified with Job's complaints of unjust betrayal and punishment by God. Finally, assessing the deeper spiritual significance of the story, they could come to see that faith is a quality that is independent of visible outcomes, that it is something you acquire because you feel compelled in that direction by a deep part of yourself, not because you get the particular outcome that you want. Translated into terms of their recovery from substance dependence, that discovery meant to them that sobriety needs to be sought for its own sake as a personal and spiritual value, not contingent upon on certain requirements such as acceptance by their family, obtaining a good job, or finding a love relationship. Archetypal myths put us in touch with basic spiritual realities and conflicts.

Jungian therapists themselves point out, however, that focusing on collective archetypes without a full exploration of the individual unconscious can have mixed results, because the patient may intellectually expand his understanding of self without significantly confronting his own pain, suffering, and sacrifice that is necessary for change. Since the 'rock bottoms' of these necessities hark back to childhood, when emotions are raw and direct, both Freud and Klein sought to regress the patient back to the earliest levels of experience. A child who is abandoned by his parents or frightened of his inner 'monsters,' for example, literally fears that he is going to die. His emotional struggles are at the most existential level. When these primal anxieties are reactivated in therapy, they provide a strong motive for working out spiritual dilemmas. These conflicts can then be resolved in the relationship to the therapist and in the context of current life experience. There are two risks inherent in this 'regressive' approach: one is that the patient may not be able to master the resources to cope with these anxieties; the other is that the focus is so much on self in the narrow 'me'/ego sense that the patient may become narcissistic and self-preoccupied rather than entering into a relationship with the world.

Jeff, a young artist, was a highly creative individual who had already accumulated a track record of artistic accomplishment. He brought to therapy a remarkable ability to vividly recall his earliest childhood experiences. This helped us to form a very good idea of the early experiences which set up his ongoing feelings of isolation and disorganization. Both parents had periods of depression, and his father had personality changes in which he would oscillate between despair and hope, so that he would inevitably fail in his enterprises, and enter another period of depression. These repetitive paternal failures fostered a split in the patient's emerging masculinity, so that he alternately felt 'castrated' by women, rejected them, and then turned to his work, where he felt omnipotent. Sometimes he felt like God and sometimes like a fallen angel, but he never felt quite human and able to relate closely with others.

His therapy soon revolved around what he had put into me as a 'container.' For example, he would think that I was rejecting him when in reality he was projecting his own anger into me. He would omnipotently control the sessions, denying my subjectivity as if I were an object he could sculpt, leaving me feeling paralyzed in my chair. Gradually, I put his anger and the 'seat' of his selfhood back into him by reflecting upon these interactions. He then became able to acknowledge his own agression and to establish healthy assertiveness.

Jeff, however, continued to 'splendidly' isolate from others, preferring to work in his studio for long hours, avoiding human contact. Then, on one serendipitous occasion, he recognized me on the street, but, not seeing him, I did not greet him. At the next session, he fumed. He was enraged and hurt that I did not say hello to him and felt as if I were cold and distant. This 'real life' event became a wedge for him to begin to recognize his suppressed need for friendship and contact with others.

Reconstructing early childhood experience brings out the early relational failures and emotionality that have been split off, projected, and repressed, but such therapy is in danger of becoming a *folie à deux*, a false relationship that substitutes for living instead of giving the patient a life, unless and until the patient has an encounter with his need to engage himself with others. Our chance meeting supplied this patient with such an encounter.

In contrast to the meticulous task of reconstructing early experience, listening empathically for emotional 'markers' has the advantage of working with what is accessible to the patient's awareness in the here and now, and it also connects these emotions directly to the therapist as a responsive other. Such an empathic phenomenological approach is especially useful in working out feelings of shame, helplessness, vulnerability, and grief. All human narratives contain such emotions, and all – except the most alienated – resonate with them. They are universal and early-evolving, so they connote multilayered synchronic elements in the psyche. Sometimes these layers are unspoken: the person tacitly 'knows.' A patient who had recently lost her daughter went through a series of sessions in which she repeatedly broke into tears. I listened contemplatively, and occasionally reflected how she must feel a terrible loss and how inconsolable she must feel. Gradually, without direct interpretation on my part, her grief and depression abated. Much later, she spontaneously offered that the loss involved not only her daughter, but also the 'death' of a part of herself, and the struggles she had with her own mother. Her grieving spiritual self 'knew' that the grief was multilayered long before she articulated it to me. She felt it as a kind of music before she wrote the libretto.

The most difficult emotional states to work with in psychotherapy are those which are 'insistent' and repeatedly unresponsive to clarifications and interpretations. The object relations theorists link these impasses and dilemmas in treatment to the earliest failures and difficulties in interpersonal relatedness, and in the transference–countertransference to the therapist's own struggles with similar issues. The psychiatrist and psychoanalyst Harold Searles (1965, 1975), in particular, worked brilliantly with such difficulties. He was capable of accessing deep layers in his own unconscious that resonated profoundly with those of the patient, and engaging himself fully in the interaction without distancing and objectifying it. In Winnicottian terms, these insistent concerns are often linked to terror of the death of the true self. This puts the spirit of the person at great risk, so he alternately retreats and engages in an attempt to locate something, anything, that will insure a possibility to 'go on being.' This can be true of both patient and therapist, whose ability to engage the patient may mean the difference between disaster and growth.

Perhaps the most 'insistent' thing a patient can do to arouse a therapist is to put his life at risk. I saw a woman, Amalie, who, after several sessions, told me she was contemplating suicide and had more than one means to do it. Since she was not at immediate risk, I could not hospitalize her involuntarily to protect her. I had to work painstakingly with her and the risk to her life for several months, often going home at night wondering if she would survive. I persisted in exploring the suicidal thoughts with her, while insisting upon repeated agreements that she would not hurt herself and contracting with her to keep the means of self-harm inaccessible.

What we gradually learned regarding Amalie's wish to demolish her self was that, throughout her life, her mother had treated her 'like a beautiful doll,' an object of adoration, a 'thing' to serve as a mirror for her mother's narcissism, rather than a whole person with feelings, needs, and imperfections. As she began to access her genuine craving for nurturance and empathic attunement, her suicidal urges abated, and she began to work out her issues without the insistent 'at risk' cry for help. I have repeatedly found that one of the greatest unmet needs of patients is to be heard and responded to as a subject rather than a 'thing' or an object. It is a spiritual need to have an 'I–Thou' rather than an 'I–It' encounter with another.

When insistent states of distress arise, it is not always sufficient to be empathic with the patient. One element, which coincides with the Judaic emphasis on life as a primary value ('Who saves a life, saves the world'), is an especially strong stance with the patient, neither to rescue nor reassure him, but to be attentively present, alert, and strongly on the side of the patient's life instinct. Andreas von Wallenberg (2000), a psychotherapist in Germany who works with Amnesty International to treat victims of political torture and abuse, emphasizes the importance of staunch attentive concern. Torture victims have often had their sense of a meaningful self severely undermined. It is necessary but not sufficient to be available and empathic. The patient will eventually reach a crisis point where he will test the therapist's total commitment to his 'going on being.'

By containing, listening, and attuning to the multilayered synchronic aspects of the patient's narrative, the therapist intuits the psychospiritual self speaking in mythic, metaphorical, and emotionally toned language about its basic struggles. This is the therapeutic context in which genuine growth and transformation can occur.

The spiritual 'journey' of psychotherapy

Thus far, we have been looking at some of the containing rituals and 'lenses' through which the therapist and patient can access the spiritual core of the self within the patient's multilayered narrative. Whether it is through universal archetypes, reconstructing childhood experience, attunement with feelings, or strongly aligning oneself with a patient's insistent cry for help, the goal is the same: to come into contact with the patient's psychospiritual task of establishing a meaningful, alive contact with his inner essences, with the world, and with significant others, thus bringing the spiritual dimension into a working relationship with daily existence.

When played out in diachronic time, this process becomes a spiritual journey in which the therapist serves as a companion and guide. In many respects, therapist and patient meet as strangers on a train who agree to accompany each other for a segment of their travels. Their destinies commingle, and then they go their separate ways. The therapist's task is to help the patient buy a 'ticket' to his next destination.

The spiritual journey itself has archetypal parallels in myth and ritual. For example, as I have already mentioned, there are rites of passage in all cultures where, by meeting certain challenges, the person becomes initiated into a discipline, religion, or society as a full-fledged member. Bar Mitzvah and confirmation are low-risk rites of passage because the dangers are represented symbolically. Some Native American tribes require that the young man go into the woods to hunt an animal, encountering real danger. Sending our young soldiers into war is likewise such an initiation rite, one with potentially horrific consequences. In Europe during the Renaissance and later, initiation of the aristocracy consisted in an actual journey to foreign cities and countries to acquire exposure to other richly endowed cultures. Yogis are given meditative and other tasks to perform successfully, including, for some, an encounter with the 'real world' from which they have sequestered themselves. Invariably, a mentor is involved as a guide and a motivator, and then the initiate is thrust into the world to apply what he has learned. Psychotherapy has become a modern rite of passage, one which emphasizes a journey through inner states of mind as well as the exploration of relationships.

The Jungian perspective views psychotherapy as a journey of individuation (Edinger, 1972; Jacoby, 1990). At birth, we are relatively helpless, incomplete and dependent on others for our survival. Our archetypal life is centered around the 'Earth Mother.' We are largely merged with Her. As we develop, we acquire the ability to separate from Her and move out into the world, but meet with 'dragons' both within and without. In a sequence of challenges, rites, and rituals, we strive to find our unique and autonomous selves while remaining connected to both our earthly and numinous sources. The myth of the birth of the hero (Campbell, 1949) typifies these challenges through which we become individual, whole persons, and our various wounds of battle become sources of inner strength and growth.

I, for one, agree with this Jungian individuation scenario, although I might elaborate it not only archetypally but also in terms what the Jungians call the 'personal unconscious' of interpersonal relations and identifications with real caregivers, the family, the peer group, and society. However, for me, the element that is underplayed in the Jungian script, not to mention most of Western psychology, is the struggle of the spiritual core to retain its pristine wholeness, goodness, and connectedness to God as it encounters the panoply of inner persecutory objects and real persons who impinge upon, deprive, and/or abandon it in varying degrees. The 'mismatch' between an all-loving God who consistently nurtures the spiritual self, and a physical body and external world which are not nearly as dependable and caring as God, yet are intuitively felt to have come from God, is a dissonance which the self must negotiate in order to find its being in the here-and-now.

Grotstein (2000, pp.37–59) emphasizes that for the self to achieve integration, it must first feel and possess the world as its own creation. The infant must play God or 'be' God in an autochthonous, self-propelling way in order to then tolerate its helplessness and vulnerability. Neglect, trauma, and abuse are factors which derail this process because the perpetrator or abandoner violates and annihilates the self, undermining the child's power before he has been able to establish trust and choice. The self's wholeness and innocence are thereby undermined rather than achieving a contained and tolerable awareness of its own vulnerability and desire. There are, of course, levels of empathic failure, frustration, and deprivation that are not abusive or traumatic, but nonetheless leave their scars as well.

In this view, development is a process not only of individuation but also of finding and refinding one's psychospiritual innocence, power, and being as they are challenged in so many ways throughout the life cycle. In such a process, the therapist is a 'night visitor,' a provider of an empathic and holding surround that allows the patient to recover and renew his autochthony, his ability to create and possess the world in a way that is consistent with his spiritual self. The therapist offers a dialectic of challenges for the patient to individuate, along with a holding context which allows the patient to discover and repossess his spiritual core. This dialectic is represented on one side or the other by diverse schools of psychoanalysis. The Jungian and Kleinian schools, for example, emphasize individuation, while the Winnicottians and the Kohutians stress wholeness and integration. Reconciliation of the two sides of the equation is necessary for the person's journey to proceed successfully.

Each life trajectory and each therapy experience is unique. They are analogous, if we can imagine it, to a moving fingerprint made up of aspects of the individual, significant others, and therapist. Like fingerprints, no two journeys are alike, and like the relationship of finger to body, each journey and each therapy experience is a part which stands for the whole. Even each session is unique and, so far as possible, should be approached unclouded with memories of the prior sessions.

Nevertheless, there are characteristic phases in the therapy journey. Not all occur in every treatment, nor do they always occur in sequence, but they provide markers to summarize what is occurring in the patient's psychospiritual development. I have called these phases somewhat arbitrarily and colorfully:

1. the meeting of strangers

2. the ascent by balloon into the stratosphere

3. the descent into darkness and disillusionment

4. walking the earth together

5. the crucifixion and resurrection

6. living and surviving in human form.

Psychotherapy begins with a meeting of two individuals who typically have had little or no prior contact with each other. The loneliness and mystery of this meeting of strangers is often obscured by a false hope for a 'magical cure' and by a need to establish a connection. Both effusively friendly and, conversely, distantly unavailable therapists tend to bypass this stage. The patient needs very much to know what it feels like to meet someone he doesn't know. For one thing, it offers an intimation of his own 'doppelgänger' or double, his shadow self. For another, it establishes an absence, a space, and a 'not knowing' which can be negotiated, filled, and emptied throughout the treatment. Without this space, the treatment becomes superficial.

This meeting of strangers contains elements of both an encounter with and alienation from God. The stranger's obscurity and origin in 'another time and place' mirrors and presages the mysterious presence of God. In the New Testament, strangers frequently appear on the scene: the curious and the devout whom Jesus meets on the road, those who come to Him for healing, the Good Samaritan, and Barabbas, a criminal whose life is spared when Jesus is chosen by the crowd to replace him on the cross. These strangers contrast strongly with Jesus' intimate disciples. They seem to represent the many faces of God throughout humanity, and at the same time the fear, confusion, and skepticism about God from which most humans suffer.

A patient who came to me shortly after a period in a mental hospital was exceedingly mistrustful and reclusive. He treated me as if I were dangerous, and I too felt unusually self-protective throughout several months of treatment. He verbalized feelings of persecution at the hands of his friends, which he quickly transferred onto me. His xenophobia (fear of strangers) was his mechanism of interpersonal survival. He treated even his family as if they were strangers. His occasional unbidden experiences of closeness with me provoked great anxiety in him. He used me to survive his own self-destructive tendencies, but his suspiciousness led him prematurely to terminate treatment. He could not trust the stranger as a potential friend and ally. He soon resumed treatment at another facility, where he would have yet another 'close encounter' with a stranger.

With the exception of such severely mistrustful individuals, however, the stranger dynamic facilitates early treatment. The therapist's anonymity and otherness help the patient to feel safer with his self-disclosures (Cohen and Schermer, 2001). The formality and awkwardness of the stranger meeting channels itself into the objectivity of the therapeutic alliance.

The 'stranger' dynamic symbolizes the infant's initial encounters with the mother's breast, an entity initially both foreign and soothing. Therapy patients often approach the stranger therapist with their neediness. This magical wish sets the stage for much of the dynamics of frustration that propel the treatment. The therapist must remain something of a stranger throughout the process. He must meet the need for nurturance in a limited, symbolic way.

The 'stranger' experience furthermore represents a confrontation with mortality and death. The Talmud says, 'As soon as a man is born, he begins to die.' To encounter death is also to encounter the wholeness of the life cycle, that it has a beginning, a middle, and an end. This awareness is in the background of the patient's narrative of his life, his reconstructing the past, his working through of grief and loss, and his living in the present with an awareness of the beginning and the end.

Death is frequently represented in dreams. One patient worked through her fear of death in a series of dreams in which significant others were in constant danger of being killed and all that she valued undermined. Her ultimate fear was the death of her spiritual selfhood, which had been stifled in childhood by her parents' need to deny and suppress their own past closeness to horror and death. A 'stranger' experience with the therapist is necessary for these death anxieties to emerge in proper context.

Following the 'stranger' encounter, which provides the momentum for the journey and often involves a working out of issues of interpersonal shame and trust, the patient often develops an enthusiasm for the therapy venture. He throws himself into self-analysis and at the same time he feels euphoric and 'cured' – his symptoms may magically disappear. During this 'flight into health,' it is as if the patient, rather than encounter the depressive awareness of his conflicts, flees 'into the light,' gaining illusory flashes of insight and idealizing the therapist. The patient's enthusiasm and idealization can serve the purpose of obtaining a bird's eye view of his issues, which is why I call it 'the ascent by balloon into the stratosphere.' Rarely, for a few gifted patients, it can be a 'journey to the mountaintop,' an existential encounter with the self, but ordinarily the ascent is merely a fantastic voyage that may prove illuminating but without substantive transformation of the self. During this phase of treatment, one patient had a dream of being a bird, flying over the city, and taking in its breadth and scope, but he also seemed to be avoiding the stark details of the abandoned houses, vacant lots, polluted rivers, and trash dumps that he might find on closer view, and images of which did indeed appear in his other dreams. Students of meditation also have periods of apparent enlightenment early in the process. During this time, they feel excitement and euphoria about the progress they are making, and the guru must encourage them to keep meditating, despite their apparent enlightenment.

Despite its illusory quality, this early phase of psychotherapy can yield two productive outcomes, which is why therapists have learned over time to treat it with respect rather than confront it as a resistance. First of all, the patient can form what Kohut calls a 'mirroring and idealizing transference' towards the therapist. That is, he will think both of them to be 'wonderful, marvelous' and very much alike.

The reader will recall that Josh, the 'grandiose' entertainer I mentioned earlier, had a difficult and deprived childhood, and portrayed me as 'one of those incredible doctors' who miraculously saved lives through their brilliant diagnoses (I did not miss the ultimate fall from grace that would come from this attribution!) and himself as an entertaining, powerful 'super-male,' able to dominate any situation with his charm and cleverness. My supervisor at the time told me to accept this state of affairs and enjoy it, and I did so, which was in fact a great effort for me. It paid off, however, since the patient's frail sense of self was strengthened and he was eventually able to tolerate a degree of disillusionment about us both and begin to work with some very painful issues.

Second, during this euphoric phase, the patient and therapist are both highly motivated to get a narrative of the patient's history, symptoms, and life problems. During such a 'flight into the light,' the diachronic narrative is highlighted, with an emphasis on 'objectivity.' The patient will relate key events in his life to the therapist, much the way two strangers will be interested in each other's background as a way of building a relationship. The patient, perhaps unburdening his guilt in a 'confessional' mode, is often eager to tell the therapist whatever he can, and there appears to be little resistance to disclosure. The therapist's anonymity and opaqueness are experienced as reassuring at this point, and he is seen as an 'expert professional' or perhaps as a kindly priest.

An astute clinician, however, will recognize that this atmosphere of co-operation and knowledge-building is based on the objectification of the narrative. It resembles the attitude of the newly converted to a religion or ideology – they are convinced they have found the 'objective' truth, and they feel it represents the solution to all ills. Similarly, the patient and therapist may believe they have an accurate picture of the patient's condition, but the reality of what has been left out may be far more important than what is said.

The next period of depth psychotherapy is ultimately the most produc-tive and also the longest and hardest part. The beginning and end point of the journey fade into the background, and the patient is now in a struggle to find himself amidst his multiplicity of thoughts, dreams, reactions, and problems. Freud, comparing therapy to the strategies of chess, called this part of the treatment the 'middle game.' He thought of this extended phase of treatment as a series of maneuvers between the patient's resistances and the therapist's overcoming them with interpretations. Such a comparison fit well with Freud's interest in military history, enjoining the struggle to take the territory occupied by the patient's symptoms, but it does not address the spiritual struggle that the patient himself must undergo.

There are times in life when we become rudely aware of ourselves in ways which are disturbing but also can be growth-enhancing. For example, the first time we have sex can be full of wonderment and pleasure, but it can also be painful emotionally (and physically, for the woman). We see that we are naked, vulnerable, full of desire, and, after the ecstatic 'near death' (*petit mort*) of orgasm, empty and exhausted. Like Adam and Eve, we have 'fallen' from our innocence. Another instance of such self-disillusionment is when, in pursuing our life's ambitions, we discover how self-aggrandizing, manip-ulative, envious, and vain we can be. Still another is when, after years of marriage, we feel unfulfilled at some level and fantasize about an affair or a life adventure. We enter a period of 'the descent into darkness and disillu-sionment' in our lives. We may be tempted by opportunities and dangerous liaisons which represent various split-off parts of ourselves that we have not integrated into our personality. In the cabalist myth of the Creation, God withdraws from the world He created, leaving many little pieces of himself behind (Berke, 1996). Some of these fragments appear to us to be 'evil' and 'destructive,' as well they may be in this splintered form. The cabalists say that the duty of humans is to gather up and sort out these pieces, which means to make ourselves and the world whole and restore God to his proper place.

Allegorically speaking, what the patient, with the help of his 'stranger' therapist, is trying to accomplish during this long descent on the journey is to pick up the pieces of the self that were 'left behind,' sometimes on account of the pressures of deciding and acting, and sometimes due to emotional failures and catastrophes that produced overwhelming anxiety.

Archetypal myths of the descent are often about the underworld and the dark side of human nature. The underworld notion goes back at least to the ancient Greeks, who, unlike the Judao-Christian ideology, considered the netherworld to be a place rich with the potential for personal growth! Their priests would gather each year at a place called Eleusis (Beach, 1995), where, with the help of intoxicants and hallucinogens, they would undergo their descent. This experience proved healing and individuating for them. The Hellenic perspective is thus very different from the concept of Hell as a place of eternal horror. The Greeks conceived of the underworld as a place where dark and mysterious beings resided. There were dangers there but also much to be learned.

For example, the Greek myth of Orpheus and Eurydice presents the underworld as a place of mystery and existential challenge. Orpheus enchants Eurydice with his music, and she falls in love with him. They marry, but under the cloud of a dire destiny in which the beautiful Eurydice, fending off the advances of the shepherd Aristeus, is bitten by a snake and dies. Orpheus, in his grief, pursues her to the underworld, where he charms its inhabitants with his lyre, and is given permission to take Eurydice back to earth with him, under the condition that he not look back at her until they complete their passage upwards. Forgetting himself, he glances at her, and she is taken back to the underworld. Prevented from returning there for her, Orpheus lives in profound grief, eventually repulsing the advances of Thracian maidens, one of whom, rejected, kills him with her javelin. In death, Orpheus is honored by the god Jupiter by placing his lyre among the stars.

This legend is about the dangers inherent in love. The therapeutic parallel is that, during the 'descent' phase of the journey, the patient 'glances back' at all the objects of his love and hate in an attempt to sort them out and see how they might affect his current relationships. This experience is painful because our early relationships are experienced ambivalently, and also because we don't want to give up these past attachments. We have to face the fact that we can never go back to them as they were. Because they are in our past, they have become 'lost ghosts' in our unconscious. We can communicate with them, but can never revive them as they were. We have to establish new relationships, even with those we have loved since childhood.

Strikingly, the ghosts and gods that inhabit the Greek underworld experience beauty, grief, and compassion upon hearing Orpheus' music. This vision of the depths differs from both the Christian notion of Hell, which is entirely filled with evil, and the Freudian understanding of the unconscious as a lifeless archaeological ruin. The Greeks realized that the dark and hidden side of our soul possesses an aliveness and a presence within us, a repository of our hurt and vulnerability as well as the potential for sin. In therapy, we not only 'remember' our past and our darkness: we commune with them, sing to them, and they respond empathically and with a grief of their own.

Sam had perpetual difficulties with relationships. One woman was too emotional and confused for him; the next was too organized and demanding. During childhood, his father was unavailable and inadequate; his mother was caring and devoted but depressed. He repeatedly expressed narcissistic rage in response to feeling misunderstood and as a reaction to his father's inadequacy as a role model. Women befuddled him because his grandiosity always failed to allure them, while their affections failed to assuage his hurt.

The patient remembered that in adolescence, there were nearby hills where he would often go for consolation after painful and fruitless arguments with family members. There he found solace and a place for his 'soul.' During therapy, as his difficult issues with women pressed upon him, he felt overwhelmed and fragmented. At one juncture, he took a vacation in the country and found himself walking deep into a valley. Above him, he saw a lone bird in flight and was taken by its grace and beauty. Hypnotized for an extended time, he was overcome with a sense of mystery and awe. Returning to therapy from his journey, he wept openly about this haunting and beautiful experience, and said he felt calmer and more content than ever before. For the first time, he began to feel that he could tolerate his differences and frustrations with women, and he began to negotiate conflicts with them rather than flee. He had found within himself a mysterious place where he could transform his demons into beautiful creatures, and thereby, in that land of magic and healing, discover himself and the women he courted to be good and adequate, even though vulnerable and flawed.

The story of Jesus has at least two periods of 'descent into the darkness.' The first occurs when he goes into the desert to face temptation. Here, he meets the challenge of conquering the evil within himself. His self-exile to confront the problem of evil parallels the Old Testament story of the scapegoat, who is sent out into the wilderness, bearing the sins of the community (Perera, 1986). Jesus struggles with temptation, and, of course, is victorious. Similarly, the patient during his 'descent' not only encounters his love objects, past and present, he also comes face to face with evil and temptation in himself. His pure and pristine spiritual self must somehow come to terms with sin.

Erik came to me at mid-life because his wife learned he was having an affair and it threatened to destroy their marriage. He loved his wife, but felt frustrated in their sex life, since she was inhibited in her sexual response. Nevertheless, he desperately wanted to maintain the marriage. In therapy, he struggled with the 'pushes and pulls' of his affair and eventually mustered the courage to end it, realizing that he was being fair to neither woman. He began to see how helpless he felt under the sway of his instincts.

He told his wife he had ended the affair, and they reconciled. Then he encountered the frustration of her continual mistrust of him. With each expression of mistrust from her, he became angry and wanted to renew his affair. I told him to be tolerant of his wife's suspicion, since he had betrayed her, and her doubts would likely persist for several months. In time, they were able to renew their marriage vows and contract for healthy changes in their relationship. By facing and renouncing his temptations, Erik was able to establish a more fulfilling partnership with his wife.

The second confrontation of Jesus with evil was his descent to Purgatory before ascending to Heaven. He is said to have gone there to free those souls that were awaiting judgement. This points to another, often unnoticed, function of the therapeutic descent. It is to repair the damage that the patient himself feels he has done to his internal and external love objects. The patient who saw the deer in the woods went there partly to free his father from the negative and demeaning 'labels' that he had ragefully attributed to him. After that experience in nature's domain, the patient was for the first time able to have warm conversations with his father and to achieve mutual forgiveness. He had found a comfort within his own darkness that allowed him to free both his father and himself from judgement.

The reparative function of the descent into darkness is facilitated by a spiritual love between the patient and therapist. This love begins with the therapist's restraint from judging or acting out with the patient, which eventually allows the patient to forgive the therapist for bringing him in contact with his 'badness,' his demons, his losses, his destructive impulses. He can then, perhaps for the first time, see the value of a type of love that includes boundaries and restraint. This Oedipal 'structuralization' of love converts the mysterious space that was initially experienced with the therapist-as-stranger into a transitional space with possibilities for imagination, intimacy, and a future. In this space, the patient's darkness, desire, and destructiveness can be converted into forgiveness, healing, and growth.

Emerging from the descent, the patient begins to regard daily life with a certain disillusionment, yet with freshness of vision. Like Lazarus returning from the dead, he experiences light-headedness and confusion, because, to some degree, he has been unconscious, asleep, dreaming in the midst of waking life.

The therapist and patient now 'walk the earth together.' That is, they explore the world around them so that the patient can learn to cope with healthier, more resilient and adaptive defenses and patterns of interaction. For a while, the patient's focus is upon everyday relationships with significant others: his partner, his business peers, his children. He works out fantasies, conflicts, and problems in a new way. His dreams take on an instructive rather than disturbing significance to him: they contain lessons. Interpersonal relations are no longer so threatening. He begins to reward himself with a vacation, a party or dinner, to validate his sense of self, and to make some plans for the future.

A gay patient, Paul, having faced in treatment the demons which made him ashamed of his homosexuality, had an overwhelmingly gratifying experience of attending a gay event and feeling joy, excitement, fun, and compassion for his gay peers. He was elected their leader. Moved to tears, he described to me every last detail of the event, down to the special mannerisms and interactions of each subgroup of gay men and women, the clothing they wore, and the various dramatic events that took place. He literally 'saw' his peer group with new eyes.

It would be easy to think that treatment is completed once the patient is accustomed to his 'walking shoes.' This is certainly the case with supportive, brief psychotherapy, where the emphasis is on improved functioning. But to complete the journey of self-transformation, I think that an additional crisis has to be weathered. It is what I call, with obvious Christian reference, 'the crucifixion and resurrection.'

In order to be fully alive, a person has to die and be reborn. The patient must, at some point in treatment, metaphorically experience a 'persecution and death' at an unconscious level. In the culture-at-large, there has always been a precarious relationship between the couple and the group, with the 'crowd' celebrating and honoring, yet envying and misunderstanding, the couple's intimacy. This tragic aspect of pairing is manifest in the story of Romeo and Juliet, who are driven to suicide by their feuding families. Therapy is an intimate personal pairing experience, and to engage in a full and deep course of treatment represents, in my view, a courageous personal and moral stance in a world gone mad. The patient is committed to working out dilemmas and concerns that most people circumvent and avoid. The therapist is committed to listening without judging and controlling. These are not commonplace social exchanges. In certain ways, it puts the patient at risk of real or imagined persecution by the envying 'crowd,' persecutory objects within and without the psyche. Sometimes the envy of the therapy couple manifests itself, as for example when a patient is discouraged from treatment by a family member who thinks the need for treatment is a sign of weakness and lack of self-reliance, or when friends pry and gossip about the patient's treatment. But I am talking more about a symbolic persecution and sacrifice the patient must endure each time he risks parts of himself in the presence of the therapist.

Because of this special commitment so distinct and apart from the 'marketplace mentality,' psychotherapy evokes in the patient the archetype of sacrifice as it is represented, for example, in the stories and lives of those who have sacrificed for their beliefs: Abraham and Isaac, Job, Jesus, Joan of Arc, Mahatma Gandhi, and Martin Luther King, for example. That is, the patient has agreed to undertake a journey that hopefully will bring him to a better place, but which also holds dangers, risks, and the possibility of misunderstanding. Most important, the patient, through a process of thorough self-examination, is risking the death of his self. He must experience this death and, paradoxically, find that he can survive and grow beyond it. This idea of 'dying in order to be reborn' is to be found in all the great religions of the world.

Such death and resurrection occurs in psychotherapy in small, though painful, ways: in mourning the passing of past loves, successes, and failures; giving up a maladaptive or compulsive pattern of behavior, while trying instead to understand its root causes; discovering that the narrative one has composed is only one of many that exist in the psyche, so that what one *thought* was one's self seems like a chimera, an hallucination. Who is the person who has been in therapy? Not 'I' but some mysterious presence. Such an uncanny sense of the process challenges many assumptions about self.

On account of the sacrifice of self, the role of the therapist takes on a new dimension of suffering with, and witnessing, for the patient his relinquishment of conventional ego or selfhood. Grotstein (2000, p.221–4) aptly calls this role the 'Pietà covenant,' because it consists of enduring the patient's 'death' with him. The resurrection allows the patient to discover himself as 'ineffable subject,' as Being itself. This is a cleansing experience in which the person regards himself in a whole new way, pristinely illuminated by the light of the core spiritual self rather than the functioning ego.

Guntrip (1986) and Little (1990), both psychoanalysts, have written about the deep level of 'regression to total dependency' they experienced in their respective treatments with Winnicott. This regressive experience can be misconstrued to imply that the patient returns behaviorally to the infantile state, as in 'rebirthing' therapies, primal scream therapy, and other deeply regressive approaches which have well-known hazards attached to them. Mary Barnes (Berke and Barnes, 1971) was an artist and formerly schizophrenic woman who literally reverted to infancy in her treatment and came out of the experience in a healing way. Ms Barnes had the combined benefit, rarely available, of a protected long-term residential living situation, a devoted psychiatrist, a team of mental health workers, and her own imaginative creativity and art work.

What Little and Guntrip were referring to was an emotional (not behavioral) regression in which the patient experiences the dependent state in the context of maternal 'holding' by the therapist. This allows the self to go on being with a new sense of aliveness and spontaneity. It is predicated on the belief that the 'basic fault' (Balint, 1979) in the self is the result of failures of maternal responsiveness during infancy. The experience of helplessness is related to fear of the loss or death of the self. During such periods of regression, the emotional availability of the analyst must be nearly absolute, for the patient fears fragmentation, dissolution, and death. The profound 'holding,' suffering, and witnessing by the analyst allows for a 'rebirth' to occur in which the personality can re-integrate rather than disintegrate.

In my opinion, such 'regressive' death and rebirth experiences must occur in order for therapy to be complete. For example, Marge had a long period of treatment in which the focus was on her relationships. She gained many insights and as a result became able to experience intimacy in a more mature and adaptive way. However, in subsequent sessions, she began to feel as if she were 'out of control' and 'falling apart at the seams.' When she finally broke up with her boyfriend of several years, the loss seemed inconsolable to her, and she felt 'as if I am dying.' I encouraged her to stay with this feeling and express it to me in words. Over several sessions, she sought to verbalize her terror, while at the same time recalling memories of abandonments by her mother and lack of empathy by her depressed father. She then reported a dream in which she was a baby in a maternity ward and her parents were viewing her through the observation window. The window represented their unavailability to 'touch' – her abandonment – but the 'baby' experience had for her a refreshing and healing quality. Soon after, she felt more comfortable with herself than ever before. She perceived her future set out before her as a welcome set of choices and options. She engaged in creative work and made plans to travel.

After the rebirth experience, the final passage in the journey of treatment is to meet the call to life. This is the original task which the core spiritual self had found so difficult – to maintain its pristine spirituality and sense of oneness while negotiating the vicissitudes of life. As a result of therapy, the patient is now hopefully better equipped to undertake this voyage, but must undergo some further 'lessons.' He must discover that, despite the temptations, suffering, loss, and harm inherent in life, the core spiritual self can remain intact. The therapist at this point may suggest that the time has come to terminate treatment, and usually adopts a benign, 'laid back' stance, trusting that the patient now has the capacity to 'hold' himself. The patient then works through the inevitable separation from the therapist, which is both mournful and exciting – exciting because life is now seen as an adventure. But what is often noticeable in the termination of a successful therapy is that the patient now possesses a certain detachment. He is no longer dependent on the therapist's holding power, but will grieve the separation because the journey they have taken together has been valuable, and an affectionate feeling has developed between them. The patient often fears that his symptoms may recur but knows he is connected to his inner self and to external resources. Most importantly, he has formed a deepened relationship with himself, his spiritual core, and the vast, mysterious Other as a benign and loving Being. He knows that life is sometimes painful and there is suffering, and yet there is someone or something one can trust, not so much a particular person or possession, but rather the totality of a self that is linked to all that is within and around it.

The psychotherapy journey that I have described here occurs in many variations. Each is unique and can be depicted within a variety of frameworks. The process could well be described, for example, in terms of transference and countertransference, interpersonal relations, attachment and loss, and any number of other vantage points. What I have tried to convey is my belief that the process is inherently spiritual, that therapy, like all of life, is propelled by 'Otherness,' by a mysterious entity that is empty yet full, infinite, at the edge of awareness. In addition, I have tried to suggest that the patient's inherent striving is to heal the damage to the spiritual self and its relation to life both as inner experience and outer reality, that the full dimensions of psychotherapy are missed unless one includes this spiritual striving.

It would be wrong, however, to surmise from this depiction that the therapist is a spiritual or religious teacher. Paradoxically, the therapist must, in fact, relinquish any pretense of being such a teacher. Instead, he must walk a path between two roles. One is to be simply human, indeed sometimes 'all too human,' walking, as it were, among the multitude as one of them. This role requires qualities of genuineness and simplicity, as well the ability to experience and verbalize what the patient is feeling because one has, somehow, somewhere, in some way been there oneself. The other is to listen in such a way that one approaches a state of 'non-self,' emptiness, openness, total concentration, and compassion. In that state, the therapist becomes a contemporary mystic, listening, as Bion said (1970, pp.33, 41–54; Symington and Symington, 1996, pp.166–184), in the absence of memory, desire, and understanding and undergoing transformations with the patient. Describing and achieving such a mode of listening and being is not an easy task, but in the next chapter I will try to say something about its dimensions and coordinates and why the listening process is in and of itself therapeutic.

CHAPTER THIRTEEN

The Therapist as Mystic
The Listening Process

While the particulars of any given treatment intervention may influence treatment outcomes, much of the positive impact of psychotherapy derives not specifically from the expertise of the psychotherapist, but from his personhood, his being, and the way in which he listens to the patient. Psychologist Carl Rogers (1951) voiced such an idea as early as the 1940s. His pioneering research on therapeutic effectiveness concluded that when the therapist attends to the patient with 'unconditional positive regard,' the result is increased rapport, self-acceptance, and self-esteem. Rogers here means that the therapist accepts the patient's whole self, rather than expecting him to meet a specific ideal. A patient may come to treatment experiencing shame, guilt, and low self-worth. By attuning to feelings, rather than judging thoughts or behaviors, the therapist helps the patient see his inherent humanity and view his shortcomings and difficulties within that perspective. Listening without judgement is very likely more crucial to good outcomes than particular interpretations and insights.

Despite Rogers' early observations, it is only in the last twenty years that the listening process has become a central focus of interest. Today, especially with the impact of self psychology and the intersubjective-relational perspective, dynamic therapists strive for empathy and attunedness comparable to the mother's ability to perceive and validate her child's needs and desires. We believe that such listening in the treatment context corrects for the deficient or disrupted 'mirroring' which many patients received from their families. Through empathic attunement with the patient's vulnerabilities, life experiences, and emotional states as they manifest in the session, we mitigate some of the profound dislocations that occur when people feel hurt, rejected, or invalidated by others. In such an atmosphere of genuine acceptance and attunement, patients are then able to resume the process of personal growth and integration.

A colleague told me about a patient whose life was disrupted by chronic drinking. He felt bereft and remorseful as he began treatment, yet helpless to stop the downward spiral of his life. The therapist was puzzled about how to aid this hapless individual, so she decided, as she put it, to 'just shut up and listen.' Gradually, the patient's shame began to lift, he stopped drinking, and his life began to come together, simply as a result of being 'held' and heard by the therapist. (I do not mean to advocate this process in itself as an approach to treating alcoholism, which is a complex psychological and physical condition.) The therapist correctly intuited that his drinking betrayed an underlying low self-esteem, and her attentive listening alleviated his shame and guilt to the point where he could take constructive measures to help himself.

In another case, a young man came to me for unbearable shame regarding a visible surgical scar. I did not try to analyze why he felt ashamed. Rather, empathizing with his plight, I realized that I might well feel the same sense of damage and self-consciousness, and might have taken the same measures of avoiding exposure, while afraid to socialize as well. I reflected these feelings of identification back to him. Empathic listening on my part helped the patient humanize his experience and risk going out on dates and swimming at a crowded beach.

Above and beyond such empathic and compassionate 'attunement,' however, there are additional psychospiritual dimensions to the listening process. Of course, it is spiritual to put oneself in another's shoes, as in the above examples, and respond to him with concern rather than blame. Such empathy is exemplified in Buddhist compassion and Judao-Christian *agapé*. Jesus stressed the spiritual value of a non-judgmental stance towards others: 'Let he who is without guilt cast the first stone!' He identified with the sick and marginalized in his society, and he felt deep love for Mary Magdalene, a prostitute. Buber (1970) held that the essence of spirituality consisted of a 'meeting' between the 'I' of one with the 'Thou' of another – a heartfelt communion between one person and another as subjective beings, rather than as objects. Empathy is what allows this meeting to occur.

Let me take the spiritual element in therapeutic listening a step further. It involves a 'quieting of the mind' akin to meditation. And it places the therapist in the role of a modern-day mystic because he becomes capable of perceiving the unspoken and the inaudible/invisible messages emanating from the patient.

To genuinely listen to a patient – to hear his unconscious longings, conflicts, and struggles as well as his great gifts and potential – is a complex process that incorporates many aspects of meditation. First, one has to make a space, akin to a religious sanctuary or an altar, away from the troubles of the world, where it is quiet, and where there is a minimum of distractions. Within that space, the therapist strives to hear the 'still, small voice' in himself and the patient. As Bion (1970, pp.33, 41–54; Symington and Symington, 1996, pp.166–184) put it, the therapist listens 'in the absence of memory, desire, and understanding.'

Once the therapist has quieted his thoughts to make a mental space for the patient, he needs to be open to whatever enters his 'empty' mind, neither judging it nor discounting it, and staying in touch with the moment. Bion perceived the potential of such an 'empty,' 'self-blinding' listening process to access the patient's unconscious and to facilitate self-transformation. He articulated this practice from the perspectives of both religion and modern scientific discourse.

In a philosophical and scientifically-minded book entitled *Attention and Interpretation*, Bion (1970, p.115) startlingly referred to the writings of the Jewish mystic, Isaac Luria, and the Christian mystic, Meister Eckhart. (It is the first time, so far as I know, in the vast psychoanalytic literature on technique, where mysticism is given as an example of how a therapist should proceed.) Bion's chief argument is that sometimes the therapist is called upon to transcend conventional ideas and think thoughts that may be disturbing and unique, even to the point where others might think him a 'lunatic.' He also suggests that the therapist-as-mystic can, in such states of awareness, access the depths of the patient's deepest self and facilitate growth and change. He quotes Isaac Luria as saying: 'I can hardly open my mouth to speak without feeling as though the sea burst its dams and overflowed. How then shall I express what my soul has received, and how can I put it down in a book?' (Quoted in Bion, 1970, p.114.)

Bion's implication here is that the experience of therapeutic listening is filled with awe and beyond words. Something happens between analyst and patient which is deeply transformative and not expressible in ordinary language. Indeed, the experience is akin to an encounter with God. It expands beyond the empathic attunement of which I have just spoken to access the horrific, the sublime, the ineffable, the infinite and the infinitely small and inarticulate in our nature. It is a state of ultimate openness to another's experience.

Bion made a continuing effort to describe the nature of this state of awareness. He said that the analyst must emotionally blind himself, and project 'beams of darkness' into the patient. That is, he must obliterate the complex of ideas and hypotheses about the patient to access another level of experience. He must exist temporarily in a 'cloud of unknowing' in order to grasp the hidden meaning and significance deeply obscured and hidden within the patient's mind. Bion held (1990b, pp.11–17) that the unconscious was a relatively new realm for humanity to understand, and, just as the discovery that the earth revolved around the sun took eons for man to make, so we now possess only the barest glimpses of unconscious communication. As with our experience of God, we see mostly 'through a glass darkly,' and only rarely 'face to face.' Bion, again with a mystical connotation and perhaps alluding to Blake's 'tyger, tyger, burning bright,' said that we have so far seen only the stripes of the tiger, but that some day, we might encounter the tiger himself (Eigen, 1998, dedication quotations).

Bion had an ironic sense of humor. It is said that he once gave a lecture to a distinguished group of psychoanalysts, and, taking his prerogative as an analyst, said nothing for one hour! On another occasion, he impishly asked a class of analytic candidates, 'What is the meaning of this cup?' He wrote a fable and allegory of psychoanalysis entitled *A Memoir of the Future* (1990a), rich with surrealistic images, in which he describes himself as 'Captain Bion,' leading the human species through 'the Dawn of Oblivion.' I think that through the cosmic laughter contained in these gestures and stories he meant to communicate the intense state of unknowingness in which we live our lives, and that, paradoxically, it is the only way in which we can ultimately grasp our true nature.

Bion, like Jung, was influenced by the philosopher Immanuel Kant (Allison, 1983), who held that the mind is a net through which reality is filtered. Our perceptions and cognitions tell us about what is captured by the net, but reality itself is unknowable. However, Kant, unlike the empiricists such as David Hume, and the modern logical positivists, such as Bertrand Russell, believed that, with mental discipline and careful intuition, we can get glimpses of the real. For Bion, the discipline for accessing emotional and mental realities consists of a persistent 'self-blinding' and emptying of self, until the reality beyond the net of the patient's mind is glimpsed. This is what establishes the therapist's kinship with the mystics and with meditative states.

A striking example of Bion's understanding of the listening process happened for me when I worked with Peter, a patient who was raised in another country and spoke a foreign language. He and his family then moved to the United States, where he learned to speak excellent English. At one point, he told me that, while his waking thoughts were in English, his dreams were in his native tongue, with the (disturbing for me) implication that his unconscious did not 'speak' English. Following Bion, I tried to 'blind' myself to everything I knew about Peter in order to try to access the foreign-speaking part of his unconscious. Soon, I began to feel that there was another patient in the consulting room, another self. I kept trying to 'get inside' that other self through the patient's dreams, which he translated into English for me, but to no avail. So I kept listening for that other self, aware of my ultimate blindness to an aspect of who he really was. Then the patient and I came to see that this was indeed his own experience of himself. He had blinded himself to himself in order to adjust to the new world he had entered.

As we explored his dreams, we came to discover that since childhood he had sequestered a sense of self that was the opposite of his conscious feelings of shame. It was based upon a fantasy of royalty, stirred by what he had learned about distant past generations of his family, that he was in fact a descendant of an aristocratic group with special gifts of intellect, creativity, and power. As this other 'self' emerged in treatment, his self-esteem was restored after years of feeling like a failure.

Based upon his increased esteem, Peter became free enough to risk marriage to someone of a different social class from himself, to have a child, and to start a new career. He completed treatment with a heightened sense of well-being and able to act on his own behalf. I felt that all of the many images, free associations, recollections, and emotions he expressed in therapy were as nothing compared with the enormity of the 'self' I initially knew nothing about, but which came into focus when I blinded my consciousness, eliminating the distractions of sense data, memory, and desire. Later I realized that the patient himself possessed an attitude of mind which helped me to attain this 'blind' state. I believe that the patient himself was a type of 'mystic,' and that he had helped me to have such an experience with him. I think that some patients possess this ability to facilitate the mysticism in their therapists.

So it may be that some of Bion's patients gave him a mystical sense of the process. The existential playwright, Samuel Beckett, was a patient of Bion, and the two also had some intellectual discussions. Beckett was certainly not a mystic, but, as an existentialist, he was acutely aware of the predominance of absurdity and 'non-sense' in our worlds. But, even more, it was perhaps the fact that Bion psychoanalyzed a number of psychotic patients that helped him to formulate his views on the listening process. Such patients think and speak in inchoate, sometimes bizarre ways. They have 'visions' and 'intuitions' which often are delusional, but which compel the analyst to abandon ordinary ideas in order to keep up with them. Sometimes, I suspect that psychotics are mystics gone awry. Undoubtedly, they make us frequently aware of how little we really know. (Again, I am not recommending deep psychoanalysis for most psychotic patients. They are at risk for deterioration and even suicide, and they need medication and support to survive and function. And I suspect that only a few analysts and psychotic patients can endure this process together. I count Bion among these few.)

What I am really suggesting here is that psychotherapy can be a form of mutual meditation, an intersubjective reverie, as it were. The therapist initiates this process by providing the space in which it can occur. Just as the yoga practitioner focuses his concentration on a candle or a mantra, and the Buddhist is taken 'out of his mind' by a Zen koan, so the therapist focuses on a mysterious detail the patient presents in the session, a perturbation in the clear lake. The patient joins him in the 'darkness,' in the 'cloud of unknowing,' while at the same time reaching out intersubjectively with further reports of images, dreams, dilemmas, and random thoughts. This leads both to catch glimpses of something Other.

Having looked at spirituality in psychotherapy from two disparate vantage points – the patient's linear narrative of his journey through life, and the mystical Otherness that is beyond words – I hope that I have generated in the reader an excitement about the possibilities that exist for a new, integrated science of mind and spirituality. This is a field of investigation that holds rich promise for psychological healing and a better way of life. The excitement and enthusiasm is not new. But the possibility for an integrated paradigm combining scientific rigor with spiritual development is first coming into clearer view through the intensifying dialogues between East and West and among scientists, philosophers, and theologians. In the next chapter, however, I temper the broad, all-encompassing, and enthusiastic vision of the circles of being with an appeal for a balanced, careful, and rigorous search for the truth and for new approaches to treatment. All rituals in the sanctuary, from the unrolling of the Torah to the preparation of the Eucharist to the Japanese Tea Ceremony, must be performed with great care. Similarly, the study of psychospirituality, spiritual states, and transformational psychotherapy must be done carefully, thoroughly, and cautiously. It is not enough to buoyantly pursue the new frontiers. It is crucial that this multidisciplinary study and practice be carried out with discipline and with a common vocabulary.

CHAPTER FOURTEEN

Conclusions
Optimistic and Cautionary

The reader will have surmised that, while I advocate a new paradigm involving a dialogue between spirituality and psychology, I am by no means zealously beating the drum for a merger of the two, nor for a psychotherapy which is, in any sense of the word, 'religious.' Some will feel that I have gone too far in the direction of spirituality and mysticism, holding that psychotherapy is primarily a secular and scientific practice and should hew closely to the naturalistic and humanistic underpinnings under which it was founded. For them, spiritual principles and practices had best be left to pastoral counselors and spiritual healers and teachers, where the 'consumer' will be well-apprised about the religious nature of the 'product' he is buying. Let secular therapists hew to their task of alleviating symptoms and treating mental illness using the biosocial perspective without invoking ad hoc and ethereal notions of a 'soul,' higher consciousness, and a Higher Power. Let us 'conquer' mental illness by scientific means, through an armamentarium of psychological techniques and medications of proven effectiveness, just as physicians treat medical conditions based upon a knowledge of physics, chemistry, and biology. Let God and the mysterious infinite remain 'placebo effects,' and leave speculative ideas to be considered by theologians and philosophers.

On the other hand, some will balk at my conservatism. The increasing numbers of therapists who engage in formal meditation practices, who offer 'faith-based' religious counseling, who have had personal experiences of past lives and the supernatural, who heal at a distance using their 'psychic powers,' or are aware of the presence of angels, spiritual beings, and inexplicable divine interventions, will think that I am sitting on the fence and playing it cagey, rather than forthrightly stating a case for bringing spiritual practices, theology, extrasensory perception, and the supernatural into the treatment process.

The answer to both sides is that I can only be true to myself. I am by both nature and nurture a thinker who likes to push the envelope – very carefully! My position on these matters has evolved slowly rather than come in a burst of insight or a series of revelations and epiphanies. All I can say with conviction is that I no longer believe that the world and the mind simply consists of 'atoms and the void' (Democritus; cf. Chown, 2001), where 'ignorant armies clash by night' (Matthew Arnold, 1867 [1997]). A purely rationalistic, cause-and-effect psychology no longer satisfies me. And it is also clear to me now that self-actualization and higher awareness are not rarities, but everyday occurrences. I am convinced that something more than ordinary experience resides within ourselves in what I have called the psychospiritual self. I believe that this realm can be studied scientifically, although some of its aspects are private, incommunicado, inarticulate, and ineffable, and so are destined to elude and transcend science. In matters regarding the empirically 'verified' existence of God (as an entity distinct from our minds and culture), supernatural phenomena, and psychic powers, I am, at best, perplexed.

In other words, the position I have put forth is not something carved in stone, but simply my own bias. It is an exhortation and a set of suggestions towards a paradigm, a work in progress, not a provable or refutable theory as such. Having said that, I will now attempt to review my position and the rationale for it. I will proceed point by point with a summary statement of the paradigm and its rationale.

1. Psychology and psychotherapy have evolved to a stage where they can productively incorporate spiritual perspectives within a scientific 'living systems' framework.

In William James' *The Varieties of Religious Experience* (James, 1997) one finds a late 'Enlightenment,' 19th-century rationale for a spiritually based psychology, namely that, as psychologists, we ought to study religious experiences empirically, because they can have positive outcomes for living and for personal growth. This important rationale was seriously overlooked by most psychologists for ninety years. Those who showed an interest in spiritual matters were relegated to subdivisions within a few psychology departments, such as those at Duke University which engage in the study of paranormal phenomena, to pastoral and chaplaincy services, and to institutions of theology. A few psychotherapists, such as Erich Fromm and Victor Frankl, who utilized religious teachings about meaning and purpose within a humanistic framework, gained some acceptance in the mainstream.

With the advent in the 1960s of the Esalen Institute and the 'encounter group movement,' Eastern spiritual teachings were given credibility as 'change agents.' This East/West dialogue led to the New Age movement and an increasing interest in spiritual teachings and holistic health, to the point where it could be said that a substantial number of therapists have become 'holistic' and 'spiritually friendly.' This emerging interest has allowed for an important development: psychologists are now beginning to do what James suggested over a century ago, namely, conducting research on the impact of spiritual beliefs and practices on 'normal' and 'positive' psychology as well as on treating mental and physical illness.

My feeling, and the basis of this book, is that we are now in a position to formulate general concepts and principles of a psychological nature about this budding research and treatment emphasis. At the same time, we must proceed with special care not to disrupt the integrity of each of the diverse disciplines and practices which contribute to it, and in particular the special provinces of religious practice and psychotherapy, each of which have their own paradigms and functions.

2. The self has dimensions and dynamics which call for a psychospiritual understanding.

The self is the defining entity of all psychology. All that is attributed to 'self' is the province of psychologists, and that which we see is outside the self is given to other disciplines such as physics and biology. The way in which we define self prescribes the scope of what we study. Religion and science have inadvertently colluded to limit our view of the self to narrow and selective regions. Religion has taken so much of our inherent human goodness and power and externalized the divine within us onto a concept of an external God who is 'non-self,' difficult to reach, and judges us unsparingly. In this schemata of unending conflict, the self is limited to its struggle between desire or 'sin' and social taboo and obedience. Freud transposed this view of the self into his structural theory of id, ego, and superego, depicting the id as the seat of impulses and desires, the superego as a harsh judge, and the ego as caught in a struggle between them. While he and his successors eventually gave expanded functions to the ego, such as creative and altruistic capacities, the self continued to be viewed as a biological and social entity, with transcendent strivings never mentioned.

Some of what evolved out of the natural and social sciences were perhaps more benign than this 'survival of the fittest,' 'conflict with nature and with God' formulation. Freud and his followers began to see the important role that self love (narcissism), relationship, cooperation, attachment, and mourning played in the development of the psyche. Sullivan (1953), Rogers (1951), Robert White (1959), and others viewed the self as seeking engagement, competence, and growth. It was acknowledged that evolution had given man the capacity for symbolization, play, and community. Culture allowed man to self-regulate the entire context of 'tools,' social 'rules,' and consensually validated meanings in which he lived. The human being possessed the capacity to go beyond his biological limitations and his conflicts to develop his potential for intimacy and creativity.

The human potential movement opened the door to including spirituality as such in the panoply of self experience. The ideas of Maslow on self-actualization, of Lilly (1985), Wilber (1983, 1997, 2000), and others on higher states of consciousness, and the writings of Capra (1975), Zukav (1979), von Bertalanffy (1968) and others suggesting that physics and biology had spiritual parallels, provided scientific rationales for transcendent potentialities in humans.

It is my sense that psychology is now positioned to develop theories and therapies which are based on a much expanded view of self in which spirituality is not merely an addendum to the self, but betokens an inner world of greater dimensionality than we have previously considered. That is, as Grotstein (2000, pp.122–125) has said, the self is a holographic entity which is capable of many more dimensions than the four (time/space) in which our bodies are housed and in which conventional psychology views the mind. In other words, the psychospiritual self is capable of expanding outside of the 'time–space box' and experiencing emotions, intuitions, and a mysterious Other on a much broader base than we have previously believed.

While, to some extent, it is possible for psychotherapists intuitively to facilitate the occurrence of such mental expansion by virtue of their openness to experience, researchers and theoreticians must face the difficult problem of how to rigorously conceptualize these other dimensions, and formulate hypotheses that can be empirically tested. This process, which needs to be disciplined to the norms of scientific exploration, can also lead to improved psychotherapy technique. A workable psychospiritual paradigm offers a beginning to such systematic dialogue and investigation

3. The world's religions, for all their many shortcomings, contain a rich lode of experience, narratives, myths, and practices which access these broader realms of the self.

It may be that, at least for now, religious and mythical expression offer the best analogs and constructs for a multidimensional spiritual understanding of the psyche. Whether we consider 'satori,' the 'Great Spirit,' the ethics of the Ten Commandments, the story of Genesis, or the notion of resurrection, we are attributing infinite and high possibilities to the self – divine and God-like possibilities, if you will. The individual experiences of such phenomena are diverse and manifold, suggesting that these spiritual ideas inhere in each of us like rays of white light which are refracted in the prism of diversity into a 'coat of many colors' that characterizes human experience. Psychologists can investigate that diversity, its sources and course of development in the life cycle, and its psychophysiological correlates (such as brainwaves, activity levels, electrical stimulation, and biochemistry). This task has already begun. It needs to be orchestrated into a coordinated set of studies within a central paradigm.

4. Religion and psychotherapy are and ought to remain distinct disciplines which overlap in some respects, but need to maintain their boundaries and integrity. Religious practice and psychotherapy should maintain a dialogue with difference in which they contribute to each other's growth.

The tendency today, as spirituality increasingly finds its way into psychotherapy, is to transform psychotherapists into quasi-ministerial practitioners and missionaries of the psyche. The therapist becomes a guru, an initiated one, a mentor of religion and quasi-religious principles. With the exception of pastoral counselors, who clearly indicate their religious orientation and their specialty, most therapists are neither trained nor certified to offer such guidance. More deeply, psychotherapy, while it has spiritual aspects, is not in itself a religious undertaking. Let me say what I mean.

The essential aspect of psychotherapy is, in my opinion, interpersonal and relational. Even cognitive and behavioral therapists, who see their results stemming from specific reinforcers and cognitive reframing, acknowledge that empathy and relatedness are potent forces in change. Otherwise, they would have to admit that they are replaceable by a book or computer software, which is not psychotherapy but 'bibliotherapy' or perhaps 'cybertherapy.' When most patients consult therapists, they are seeking, among other things, a very special kind of interpersonal relationship that can be useful to them.

By contrast, the essential aspect of religion is *trans*personal. The minister, the congregation, the sanctuary are merely vessels and messengers for the 'big picture,' whether Talmudic teachings, Christ, or Buddhist Enlightenment. The holiness of this enterprise stems from its subordination to this transpersonal project.

When we seek to utilize spiritual principles in psychotherapy, we should do so with this distinction in mind. The therapist may bring a sense of mystery and awe into the session. He may seek an 'I–Thou meeting.' He may help the patient access transcendent states of consciousness and encourage spiritual values. But he offers these provisions within the framework of an interpersonal relationship and contract. That is, he offers himself and his methodology to the patient – not 'God,' theology, or a transcendent state as such. In actual practice, we have sometimes seen the unfortunate results both of psychotherapists who pose as prophets and gurus and of spiritual leaders who offer 'therapy' to their flock.

What I can legitimately offer the patient in a spiritual sense is a relationship, defined both by my training and by each of our personal characteristics, that may be healing for him and, by healing, may or may not lead him on a specifically spiritual quest. It is perfectly acceptable for people to pursue life within an atheistic or humanistic framework. Indeed, such a framework may be 'filled' spiritually if the person is deeply in touch with himself and others. A religious teacher or guru would be unlikely to take the same position, although he might be open to such an individual participating in his congregation or spiritual practicum. Unlike a therapist, the purpose of a religious teacher is to convey a specific set of beliefs and practices of a spiritual nature.

5. In the end, our theories and beliefs are only a limited part of the process. Who we are may be more important than what we say or think. To learn is to grow, to be convinced is to stagnate. The application of spirituality to psychology and psychotherapy should be conducted in this spirit of dialogue rather than as a new enthusiasm.

Much, if not most, of human spirituality is 'beyond words.' Our basic personality is formed prior to the acquisition of a language other than the most simple monosyllabic utterances and cries. Words and concepts may point to, but can never describe or delineate, spiritual experiences, because the latter are too complex to operationalize in this way. When we enter the realm of psychospirituality, concepts and theories become more fluid and evolving than with respect to other areas of psychological functioning. Theories themselves become ephemeral, chaotic, and complex. They are moving targets rather than fixed truths. We use them only to discard them; we wear the garment loosely.

Our nervous systems are inevitably more complex and multifaceted than our theories, which are, after all, merely products of our nervous systems. Psychospirituality consists of opening ourselves up to the totality of our neural networks, and flowing with them. I am concerned about recent attempts to locate specific brain areas where 'God-experiences' reside. There may be locations in the brain which stimulate particular awakenings and awarenesses. But spirituality itself is holistic and polydimensional. The entire nervous system, and perhaps more, must be involved. In the living systems paradigm I have developed here, God could be present in a single nerve impulse and a single cell and also in the confluence of memories, thoughts, images, and emotions involving the brain and all aspects of the environment which we can potentially access. There is no single 'location' of God, and no single theory that can encompass all of that which is God-awareness.

Thus, I would urge us to be cautious in ushering in a new era of spirituallybased psychology and psychotherapy as such. Whatever it is that we profess to be the new psychology will inevitably represent only a small part of the picture. My mentors, peers, and I have already lived through several eras of enthusiasm for psychoanalysis, family therapy, behaviorism, cognitive therapy, and still other approaches which seemed to provide definitive treatments for mental illness and then been proven to have feet of clay. Spiritually based approaches from Zen therapy to rebirthing are today being similarly acclaimed and proclaimed by their proponents. Inevitably, the shortcomings of these methods will be uncovered.

Instead of enthusiasms, what I advocate is a new openness to experience and expression combined with a careful weaving together of diverse threads into a richer fabric of research, understanding, and practice. This is going to be a multidisciplinary effort, bringing together systems and quantum theorists, neuroscientists, research psychologists, psychotherapists, psychoanalysts, cultural anthropologists, theologians, philosophers, and others in a quest for integration and the opening of new paths to explore. Whether it will be God, ourselves, a neural network, or the limits of our own knowledge that we ultimately discover is difficult to estimate. My own guess is that, by that time, such distinctions will have little meaning. We will simply be living in a new, expanded, emotionally richer, and hopefully more gracious psychological space than we now occupy.

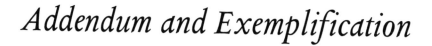

Addendum and Exemplification

Spirituality, the Twelve-Step Model, and Psychotherapy

As I mentioned early in this work when discussing the sources of my interest in and enthusiasm for spiritually based psychotherapy, I have been impressed by the utility of twelve-step programs in treating addictive and compulsive disorders. Even with the spate of popular books on alcoholism, addiction, and the recovery process, many counselors, psychotherapists, and psychoanalysts, and the public in general, are only vaguely familiar with the 'steps' of these programs and how they incorporate spiritual principles in a course of self-transformation which can lead to a remission of the powerful craving for and attachment to substances and compulsive behaviors. For this reason, I have added the following discussion of the Twelve Steps of Alcoholics Anonymous with particular attention to a depth psychological understanding of their inner workings. Such an exploration will also serve to exemplify how the psychospiritual paradigm is manifest within a support program which has had a healing impact on a large cadre of individuals, a much larger number than those who have been reached by professional psychotherapy as such.

The Twelve Steps of Alcoholics Anonymous would appear initially to diverge from the dynamic/developmental/systems model which forms the backbone of this book. Some readers may be surprised and taken aback by my including it here, much less by my enthusiasm for it, given my psychoanalytic orientation. Indeed, it was an anomaly that a clinician with my bias was hired to work at an inpatient substance abuse facility based on twelve-step principles. (It is a fact that only a very small number of psychoanalysts treat substance abuse as a specialty, the most noteworthy of them being Dr Leon Wurmser (1978) whose book, *The Hidden Dimension*, is a classic.) This experience of being 'a stranger in a strange land' was, for me, challenging and enlightening. In retrospect, I think that every aspiring therapist ought to 'do time' in a setting with a philosophy and treatment approach radically different from his own. Indeed, at every moment, and with the gift of a knowledgeable, clinically sound, and ethical supervisor (Dr Robert Pomerantz), I was challenged to rethink all that my extensive training had taught me.

For example, I quickly learned to be far more careful about diagnoses than I had been up to that time. It would have been easy for a psychoanalytic therapist like myself to regard many of these addictive patients as borderline (i.e. having disorganized and psychotic features), antisocial personalities (individuals, sometimes but not always hyper-aggressive, who violate societal norms and isolate from others, incapable of forming close ties with significant others), and/or chronically and clinically depressed. However, their improvements within days, weeks, and months convincingly demonstrated that their symptoms, while resembling those of major mental illnesses, often were direct effects of both acute and chronic substance abuse. Life on this alcoholism unit was full of surprises and 'miracles' of recovery. The creativity, generosity, and inner strength of these patients, as they found a way out of their addiction, was emotionally moving and highly gratifying to me.

I think it is noteworthy that support programs like Alcoholics Anonymous (AA), were originally developed by the patients themselves, and at points in their lives where they were given up for lost by the medical community. What bravado that they should have believed they could do what many brilliant physicians, psychoanalysts, and clergy could not achieve with all their intelligence and credentials! And what humility and far- sightedness they displayed in 'giving away' the AA program to alcoholics-at-large as a non-fundable and non-professional 'fellowship,' thus separating the program from money-making ventures and social reformers, and giving access to anyone who wishes to join.

As best as I can reconstruct it from the AA literature, the founding members of AA sought out and utilized whatever they could about spirituality, medicine, and psychotherapy, and stirred it into the pot of their collective experience to discover pragmatically what might keep them sober (Alcoholics Anonymous World Services, 1957). Then, in 1939 *ibid.* p.159–160), four years after their inception in 1935, they formulated their combined knowledge into systematized 'steps' towards sustained recovery.

It is significant that one of the co-founders of Alcoholics Anonymous, Bill Wilson, became sober through a process of spiritual awakening, having benefitted from the insights of a friend and a supportive physician. The friend had sobered up by applying the principles of the Oxford Movement, a non-sectarian, spiritually based group. The doctor supported Bill in taking his spiritual experiences seriously (Alcoholics Anonymous World Services, 1957, pp.1–48.) So the cornerstone of the steps was spiritual: an unconditional surrender to a higher power. The AA path invokes the inherent spirituality of each individual, leading to inner change and a non-addictive way of life. Although it borrows freely from various spiritual sources, the AA program is not religious in the sense of espousing a particular doctrine or belief system. While God is mentioned many times in the steps, it is clear that it is the God of one's choosing, 'as we understand him,' and the concept of a 'higher power' is still more open, allowing the recovering person to utilize the AA group, nature, the higher self, or a concept like universal love as a power greater than himself to whom he surrenders his ego. The important ingredient in the choice of a higher power, as far as I can tell, is that it be transpersonal, not a single person – since alcoholics are prone to form overdependent relationships with significant others. In addition, the power that is called upon must be a force for the general good, since an ethical, responsible life is essential to recovery. The shame, guilt and temptations of living can otherwise drive a person back to 'the drink.'

How AA works

It is not my purpose here to provide a thorough discussion or evaluation of Alcoholics Anonymous. What I wish to do is to place the steps in the context of a dynamic psychospiritual paradigm. Building that bridge will, I believe, illustrate one way in which spiritual principles have attained proven effectiveness in healing a psychiatric disorder. While AA is not psychotherapy as such, it serves many quasi-therapeutic functions and its ideas have been frequently utilized by addictions counselors. Therefore, it should be possible to find therapeutic parallels to the tasks and principles set forth in the steps.

It is important to note that AA does not offer the steps as a prescription for change without support and guidance. Rather, the steps are utilized in the context of a community of recovering individuals linked by a common purpose. The support group concept is itself spiritually based upon the principle of unconditional mutual love and is aimed not only at symptom alleviation but also at restoring order, esteem, meaning, and purpose in its members. Experience has convincingly shown that such support groups are helpful for a wide range of disorders, including sexual compulsivity, eating disorders, gambling, and severe physical illnesses. The support group provides the context and the human relationships within which change can occur.

The crucial discovery of AA, which ultimately led *Time* Magazine (Cheever, 2000) to declare co-founder Bill Wilson one of the one hundred greatest personages of the 20th century, was that one alcoholic could help another when no one else could. This principle of mutual identification, which is also the basis of group psychotherapy (Foulkes and Anthony, 1965; Scheidlinger, 1955), incorporates the spiritually connecting principles of Christian *agapé*, Buddhist compassion, and Judaic I–Thou relatedness. It also utilizes the notion of the 'wounded healer,' namely that the physician is someone who is striving to heal himself. It resembles Native American medicine, in which the shaman treats illness by acquiring and curing it in himself. In my view, such mutual healing principles are beginning to enter dynamic psychotherapy through the intersubjective and relational approaches, which place the parties to therapeutic interaction on a more equal plane, recognizing the vulnerability of both therapist and patient. In AA, powerful healing happens when two people, usually one of whom is recovering from alcohol addiction and the other having reached a point of helplessness and desperation, meet to discuss their common plight. The depths of despair, which was given theological and philosophical importance by Kierkegaard (1843 [1988]), are a key motivating factor for recovery. Mechanisms of denial and psychophysical cravings are so powerful in addiction, that a point of despair must be reached before a radical change can occur. At the nadir of the alcoholic 'bottom,' a moment of sanity may occur, and a person who has achieved sobriety can then offer hope to one who is ready to receive it.

AA support groups and networking

AA meetings are believed by its members to have an almost magical healing power. Individuals experiencing severe anxiety and agonizing depression often find that they leave a meeting feeling relieved and able to function effectively. Partly, this relief derives from confessional opportunities. Members share their feelings and concerns, finding recognition and acceptance rather than harsh judgement. Often, a recovering speaker will tell his story at length, offering a narrative that places the members' suffering in perspective and makes their mutual experience meaningful and purposeful.

Meetings also provide an environmental context which surrounds the members with hopefulness, good humor, and well-being. This context, and the ubiquitous availability of the membership to each other, parallels and recapitulates the mother's nearly total accessibility to the infant. Winnicott

(1963a) wrote about what he called the 'environment mother,' the aspect of mothering in which her presence surrounds the infant with a context in which it feels held and supported. AA meetings generate similar feelings of being safely 'held' in a favorable environment.

There is also a psychospiritual reason why AA meetings can become vital for people with alcohol problems. It is the need for ongoing contacts which restore the sense of wholeness. People who misuse substances often come from families where consistent mirroring and love is lacking. Their families have perhaps provided them with material necessities, caring, and concern, but may lack the internal resources to foster the development of self-esteem and wholeness. Alice Miller (1996), Margaret Mahler (Mahler, Pine, and Bergman, 1975), and Kohut (1977) have pointed out the need of such vulnerable offspring to 'refuel' their esteem throughout adulthood in order to regulate feelings of fragmentation and depression. Miller identified the parents' narcissism as limiting their ability to nurture their child's strengths and gifts. Mahler identified the difficulty such individuals encounter in retaining the warm, symbiotic feelings of early mothering as they separate and individuate from the maternal orbit. Kohut considered that the parents' failures to empathize with the child's feelings and self states produced a 'selfobject' deficit in which the individual frequently needs reinforcement of self-esteem and self-cohesion to shore up a depleted self system.

Those with alcohol problems may require such refueling of the self throughout their lifetimes. Many of them find such 'mirroring' and life-affirming 'selfobjects' late in the game, and after a battle with alcoholism, so they require repeated doses of their recovering peer group. The experiences of 'mirroring,' 'merger,' and 'twinship' (Wolf, 1988, pp.56–57) that they find with others who share a similar condition is crucial to them.

So the AA support group provides a powerful replica of the early maternal context that allows one to 'go on being,' rather than succumbing to a self-destructive impulse. This, in turn, is necessary for the sustenance of the core spiritual self in its struggles to actualize as it encounters inner conflict and a world which is not always caring.

The steps offer a way of life in which spirituality and ethical behavior become the individual's main priority. The steps are radical in that they ask the alcoholic to prioritize sobriety and spirituality above material and personal rewards. The success of the steps in addressing the physical, emotional, and spiritual aspects of alcoholism poses, in my opinion, a profound challenge to the ethos and goals of conventional psychotherapies. Very few therapists advise their patients that they may have to give up everything they have desired and achieved, in a state of surrender to God, in order to get well.

Because of the possibilities and challenges the steps offer for psychotherapy, I wish now to review them and offer a dynamic understanding in keeping with the psychospiritual paradigm set forth in this book. My purpose, once again, is to build bridges between spirituality, psychology, and psychotherapy through the vehicle of a specific approach to healing.

A psychospiritual understanding of the Twelve Steps of Alcoholics Anonymous

In the addictions program where I served as psychotherapist, the 'twelve-step philosophy' of Alcoholics Anonymous was frequently discussed in educational sessions with the patients, who also attended AA meetings held 'on campus.' It was in that educative context that I began to explore the dynamics of AA and to strive to make my approach to treatment of substance abuse consistent with its precepts. Initially, I was a benevolent skeptic. In time I saw that, while the steps are not psychotherapy as such, they do suggest a way of understanding addictions, compulsions, and psychotherapy which is based upon spiritual ideas. Since many counselors and psychotherapists encounter patients who are involved in twelve-step programs, and since the principles contained in the AA steps are applicable to some disorders other than substance abuse, I felt that a discussion of their therapeutic significance could be fruitfully undertaken in the present context.

I hasten to add that the therapist needs to assess whether the AA steps are relevant to any particular patient. Unfortunately, some counselors are over-zealous and apply them willy-nilly to any and all patients, with virtually any diagnosis. A bipolar or schizophrenic patient, for example, requires a decidedly different set of interventions than are implied in the steps, although they may be useful in addressing a 'co-morbid' substance abuse disorder. Enthusiasms for a particular approach are legion in the history of psychotherapy, and often lead to misguided, ineffective treatment.

That the steps bear striking parallels to modern psychotherapies is no accident. The early AA members communicated extensively with psychiatrists and psychotherapists. Jung, in fact, exchanged brief letters with AA co-founder Bill Wilson, after the latter learned about Jung's work from a friend. In addition, a few years after he became sober, Wilson entered into extensive treatment with Dr Harry Tiebout, a psychiatrist who supported and influenced AA in its early days. (AA was founded in 1935.) Tiebout (1943) wrote about a 'conversion experience' undergone by AA members, in which the realization of total powerlessness and the necessity to 'surrender' led to remarkable personality changes and long-term sobriety.

Prolonged sobriety was an extremely rare phenomenon at the time, and many of those professionals who worked in the field of alcohol abuse were startled and gratified by the successes of AA. In addition, Dr Bob Smith, a co-founder of AA, was a physician who doubtless had some exposure to psychiatry. The early AA members frequently spoke with clergymen, psychotherapists, physicians, and others as they sought to understand the nature of their condition and how to achieve healing. The steps, although spiritual at their core, reflect the historical emergence of psychological therapy as an influential force in medicine, society, and religion in the 20th century.

The steps constitute an orderly summary of what early AA members found helpful in maintaining their sobriety and developing a satisfactory way of life. They were inspired in part by the Oxford Movement, which offered a non-denominational spiritual lifestyle for its participants. AA members offered their own experience in developing the steps, and Bill Wilson documented them in the order in which they have been handed down to the present day. The steps have four psychospiritual components:

1. The first, which is controversial in psychotherapy circles, is to *accept 'powerlessness' over the problem, acknowledging that 'surrender' of one's 'life and will' is necessary* to achieve long-term remission of alcoholism. AA holds that alcoholism is an illness with physical, emotional, and spiritual dimensions. (Medical authorities such as the American Medical Association voice agreement with the 'disease' model of alcoholism.) The power of the addiction is so strong that the individual ego cannot overcome it. It therefore needs to be surrendered to a 'higher power,' which in some respects is reminiscent of the Jungian 'collective unconscious.'

2. The second aspect of the steps is *an overhaul of one's life: a combination of moral inventory, constructive action, and character building.* It is suggested that the AA member conduct a thorough evaluation of his assets, liabilities, and defects of character, share the inventory with another, develop humility as a basis for living, strive to make amends for harms done to others, and continue to evaluate his problems and resources on a daily basis.

3. The third component is *prayer and meditation*. Again, the philosophy is non-denominational. The raising of spiritual awareness is considered essential to psychological development that sustains sobriety. Universal love and a belief in miracles (not in a supernatural sense, but as unexpected, gratifying changes that can only be explained as a manifestation of something greater than the personal ego) characterize the spiritual awareness that AA members are seeking. The 'miracle' incorporates the mysterious element of healing that I have emphasized throughout this book. However, the steps make clear that sudden spiritual awakenings and sea-changes are rare, and that spirituality comes to most through laborious efforts over an extended time period.

4. The fourth imperative is *'helping others.'* By aiding the recovery of others facing the problem of alcoholism, the AA member is reminded of the nature of his condition, is able to transcend the narrow bounds of self-preoccupation, and develops a lifestyle in which service to others is paramount.

All of these principles are consistent with religious practices and beliefs. On the other hand, they initially appear to contradict the traditional secular psychotherapies which emphasize personal independence and autonomy, overcoming shame and guilt, and self-interest over altruistic and self-sacrificial aims. These differences could perhaps be accounted for on the basis that, as has often been argued, people who misuse alcohol are anti-social personalities with a deficient superego or moral conscience, and so require a moral treatment as distinct from one which reinforces ego strength and choice. Extensive and repeated research, however, has shown that there is, at best, a complex relationship between addictions and person-ality disorders (see, for example, Trull, *et al.*, 2000). While a segment of the addicted population manifests sociopathy in the premorbid stage, many if not most have harsh, restrictive superegos rather than a deficient moral fiber (Vaillant, 1983). Indeed, an overweening conscience may initially drive them to drink. Their 'co-morbid' diagnoses vary considerably. The emphasis on morality and spirituality in AA is not so much to shore up a deficiency of character, as it is designed to aid recovery from the chaotic lifestyle generated by chronic drinking, strengthen the individual's connection to society, and prevent a drinking relapse by reducing the rationalizations, denial, and painful conflicts which lead to it.

What I would propose in lieu of the 'antisocial superego-deficient' characterological basis for the steps is that AA is surprisingly more advanced than psychotherapy in its use of paradox. Specifically, the difference between the AA steps and 'conventional' psychotherapies rests in the paradox that, if you admit powerlessness over that which you genuinely cannot change, and allow that change to occur by going with the flow of the 'larger system' of life-as-a-whole or a higher power, then you are in a better position to 'change the things you can,' i.e. your present circumstances and yourself. That is, AA is an 'ecosystems approach' to recovery (cf. Bateson, 1972), placing the individual ego in the perspective of being a part of a larger context which has its own, often inscrutable, laws ('God's will'). Furthermore, the altruism and moral principles of the steps are presented, not as a form of religious salvation, but as a practical means to sobriety, a 'clean pattern of living,' and healthy relationships and family life.

In this respect, the apparent contradiction between spiritual objectives and personal desires is resolved. While many AA members do pursue psychotherapy, focusing on cognitive and behavioral changes, achieving personal ambitions and life goals, resolving psychological trauma, and, in some cases, making an in-depth psychoanalytic self-examination, the key to understanding the steps is the emphasis they place on whole systems versus the individual ego. When therapy emphasizes the primacy of the ego, it can lead patients into therapeutic impasses and failures. I am of the opinion that almost any brand of therapy can be done with a 'systems awareness' and a consciousness of context and the search for meaning and wholeness.

The Twelve Steps of Alcoholics Anonymous are specifically stated as follows (Alcoholics Anonymous World Services, 2001, pp.59–60):[1]

1. We admitted we were powerless over alcohol – that our lives had become unmanageable.

2. Came to believe that a power greater than ourselves could restore us to sanity.

3. Made a decision to turn our will and our lives over to the care of God *as we understood Him.*

4. Made a searching and fearless moral inventory of ourselves.

5. Admitted to God, to ourselves, and to another human being the exact nature of our wrongs.

6. Were entirely ready to have God remove all these defects of character.

7. Humbly asked Him to remove our shortcomings.

8. Made a list of all persons we had harmed, and became willing to make amends to them all.

9. Made direct amends to such people wherever possible, except when to do so would injure them or others.

10. Continued to take personal inventory and when we were wrong promptly admitted it.

11. Sought through prayer and meditation to improve our conscious contact with God *as we understood Him*, praying only for the knowledge of His will for us and the power to carry that out.

12. Having had a spiritual awakening as a result of these Steps, we tried to carry this message to alcoholics, and to practice these principles in all our affairs.

The steps are framed in such a way that their purpose is simple: to help the person achieve continuous sobriety by developing a 'one day at a time' set of practices. Changes are made in the here and now, in place of intentions and self-promises. Life, in all its potential difficulty, suffering, and disruption goes on. No special status or exemptions are granted. The person simply becomes capable of having a worthy life. In this respect, the steps, although framed in terms of Western beliefs, also have a Buddhist thrust, emphasizing reduced ego control and the value of the present moment, so that, as the Zen saying puts it: 'Before Enlightenment, chop wood, carry water; after Enlightenment, chop wood, carry water.' Everything changes, and everything remains the same.

The first three steps can be given a dynamic therapeutic interpretation as follows. The sufferer has formed a self-defeating 'transference' relationship, not to a person, but to a substance, alcohol. For him, the drink is a 'self object,' in that he turns to the chemical (and, not incidentally, the various rituals around it, such as the superficial narcissistic contacts at a bar or party) to bolster and restore a spurious wholeness and self-esteem, find pleasure and relief from frustration, and relieve feelings of loneliness and rejection. Initially using the substance and its 'ceremonial chemistry' (Szasz, 1985) as an 'all-good, all-powerful, all-giving' selfobject, the alcoholic gradually finds this magic elixir to be increasingly demanding, controlling, and destructive, analogous to the deleterious impact of a 'bad,' traumatizing parent. So when the person finally joins AA, surrendering his life and will to a higher power is akin to finding an all-powerful parent who is benign, consistently loving, and just. My point here is that 'surrender' can be understood in psychodynamic terms of transference, just as Freud, a century ago, held that the idealizing transference to the therapist facilitates the therapeutic alliance. Freud (1927) was quite aware of the aspect of God as a 'transference phenomenon,' although, as a stoic and a non-believer, he looked skeptically upon such religious transference.

Steps Four through Ten resemble the process of 'character analysis', developed by Wilhelm Reich (1980). The recovering person, who now has found support to sustain him through the difficult task of facing himself, is confronted with his 'character armor,' the layers of self-protective maneuvers he has developed over a period of years. Through a 'searching and fearless moral inventory' and its disclosure to a trusted other, he is then stripped of his armor-plating of character 'defects' but is afforded the validation of AA members and a benign deity. He then seeks a new way to live in which he can be vulnerable, fully conscious, and related to others.

Cognitive therapy incorporates similar features of character building by questioning the patient's 'cognitive distortions,' and behavioral therapies strive to achieve similar objectives through 'homework assignments,' i.e. contracts for change. Paradoxical therapy (Weeks, 1991) puts the patient in a position where any option he chooses leads to a change for the better, just as the steps are arranged so that, once the person accepts the basic premises of Step One, the remaining steps seem to follow, and there is no going back.

Steps Six and Seven are about inner change, and Eight and Nine are about restitution. These steps present important challenges to conventional psychotherapies in ways that I now wish to elaborate.

AA's program of inner change is different from the way we therapists ordinarily think about change. Therapists see inner change as resulting from proactive changes in thinking and behavior. The patient 'chooses' to adopt new attitudes and new behaviors towards himself and others. The therapist encourages patients to make these healthy choices, and reinforces them with 'rewards,' even if it only be a word of praise, a nod of approval, or a useful interpretation. The psychoanalyst, for example, believes that once the patient understands his problem in depth, he will, on his own accord, make better decisions based on his inherent desire to survive and thrive. Cognitive and behavioral therapists actively contract for changes in thinking and behavior. As a result of the new behaviors, and the positive feedback they engender, the patient experiences increased self-esteem and assertiveness. The therapist supports the patient in attributing these changes to the latter's own efforts.

AA takes an entirely different tack on this problem of change, although, as I shall suggest, the difference may be more superficial than deep. The member, instead of 'changing his ways,' becomes 'entirely ready' to have God remove his defects. (I find the word 'defects' problematical. I understand that term to include anything from maladaptive habits to deep-seated conflicts and self-destructive tendencies. Further, it implies a moral weakness, which I don't think is intended, although 'moral responsibility' is certainly implicit in the AA literature.) In simple biblical terms, how can God remove character defects if he has given man choice as to how he shall behave? Surely, man must decide his own behaviors, turning perhaps to God for guidance. In psychological terms, how can a person willingly surrender his own personality? That would be tantamount to cultism and brainwashing. But that is not what AA means.

'Becoming entirely ready' can be related to the psychoanalytic notion of 'resistance.' A patient encountering a block in the flow of thoughts, or an attitude, behavior, or defense mechanism which obstructs the analytic task is said to be 'in resistance,' that is, he often avoids the task of uncovering his complexes, coming face-to-face with himself, and proceeding with the analysis. He resists the insights and changes towards which he is inevitably moving. He becomes 'entirely ready' to give up these resistances only when he clearly perceives how they obstruct his conscious purposes. Similarly, the sixth step of AA encourages the member to come to grips with that in him which avoids growth and change. 'Being entirely ready' does not mean succumbing to a belief system or giving up one's personality. Rather, it is to embrace the struggle to overcome resistances to change. In object relations terms, the patient needs to grieve the loss of the love objects that failed him in life, and seek a new object relation unencumbered by deleterious past experiences. He starts to 'resolve the negative transference.'

Step Six is full of challenge, using phrases like 'this step separates the men from the boys,' and stating the goal of spiritual 'perfection' which is never achieved but serves as a compass point for development. Such indeed is the challenge of all spiritual quests, exemplified for example by Oedipus' self-blinding and his journey to Colonus, the Jews' and Moses' journey through the desert, Jesus' retreat from the city to encounter his demons, and Siddhartha's quest for Enlightenment.

Having God 'remove these defects of character' is by no means a passive process. It implies, rather, that our resistances to change can be as powerful as addictions themselves. We are in love with our defects and defenses – they protect us and relieve us temporarily of difficult dilemmas and situations. They are more than 'bad habits' that we can change at will. In this sense, we are powerless over them. Therefore, we need to access something beyond our limited egos to remove them.

What is it that removes defects of character? Step Six implies that this question is tantamount to asking 'Who or what is God?' There is mystery here – and I think that being available to mystery is an attitude that promotes healing. For example, I walk along a deserted beach, look at the stars at night, meditate in an ashram, look at a beautiful work of art, and I am moved to mystery and awe by the largeness and the miracle of the experience. Genuine mystery is infused with love, and so begets compassion, so when I return to 'everyday life,' I am a bit kinder to my wife, my child, a stranger. There are moments of mystery in psychotherapy as well. When a patient becomes aware of the unknown in himself, when he experiences caring and concern from others, when he releases an emotion, he senses something mysterious at work – even if we label that mystery naturalistically as 'the unconscious' or a 'good object.' He becomes more accessible to his own and others' humanness.

In that sense, God (as eternal mystery) is available everywhere and at every moment. Preparing ourselves to receive that mystery is a key to healing defects of character. Thomas Merton said 'God is Love,' as a divine principle of all life and all the universe. Often this love, this *agapé*, this I–Thou relation, is the basis of the patient's ability to change at a deeper level.

Overcoming resistances to change requires accessibility to loving and being loved. Step Six makes it clear that achieving such a goal, while it involves 'letting go' rather than self-control, is supremely difficult. One must relinquish festering resentments, practice altruistic love in the face of pressures against it, come to know oneself and one's motives at deeper levels, and live firmly according to moral precepts. 'Entirely ready' is thus wisely phrased as a striving rather than an end state.

Therapists usually have more limited treatment goals than those of Step Six. Yet, at the same time, we can recognize a correlation between the sixth step and our implicit values as psychotherapists. Therapeutic values, of course, derive from the Judao-Christian tradition, and, more recently, from the diversity of Eastern and Western spiritual orientations. When a psychoanalyst asks a patient to abstain from action and instead verbalize his wishes and conflicts (the so-called 'abstinence rule'), a contextual family therapist negotiates 'fairness' and 'exoneration' among parents and siblings, or a cognitive therapist challenges 'cognitive distortions,' elements of renunciation, sacrifice, altruism, and truthfulness are implicit in our methodology. The fact that the Twelve Steps so forthrightly state these values is indeed refreshing.

Step Seven makes it still more plain that AA represents a different system of thought from conventional psychotherapy. This step proposes, contrary to the modern ethic, that humility is the basis of growth and change, a theme which was also taken up by M. Scott Peck (1978) in his book *The Road Less Traveled*, a significant departure from the tendencies towards hedonism and narcissism which permeate our society and our treatment approaches.

I can understand why some readers might object to humility as a path to growth and change. While there are patients, especially those with narcissistic personality disorder, who come to us with an arrogance and pride which may be helped by a sense of proportion, modesty, and circumspect self-assessment, most therapy patients are initially full of shame, guilt, suffering, and low self-esteem. To exhort them to be humble would constitute arrogance on the therapist's part, a countertransference response, the awareness of which I suspect led Kohut to some of his formulations about 'healthy narcissism.' Yet, I think there is a way to understand humility which does not consist of an assault upon an already frail self.

The seventh step tries to address this problem. It makes a distinction between 'humiliation' and 'humility.' Many of us are all too familiar with humiliation, where our mistakes and failures are harshly judged. Humiliation de-humanizes the individual, and takes away from his self-esteem and connectedness to others.

People with alcohol problems have been humiliated by their 'shame-based' families of origin and by their own alcoholic behaviors. Step Seven suggests paradoxically that they can avoid further humiliation by practicing humility. The step suggests that the alcoholic see his substance-induced humiliations (such as making inappropriate remarks when drunk, or being arrested for vagrancy) as a basis, no longer for shame, but for realistic self-appraisal.

Therefore, I do think that humility need not necessarily lead to guilt or shame, but rather to accuracy of self-perception, a proportionate assessment of self. It can be a relief to learn that one is flawed and imperfectly human. For one thing, our limitations and shortcomings enable us to feel connected to our fellows rather than 'above and beyond' them. For another, humility allows us to proceed realistically towards our goals, instead of stumbling over our unfulfilled daydreams and delusions of grandeur.

Humility also entails a willingness to be vulnerable and open to experience. In psychoanalysis, a patient's humility can be found in his regression to childhood levels in order to learn more about himself and his development, in his persistent focus on himself and his own issues, in following a fee and appointment schedule, and, above all, in his acceptance that he needs help.

Readiness to change and humility as described in Steps Six and Seven are attitudes and mindsets. What follows upon them are specific actions towards accepting responsibility for one's actions and rectifying misdeeds. Step Eight suggests making a list of amends and Step Nine consists of active restitution for harms done. Certainly, individuals with alcoholic and other addictive disorders often leave behind them a trail of catastrophes, hurt, and alibis that may put their families, their employers, their lovers close to ruin. This is less true of our 'non-addictive' patients with anxiety and depressive disorders, who have mostly hurt themselves, and so there are few schools of psychotherapy which advocate specific 'amends' to others. One is Boszormenyi-Nagy's contextual family therapy (1984), in which righting wrongs, fairness, 'merited trust,' and exoneration are primary goals of treatment. Nagy's contextual approach regards symptoms as resulting partly from unresolved ethical problems in the family. Interestingly, his is the only therapeutic school which includes reducing potential harm to future generations as a central goal of the treatment process. In general, family therapy appears to be more attuned to the natural and social ecology than does individual treatment.

In Japanese society, which places the family and the group over individualism, a form of treatment called 'Morita therapy' (Chihiro, 1984) incorporates character development and correct action in the here-and-now, including 'amends.' The overall thrust of Morita therapy is to bring the mentally ill patient back into full connection with himself, the world, and society. (It has long been recognized that social isolation and marginalization are prime causes and effects of mental illness.) Making restitution rounds out the process of re-socialization, and restoring self-respect and the respect of one's fellows. It is no accident that Morita therapy, which is spiritually based in Zen Buddhism, is often used to treat alcoholics in Japan.

A still more stringent vantage point was advocated by Mowrer (1980), who held, controversially, that patients' guilt feelings were often well justified. He believed that, no matter how sick, mental patients remained morally culpable and needed to rectify the harm they had done. I've always felt that Mowrer's position was overstated, that we cannot blame someone for having a condition which makes it difficult for him to behave in a fully responsible manner. I have also observed that patients' disorders are sometimes massive acts of heroism, attempts to save significant others from a worse fate. An example might be a sexually abused child who protects the abusing parent by not disclosing the incest. Another instance is the schizophrenic who 'goes crazy' to prevent the family from fragmenting. Thus, while we want patients to develop a sense of responsibility for their actions, we certainly don't want to reinforce their own feelings that they are purveyors of harm.

Within the therapeutic interaction itself, reparations and amends occur both overtly and through subtle, unspoken gestures. Although therapy allows wide latitude for thought and emotion, neither patient nor therapist is above apologizing for disturbing behaviors. Patients may realize that they have been unnecessarily rude to their therapist, for example, and therapists may acknowledge an erroneous or tactless statement about the patient. Such apologetic 'corrections of course' may seem superfluous etiquette in a setting where free emotional expression is given primacy, but experience has shown that, in addition to reinforcing moral values, they can help clear the air and restore the frame of treatment.

But the amends which are most noteworthy yet often overlooked are those which occur tacitly via unspoken gestures of goodwill. For example, a therapist's merciful and compassionate phrasing in an otherwise disarming confrontation of a patient's character armor contains a 'reparation' and restitution within it, for the therapist has avoided the temptation to attack and undermine the patient's defenses. A patient's providing of associations, memories, and imagery for the therapist's use heals the inevitable gap between them. His very engagement in the therapy process constitutes amends and atonement for the inevitable damage done by the tear in the fabric of his frail selfhood. This subtle thread of reparation and restitution runs through all healthy human relationships and can be seen, for instance, in the merciful mutual empathies of parent and child that maintain the tenderness between them. Without such kindnesses and reparative acts, therapy, like all interpersonal relationships, would be jeopardized. We hardly realize that such 'amends' occur frequently in our lives, but their absence can be seen in situations where hostility breaks forth. Amends are soothing and healing, and they provide corrective clarification and feedback.

Following specific tasks designed to heal the damage wrought by years of problem drinking, Step Ten – the daily inventory – initiates 'maintenance' practices to enable the recovering person to sustain a positive quality of life. These practices begin with periodic self-inventories to defuse, debrief, and resolve problems resulting from untoward emotional reactions. Step Eleven recommends daily meditation and prayer. Step Twelve emphasizes a continued practice of service, as well as accepting the joys and gifts of sobriety with gratitude and equanimity.

The so-called 'action steps' (Four through Ten) are followed paradoxically by an exhortation to quietude and contemplation. Step Eleven suggests that the AA member develop a practice of meditation and prayer to achieve 'conscious contact with God as we understand Him.' As I have emphasized before, such a practice stimulates mental processes which parallel those which occur in dynamic psychotherapy. The individual is invited to go inward, to listen to his inner self. It is suggested that he reserve space for new experience by suspending judgement. The step advocates that specific requests, desires, and wishes from God must often be renounced so that the person's relationship to God may become a mature and non-demanding partnership. Eventually, the AA member may come to 'see' God as He really is, just as a patient in analysis may gradually come to see the therapist as a real person, not as a transference object of his childish fantasies and wishes.

Earlier, I pointed out that Eigen (1998) believes psychotherapy itself to be a form of meditation and prayer. Ogden (1994) postulated that in therapeutic communication there eventuates an analytic third, an Other who is the result of the dyadic interaction. This Other also, I suspect, consists of ethical and spiritual values, the background against which all therapy takes place. When patient and therapist step back and seek a new understanding and empathic connectedness, they look towards this Other for guidance and support. They open up to the unknown, the ineffable, the benevolent yet challenging Other, the widest Circle of Being. Such a process can be understood as a form of meditation and prayer.

Step Twelve is about 'living the life' of the recovering alcoholic. It has two components: helping others and experiencing the joy of living. Helping other alcoholics is considered the foundation of all recovery in AA. The discovery that led to the founding of Alcoholics Anonymous was the serendipitous meeting between Bill Wilson and Dr Bob Smith in Akron, Ohio in 1935, when they learned that they could help each other to achieve lasting sobriety. They then proceeded to help other alcoholics as an integral part of their own recovery process, and this is how AA was born.

In traditional psychotherapies, there is an 'asymmetry' (Cohen and Schermer, 2001) in which the helping 'arrow' flows mainly one way: from the therapist to the patient. This role complementarity reflects the professional contract in which an 'expert' with specific tools and strategies assists a 'client' who has specific symptoms and needs. Role asymmetry should not, however, preclude a recognition of the mutuality of the therapy process. Therapy is not an 'equal' symmetrical relationship as in AA, but mutuality of human experience is a part of how therapy works. The AA principle of mutual help parallels Sullivan's notion of 'participant observation' which advocates engagement and use of the therapist's self in the healing process. Interestingly, both have roots in small-town America (Sullivan grew up in a small town in New York State; Bill Wilson and Bob Smith were both reared in Vermont) and both emphasize 'cracker-barrel' plain talk in the healing process. 'Small town' mutuality and fellowship are very much a part of psychotherapy. It just must be accomplished with careful attention to the specific roles, boundaries, and duties of the therapist.

Group psychotherapy, of course, closely approximates to the mutuality and fellowship of AA. Mirroring and identification are known to be key ingredients of successful group therapy (Foulkes and Anthony, 1965; Scheidlinger, 1955). The group members benefit from perceiving aspects of self in others and from sharing a common dilemma. Feedback given in the form of 'What you say and what I observe about you reminds me of myself' is better received than objectified 'you' statements. Cohen (2000) has emphasized that such 'intersubjective feedback' about self is more beneficial than 'cybernetic feedback' in which members point out what they observe in others. AA members have known for decades that sharing their own experience is the most helpful way of responding to another's pain and difficulty. Only recently have psychoanalysts come to recognize the value of their own selective self-disclosure (Cohen and Schermer, 2001).

Step Twelve, then, describes a process which in psychoanalysis is called 'working through.' The AA member repeatedly subjects his experience to the insights he has acquired until the changes have become secure. He finds that, while his recovery was initially confined mostly to the AA meeting room, he is now putting what he has learned to use in many areas of his life. The twelfth step encourages the application of the steps in daily life and with significant others. AA emphasizes the active component of spirituality, that 'faith without works is dead.' Similarly, successful therapy is never a 'five-finger exercise' meant for the consulting room only – it moves outward in ever-widening circles to significant others and the world at large.

Finally, Step Twelve states a goal and a reward for recovery, namely, 'the joy of living.' All healing has an end state in mind. There are subtle and unsubtle differences in what is considered to be 'wellness.' Freud held that the goal of psychotherapy was to enhance the patient's ability 'to love and to work.' By sharp contrast, Reich viewed ecstatic orgasm as the chief goal of treatment! Maslow's humanistic psychology seeks self-actualization. Spiritual practices promise bliss, transcendence, redemption.

Obviously, relief and contentment are implicit in all these end states. AA's promises stand somewhere between the stoicism of Freud's functionality and the ecstasy, self-fulfillment, and bliss promised by other approaches. The 'joy' offered by AA is a 'lightness of being,' Lacan's (1977, p.23) *jouissance*, serenity, and contentment in the midst of life's difficulties. It is also a freedom to choose, a victory that comes from no longer being a slave of compulsion, and this freedom extends to the whole of life. The thrust of AA is towards spontaneous and serene living in accord with spiritual principles. In this respect, AA is self-actualizing. I know, for example, of a physician who chose to become an artist in his recovery. AA members become more comfortable with their innate sexuality. They choose friends who are supportive rather than manipulative. They often seek a better way of life than that portrayed in conventional society and the social neurosis. Paradoxically, AA utilizes the 'dictator' alcohol as a wedge for a 'conspiracy of good will' and the authority of a loving God to redeem the individual and bring him to the grace of freedom as a human being. In this respect, AA has its own grace. Therapy too, when well pursued, has its grace. It is the grace of helping to transform a human being into who and what he is and what he was intended to be. That is the true 'grace of God' of which all healing partakes.

How the Twelve Steps challenge conventional psychotherapy

While the AA Twelve Steps are imbued with psychotherapeutic understanding, certain aspects of their spiritual orientation present significant challenges to conventional therapeutic modalities. I would like now to be more specific about these differences.

Psychotherapy aims to enhance the patient's sphere of ego control: when the sensible and intelligent ego is in the driver's seat, all will be well. The Twelve Steps fly in the face of this emphasis on rationality and control. Their basic contention is that there are behaviors and thoughts that cannot be controlled, alcoholic drinking being one. With alcoholism at the helm, the more one strives to think and decide one's way out of the alcoholic maze, the more the drinking swings out of control. The 'disease' pulls one down, just as a drowning person is pulled down by an undertow in proportion to his struggle, when letting go might lead to a righting of the situation by the natural forces of the ocean itself.

The First Step advocates an admission of powerlessness. Yet, if a therapy patient were to say he were powerless, helpless, and dependent, a victim of an unmanageable condition, the therapist might surmise that he is 'rationalizing and excusing his condition,' 'characterologically defective,' 'avoiding reality,' and 'externally' rather than 'internally' controlled. The therapist would hold that the patient needs to know that he is in the driver's seat. There might be some 'exclusionary clauses' to this rule, for example, the patient may have been exposed to adverse family or life circumstances, or suffer from a serious physical illness. But ultimately, even with such exceptions, the therapist would hold that the patient can use the 'executive' part of his ego to 'choose' a course that is more fruitful than the one he had been following. The task of therapy is to help the patient to make such choices – a matter of volition. Step One, on the contrary, contends that the alcoholic is totally powerless over his drinking and that will-power is of no avail.

Steps Two and Three, advocating first faith and belief, and then surrender of will, challenge the contemporary skepticism on which much psychotherapy is based. Modern therapists lean towards secular progressivism in which both the individual and society are capable of unlimited successes through the application of knowledge, and therapy poses itself as a knowledge base for reaching personal goals, whether relief from anxiety and depression, a more satisfying marriage, or greater self-esteem. Therapists are generally not favorable to having patients 'surrender' to anything, much less a God whose existence cannot be scientifically verified. Instead, they want to form a working relationship based upon their knowledge and expertise, whereby the patient can achieve visible, measurable results. Therapists seek predictability based on observation. Reliance on intangible, invisible, mystical, higher realities and miracles is anathema to them. AA, by contrast, tells the member that 'no human power could have relieved their alcoholism' (Alcoholics Anonymous World Services, 2001, p.60). The answer, they contend, lies in faith in an entity beyond their ability to perceive and control.

Steps Four and Five suggest a 'moral inventory' of one's conduct. Modern therapy eschews morality as such. Instead, it is concerned with feelings, thoughts, and their consequences. Therapists rarely phrase patients' problems in terms of genuine ethical dilemmas. If a patient engages in promiscuity or hurts others in the relentless pursuit of ambition, there is no right and wrong about it. If he can negotiate these treacherous paths successfully, they are left untreated. If he gets into difficulty, he must seek more adaptive patterns. The consequences are what matter, not the ethics. By contrast, AA states unequivocally that the alcoholic must place his entire life on a sound ethical basis. He must be 'rigorously honest' and make others aware of his wrongdoings. Even minor transgressions cannot be overlooked.

Furthermore, the search for perfection and humility in this life, as Steps Six and Seven implore, are rarely goals which therapists set with their patients. These purposes are seen stereotypically as leading to self-effacing martyrdom. Admittedly there have been a few therapists, such as Jaspers (1951), Frankl (1998), and Fromm, who have advocated the goal of a righteous life well lived, with the welfare of others equal to one's own. But by and large the ethos of therapy has been that of achieving personal satisfaction. Self-sacrifice is underplayed at the expense of 'feeling good,' which is actually the title of a popular book on overcoming depression (Burns, 1999). AA holds that the best path to 'feeling good' is not self-seeking, but 'loss of self' in a larger purpose and context.

Therapy usually encourages patients to put the past in perspective and move on. So does AA, but with the exception that amends should be made for past wrongdoings. Again, very few therapists contract with their patients to make amends. As the famous saying from Erich Segal's *Love Story* goes, love means never having to say you're sorry. You cut your losses and go on from there. There is no need to rectify past mistakes. Only in Kleinian and Winnicottian object relations theories is there any implication that 'reparation' (Klein, 1977a) and 'the capacity for concern' (Winnicott, 1963a) are important elements of human development. Most developmental formulations are about the 'self' in the narrower sense, the needy, greedy self at war with the superego that sets injunctions and metes out punishments. Amends, on the contrary, acknowledge realistic guilt and allow for forgiveness, exchange, and equity. They require a larger perspective than our narrow struggles with survival and acquisition.

AA encourages meditation, solitude, and prayer. Conventional therapy emphasizes verbiage and activity. Maslow's (1954) ideas about the importance of 'being' over 'doing' are mostly ignored in conventional therapies. The idea of 'lifting up the mind' to higher things is also neglected in therapies which urge us to narrow our focus to that which is visible and palpable. While such a practical focus has its merits, it also can result in a stultified vision of life in which higher aims and visions are avoided.

Finally, AA challenges the therapist's time-honored neutrality and expert authority. Fellowship and mutual recognition are healing factors with untold powers. So much of the training of therapists places the therapist above and beyond the patient. In one training experience in family therapy, we, the trainees, were positioned in a conference rooom one floor above the consulting room, watching a 'live' television screen showing the family and therapist at work. The therapist periodically called us on the house phone to ask us what interventions we would suggest. The father of the family, with dour humor, persisted in correctly predicting what we would say! But you could sense his and our unease. He felt shame and we felt guilt. Who were we, placed above and beyond being present and human, to make these judgements about our fellows? In a less literal sense, therapists often impose an impenetrable barrier that separates them from their patients. AA poses a challenge to therapists to descend from their heights and admit that they, too, are frail and human 'wounded healers.' As an anonymous Christian clergyman once said, 'Be like God; become a human being.'

The AA Twelve Steps are important to the purposes of this book because they set forth a system of processes which have proven healing potential and which place spiritual principles at their center. I have included a discussion of them because, although they do not purport to represent a school of psychotherapy, they contain many elements of spiritually based treatment: holistic and systems-oriented rather than rationalistic; the utilization of paradox; a moral basis for living; mutuality of experience. While AA and psychotherapy are distinctly different enterprises that ought to maintain clear purposes and boundaries, I do think that a dialogue between the two could provide a fruitful vehicle to enrich the synergy of spirituality and psychotherapy which is occurring today. I hope that what I have written here will stimulate others to pursue that dialogue further.

Endnote

1   The Twelve Steps are reprinted with permission of Alcoholics Anonymous World Services, Inc. (AAWS). Permission to reprint the Twelve Steps does not mean that AAWS has reviewed or approved the contents of this publication, or that AAWS necessarily agrees with the view expressed herein. AA is a program of recovery from alcoholism *only* – use of the Twelve Steps in connection with programs and activities which are patterned after AA, but which address other problems, or in any other non-AA context, does not imply otherwise.

References

Alcoholics Anonymous World Services (1957) *Alcoholics Anonymous Comes of Age: A Brief History of AA.* New York: Alcoholics Anonymous World Services.

Alcoholics Anonymous World Services (2001) *Alcoholics Anonymous: 'The Big Book.'* (Fourth edition.) New York: Alcoholics Anonymous World Services.

Allison, H. E. (1983) *Kant's Transcendental Idealism: An Interpretation and Defense.* New Haven, CT: Yale University Press.

Amacher, P. (1965) 'Freud's neurological education and its influence on psychoanalytic theory.' *Psychological Issues, 4,* 4, Monograph 16. New York: International Universities Press.

Arnold, M. (1997) 'Dover Beach.' In *New Poems.* (First published 1867.) Toronto: University of Toronto Press.

Ashbach, C. and Schermer, V. (1987) *Object Relations, the Self, and the Group.* London: Routledge.

Austin, J. (1999) *Zen and the Brain.* Cambridge, MA: MIT Press.

Balint, M. (1979) *The Basic Fault.* (First published 1968.) New York: Brunner-Mazel.

Basch, M. (1988) *Understanding Psychotherapy: The Science Behind the Art.* New York: Basic Books.

Bateson, G. (1972) *Steps to an Ecology of Mind.* New York: Ballantine Books.

Beach, E. (1995) 'The Eleusynian Mysteries.' *The Ecole Inititiative.* [World Wide Web URL: http://www.erols.com/nbeach/eleusis.html]

Benjamin, J. (1990) 'Recognition and destruction: An outline of intersubjectivity.' *Psychoanalytic Psychology, 7* (suppl.), 33–47.

Benson, H. and Proctor, W. (1985) *Beyond the Relaxation Response.* New York: Berkley Publishing Group.

Benson, H. and Stark, M. (1996) *Timeless Healing: The Power and Biology of Belief.* New York: Simon and Schuster.

Berke, J. (1996) 'Psychoanalysis and Kabbalah.' *Psychoanalytic Review, 83,* 6 (December).

Berke, J. (1997) 'Womb envy.' *Journal of Melanie Klein and Object Relations 15,* 3.

Berke, J. and Barnes, M. (1971) *Mary Barnes. Two Accounts of a Journey through Madness.* London: MacGibbon & Kee. (London: Free Association Books 1991.)

Bertalanffy, L. von (1968) *General Systems Theory.* New York: Georges Braziller.

Bettelheim, B. (1983) *Freud and Man's Soul.* London: Chatto and Windus/Hogarth.

Bick, E. (1968) 'The experience of the skin in early object relations.' *International Journal of Psycho-Analysis, 49,* 484–6.

Bion, W. R. (1959) *Experiences in Groups.* London: Tavistock. (New York: Ballantine Books, 1974.)

Bion, W. R. (1970) *Attention and Interpretation.* London: Tavistock.

Bion, W. R. (1977) *Two Papers: The Grid and Caesura.* Rio de Janeiro: Imago Editora.

Bion, W. R. (1990a) *A Memoir of the Future.* London: Karnac Books.

Bion, W. R. (1990b) *Brazilian Lectures.* London: Karnac Books.

Blake, W. (1698) 'There is no natural religion.' In M. Eaves, R. N. Essick and J. Viscomi (eds) *The Illuminated Books of William Blake. Volume 3: The Early Illuminated Books.* Princeton, NJ: Princeton University Press, 1998.

Bleandonu, G. (1994) *Wilfred Bion: His Life and Work: 1897–1979.* London: Free Association Books; New York: Guilford Publications.

Blos, P. (1979) *The Adolescent Passage.* New York: International Universities Press.

Bollas, C. (1987) *The Shadow of the Object: Psychoanalysis of the Unthought Known.* London: Free Association Books.

Boszormenyi-Nagy, I. (1984) *Invisible Loyalties: Reciprocity in Intergenerational Family Therapy.* New York: Brunner/Mazel.

Bowen, M. (1978) *Family Therapy in Clinical Practice.* New York: Jason Aronson.

Bowlby, J. (1969) *Attachment and Loss* (Volumes 1 and 2). New York: Basic Books.

Brazelton, T. B. and Als, H. (1979) 'Four early stages in the development of mother–infant interaction.' *The Psychoanalytic Study of the Child, 34:* 349–371.

Bromberg, P. (1998) *Standing in the Spaces: Essays on Clinical Process, Trauma, and Dissociation.* Hillsdale, NJ: Analytic Press.

Buber, M. (1950) *The Way of Man According to the Teaching of Hasidism.* London: Routledge and Kegan Paul Ltd. (Reprinted in paperback: Secaucus, NJ: Citadel Press, 1966.)

Buber, M. (1970) *I and Thou.* (transl. Walter Kaufinan) New York: Scribner's.

Burns, D. (1999) *Feeling Good: The New Mood Therapy.* New York: Avon.

Campbell, J. (1949) *The Hero With a Thousand Faces* (Bollingen Series XVII). Princeton, NJ: Princeton University Press.

Campbell, J. (1997) (ed Anthony Van Couvering) *The Mythic Dimension: Selected Essays 1959–1987.* San Francisco, CA: HarperSanFrancisco.

Capra, F. (1975) *The Tao of Physics.* (25th anniversary edition, 2000) Boston, MA: Shambhala.

Capra, F. (1997) *The Web of Life: A New Understanding of Living Systems.* New York: Doubleday.

Cheever, S. (2000) 'The healer: Bill Wilson.' *Time.* Webpage: http://www.time.com/time/time100/heroes/profile/wilson01.html

Chihiro, F. (1986) *Morita Therapy: A Psychotherapeutic System for Neurosis.* Tokyo: Igaku-Shoin Medical Publications.

Chopra, D. (1990) *Quantum Healing: Exploring the Frontiers of Mind/Body Medicine.* New York: Bantam Doubleday Dell Publishing Group.

Chown, M. (2001) *The Magic Furnace: The Search for the Origin of Atoms.* Oxford: Oxford University Press.

Cohen, B. D. (2000) 'Intersubjectivity and narcissism in group psychotherapy: How feedback works.' *International Journal of Group Psychotherapy, 50,* 163–179.

Cohen, B. and Schermer, V. L. (2001) 'Therapist self disclosure in group psychotherapy from an intersubjective and self psychological standpoint.' *Group, 25,* 2 (June), 41–57.

Coltrane, J. (1965) *Meditations.* Recorded 23 November 1965. Re-released 1996 as Impulse CD IMPD-199.

Combs, A. (1995) *The Radiance of Being: Complexity, Chaos, and the Evolution of Consciousness.* St. Paul, MN: Paragon House.

Cox, G., Bendiksen, R. A., and Stevenson, R. (eds) (2001) *Complicated Grieving and Bereavement: Understanding and Treating People Experiencing Loss.* Amityville, NY: Baywood Publishing Co.

Damasio, A. (2000) *The Feeling of What Happens: Body and Emotion in the Making of Consciousness.* Fort Washington, PA: Harvest.

DeGeorge, R. and DeGeorge, F. (1972) *The Structuralists from Marx to Levi-Strauss.* Garden City, KS: Anchor Books (Doubleday).

DeMartino, R. (1971) 'Dialogues, East and West: Conversations Between Dr Paul Tillich and Dr Hisamatsu Shin'ichi.' *Eastern Buddhist, IV,* 2 (1971), 89–107; *V,* 2 (1972), 107–127; *VI,* 2 (1973), 87–114.

Dilts, R. (1983) *Applications of Neuro-Linguistic Programming.* Cupertino, CA: Meta Publications.

Edinger, E. F. (1972) *Ego and Archetype: Individuation and the Religious Function of the Psyche.* New York: Putnam.

Eigen, M. (1985) 'Toward Bion's starting point: between catastrophe and faith.' *International Journal of Psycho-Analysis, 66,* 321–330.

Eigen, M. (1998) *The Psychoanalytic Mystic.* London: Free Association Books.

Erikson, E. (1950) *Childhood and Society.* New York: W. W. Norton, 1993.

Erikson, E. (1959) 'Identity and the life cycle.' *Psychological Issues Monograph 1.* New York: International Universities Press.

Erikson, E. (1968) *Identity, Youth, and Crisis.* London: Faber and Faber.

Erikson, E. (1969) *Gandhi's Truth: On the Origins of Militant Non-Violence.* New York: W. W. Norton.

Fairbairn, R. W. D. (1952) *Psychoanalytic Studies of the Personality.* London: Routledge and Kegan Paul.

Feynman, R. P., Leighton, R. B., and Sands, M. (1989) *The Feynman Lectures on Physics, Vol. 1.* Redwood City, CA: Addison-Wesley.

Flores, P. (1997) *Group Psychotherapy with Addicted Populations: An Integration of Twelve-Step and Psychodynamic Theory.* (Second edition.) New York: The Haworth Press.

Foulkes, S. H. and Anthony, E. J. (1965) *Group Psychotherapy. The Psychoanalytic Approach.* London: Penguin Books.

Fox, M. (2000) *Original Blessing: A Primer in Creation Spirituality Presented in Four Paths, Twenty-Six Themes, and Two Questions.* New York: Putnam.

Frankl, V. (1998) *Man's Search for Meaning.* New York: Washington Square Press.

Freud, A. and Dann, S. (1951) 'An experiment in group upbringing.' *Psychoanalytic Study of the Child, 6:* 127–168.

Freud, S. (1900) *The Interpretation of Dreams.* New York: Avon, 1965.

Freud, S. (1905) 'Fragment of an analysis of a case of hysteria.' In *The Standard Edition of the Complete Psychological Works of Sigmund Freud, Vol. 7,* 3–122, London: Hogarth Press, 1981.

Freud, S. (1908) 'Character and anal eroticism.' In *The Standard Edition of the Complete Psychological Works of Sigmund Freud, Vol. 9,* 167–176, London: Hogarth Press, 1959.

Freud, S. (1915) 'The unconscious.' In *The Standard Edition of the Complete Psychological Works of Sigmund Freud, Vol. 14,* pp.161–215, London: Hogarth Press, 1957.

Freud, S. (1920) 'Beyond the pleasure principle.' In *The Standard Edition of the Complete Psychological Works of Sigmund Freud, Vol. 18,* 3–64, London: Hogarth Press, 1975.

Freud, S. (1923) 'The ego and the id.' In *The Standard Edition of the Complete Psychological Works of Sigmund Freud, Vol. 19,* 13–66, London: Hogarth Press, 1961.

Freud, S. (1927) 'The future of an illusion.' In *The Standard Edition of the Complete Psychological Works of Sigmund Freud, Vol. 21*, 3–58, London: Hogarth Press, 1961.

Fromm, E. (1970) *The Crisis of Psychoanalysis.* New York: Fawcett.

Fromm, E. (2000) *The Art of Loving.* New York: HarperCollins.

Gergens, K. (1991) *The Saturated Self.* New York: Basic Books.

Giovacchini, P. L. (ed) (1990) *Tactics and Techniques in Psychoanalytic Therapy III: The Implications of Winnicott's Contributions.* Northvale, NJ: Jason Aronson.

Gleick, J. (1987) *Chaos.* New York: Viking.

Gottlieb, D. (2001) 'Chairperson. Panel interview of three psychotherapists who utilize spiritual principles in their practice. With Drs Phillip Bennett, Haim Horowitz, and Molly Layton' At conference on *The Sacred Space and the Journey Within: Psychotherapy and Spirituality,* 28 October 2001, Thomas Jefferson University, Philadelphia, PA.

Grof, S. (1988) *The Adventure of Self-Discovery* (2 volumes). Ithaca, NY: State University of New York Press.

Grof, S. and Grof, C. (1989) *Spiritual Emergency: When Personal Transformation Becomes a Crisis.* Los Angeles, CA: J. P. Tarcher.

Grosskurth, P. (1986) *Melanie Klein: Her World and Her Work.* New York: Alfred A. Knopf.

Grotstein, J. S. (1978) 'Inner space: Its dimensions and coordinates.' *International Journal of Psychoanalysis, 59,* 55–61.

Grotstein, J. S. (1985) *Splitting and Projective Identification.* New York: Jason Aronson.

Grotstein, J. S. (1990) 'The "black hole" as the basic psychotic experience: Some newer psychoanalytic and neuroscience perspectives on psychosis.' *Journal of the American Academy of Psychoanalysis, 18,* 1, 29–46.

Grotstein, J. S. (2000) *Who is the Dreamer Who Dreams the Dream? A Study of Psychic Presences.* Hillsdale, NJ: The Analytic Press.

Grotstein, J. S. (2001) 'Who is the dreamer who dreams the dream? The numinous nature of the unconscious.' Lecture given at conference on *The Sacred Space and the Journey Within: Psychotherapy and Spirituality.* 28 October 2001, Thomas Jefferson University, Philadelphia, PA.

Guntrip, H. (1961) *Personality Structure and Human Interaction.* New York: International Universities Press.

Guntrip, H. (1971) *Psychoanalytic Theory, Therapy, and the Self.* New York: Basic Books.

Guntrip, H. (1986) 'My experience of analysis with Fairbairn and Winnicott. (How complete a result does psycho-analytic therapy achieve?)' In Buckley, P. (ed) *Essential Papers on Object Relations.* New York: New York University Press.

Hawking, S. (2001) *The Universe in a Nutshell.* New York: Bantam Doubleday Dell.

Hayman, R. (1999) *A Life of Jung.* New York: Norton.

Hopper, E. (1991) 'Encapsulation as a defence against the fear of annihilation.' *The International Journal of Psycho-Analysis, 72,* Part 4, 607–624.

Hopper, E. (1997) 'Traumatic experience in the unconscious life of groups: A fourth basic assumption.' *Group Analysis, 30,* 439–470.

Horney, K. (1994) *The Neurotic Personality of our Time.* New York: W. W. Norton.

Jacoby, M. (1990) *Individuation and Narcissism: The Psychology of the Self in Jung and Kohut.* London: Routledge.

James, J. (1992) 'Emotion.' In *William James: Writings 1878–1899.* New York: The Library of America, 350–365.

James, W. (1997) *The Varieties of Religious Experience*. (First published 1902) New York: Scribner.

Janet, P. (1886) 'Les actes inconscients et le dedoublement de la personalité pendant le somnambulisme provoqué.' *Revue Philosophique, 22*, II, 577–792.

Janoff-Bulman, R. (1992) *Shattered assumptions: Towards a New Psychology of Trauma*. New York: The Free Press (Macmillan).

Jaspers, K. (1951) *Way to Wisdom*. New Haven, CT: Yale University Press.

Jourard, S. (1980) *Healthy Personality: An Approach from the Viewpoint of Humanistic Psychology*. New York: Macmillan.

Jung, C. (1933) *Modern Man in Search of a Soul*. New York: Harcourt Brace.

Jung, C. (1934) 'A review of the complex theory.' In *The Collected Works 8* (Bollingen Series XX) Hull, R.F.C. (transl.); Read, H., Fordham, M., and Adler, G. (eds) Princeton, NJ: Princeton University Press.

Kagan, J. (1994) *The Nature of the Child*. (10th anniversary edition) New York: Basic Books.

Keats, J. (1817) *The Complete Poems and Selected Letters of John Keats*. Princeton, NJ: Princeton Review, 2001.

Keats, J. (1817) *The Letters of John Keats: A Selection*. Edited by R. Gittings. Oxford: Oxford University Press, 1970.

Kierkegaard. S. (1988) 'Fear and trembling.' In E. H. Hong, and H. V. Hong (eds) *Kierkegaard's Writings, Vol. 6*. Princeton, NJ: Princeton University Press.

King, P. and Steiner, R. (1991) *The Freud–Klein Controversies: 1941–45*. London: Routledge.

Klein, M. (1946) 'Notes on some schizoid mechanisms.' *International Journal of Psycho-Analysis, 27*, 99–110.

Klein, M. (1977a) *Love, Guilt, and Reparation and Other Works: 1921–1945*. New York: Delta.

Klein, M. (1977b) *Envy and Gratitude and Other Works: 1946–1963*. New York: Delta.

Klein, R. H. and Schermer, V. L. (2000) *Group Psychotherapy for Psychological Trauma*. New York: The Guilford Press.

Knafo, D. and Feiner, K. (1996) 'The primal scene: Variations on a theme.' *Journal of the American Psychoanalytic Association, 44*: 2, 449ff.

Kohon, G. (1971) [1997] *The British School of Psychoanalysis: The Independent Tradition*. (Reprint edition) London: Free Association Press, 1997.

Kohut, H. (1971) *The Analysis of the Self*. New York: International Universities Press.

Kohut, H. (1977) *The Restoration of the Self*. New York: International Universities Press.

Lacan, J. (1977) *Ecrits: A Selection*. (transl. A. Sheridan) New York: W. W. Norton.

Langs, R. L. (1976) *The Bipersonal Field*. New York: Jason Aronson.

Levi-Strauss, C. (2000) *Structural anthropology*. New York: Basic Books.

Levin, J. S. and Chatters, L. M. (1998) 'Research on religion and mental health: An overview of empirical findings and theoretical issues.' In H. G. Koening (ed) *Handbook of Religion and Mental Health*. New York: Academic Press.

Lewin, K. (1951) *Field Theory in Social Science*. New York: Harper & Row.

Lewis, H. B. (1971) *Shame and Guilt in Neurosis*. New York: International Universities Press.

Lichtenberg, J. (1983) *Psychoanalysis and Infant Research*. Hillsdale, NJ: Analytic Press.

Lilly, J. C. (1985) *The Center of the Cyclone: An Autobiography of Inner Space.* New York: Random House.

Little, M. I. (1990) *Psychotic Anxieties and Containment: A Personal Record of an Analysis with Winnicott.* Northvale, NJ: Jason Aronson.

Lockwood, M. (1989) *Mind, Brain, and the Quantum.* Oxford: Basil Blackwell Ltd.

Mahler, M., Pine, F., and Bergman, A. (1975) *The Psychological Birth of the Human Infant.* New York: Basic Books.

Mann, A. T. and Lyle, J. (1995) *Sacred Sexuality (Sacred Arts).* London: HarperCollins–UK.

Maslow, A. H. (1954) *Toward a Psychology of Being.* New York: Van Nostrand Reinhold.

Matte-Blanco, I. (1975) *The Unconscious as Infinite Sets: An Essay in Bi-logic.* London: Duckworth.

Maturana, H. (1980) *Autopoesis and Cognition: the Realization of the Living.* Brodrecht, Holland: D. Reidel.

McMullin, R. E. (2000) *The New Handbook of Cognitive Therapy Techniques.* New York: W. W. Norton.

Meissner, W. W. (1986) *Psychoanalysis and Religious Experience.* New Haven, CT: Yale University Press.

Miller, A. (1996) *The Drama of the Gifted Child.* New York: Basic Books.

Milton, J. (1667) 'Paradise Lost.' In Quiller-Couch, A. T. (ed) *The Oxford Book of English Verse.* Oxford: Clarendon, 1919.

Mitchell, S. (1988) *Relational Concepts in Psychoanalysis.* Cambridge, MA: Harvard University Press.

Mowrer, O. H. (1980) *Learning Theory and Personality Dynamics: Selected Papers.* Melbourne, FL: Krieger Publishing Company.

Mullahy, P. (1948) *Oedipus: Myth and Complex.* New York: Hermitage Press.

Nathanson, D. (ed) (1987) *The Many Faces of Shame.* New York: Guilford.

Newsom, M. And Cook, V. (eds) (1996) *Chomsky's Universal Grammar: An Introduction.* Oxford: Blackwell Publications.

Ogden, T. H. (1982) *Projective Identification and Psychotherapeutic Technique.* New York: Jason Aronson.

Ogden, T. H. (1994) 'The analytic third: working with intersubjective clinical facts.' *International Journal of Psycho-Analysis, 75,* 3–20.

O'Hanlon, W. (1987) *Taproots: Underlying Principles of Milton Erikson's Therapy and Hypnosis.* New York: W. W. Norton and Company.

O'Leary, J. (2001) 'The postmodern turn in group psychotherapy.' *International Journal of Group Psychotherapy, 51,* 4, 473–488.

Pearlman, L. A. (2001) 'Treatment of persons with complex PTSD and other trauma-related disruptions of self.' In Wilson, J. P., Friedman, M. J., and Lindy, J. D. *Treating Psychological Trauma and PTSD.* New York: Guilford, pp.205–236.

Pearlman, L. A., and Saakvitne, K. W. (1995) *Trauma and the Therapist: Countertransference and Vicarious Traumatization in Psychotherapy with Incest Survivors.* New York: W. W. Norton.

Peck, M. S. (1978) *The Road Less Traveled: A New Psychology of Love, Traditional Values, and Spiritual Growth.* New York: Simon and Schuster.

Pentikainen, J. and Poom, R. (transl.) (1999) *Kalevala Mythology (Folklore Studies in Translation).* Bloomington, IN: Indiana University Press.

Perera, S. (1986) *The Scapegoat Complex.* Toronto: Inner City Books.

Phillips, M. and Frederick, C. (1995) *Healing the Divided Self: Clinical and Eriksonian Hypnotherapy for Post-traumatic and Dissociative Conditions.* New York: W. W. Norton.

Piaget, J. and Inhelder, B. (1969) *The Psychology of the Child.* New York: Basic Books. (First published 1966.)

Polanyi, M. (1974) *Personal Knowledge: Towards a Post-Critical Philosophy.* Chicago, IL: University of Chicago Press.

Porter, L. (1999) *John Coltrane: His Life and Music.* Ann Arbor, MI: The University of Michigan Press.

Rando, T. (1993) *Treatment of Complicated Mourning.* Chicago, IL: Research Press.

Reich, W. (1973) *The Function of the Orgasm.* New York: Farrar, Straus, and Giroux.

Reich, W. (1980) *Character Analysis.* (Third reprint) New York: Noonday Press.

Ricoeur, P. (1970) *Freud and Philosophy.* New Haven: Yale University Press.

Rieff, P. (1979) *Freud: The Mind of a Moralist.* (Third edition) Chicago, IL: The University of Chicago Press.

Rodman, F. R. (1990) 'Insistence on being himself.' In P. L. Giovacchini, (ed) *Tactics and Techniques in Psychoanalytic Therapy, III: The Implications of Winnicott's Contributions.* Northvale, NJ: Jason Aronson, pp.21–40.

Rogers, C. (1951) *Client-Centered Therapy: Its Current Practice, Implications, and Theory.* Boston, MA: Houghton Mifflin.

Rosenau, P. M. (1992) *Post-Modernism and the Social Sciences.* Princeton, NJ: Princeton University Press.

Rossi, E. L. and Erickson, M. H. (1989) *The Collected Papers of Milton H. Erickson on Hypnosis.* (Four volumes) New York: Irvington Publications Inc.

Sarkar, S. (ed) (1996) *The Legacy of the Vienna Circle: Modern Reappraisals.* New York: Garland Publications.

Sarnoff, C. (1976) *Latency.* New York: Jason Aronson.

Sarup, M. (1992) *Jacques Lacan.* Toronto: University of Toronto Press.

Schachter, S. and Singer, J. (1962) 'Cognitive, social, and physiological determinants of emotional state.' *Psychological Review, 69,* 379–399.

Scheidlinger, S. (1955) 'The concept of identification in group psychotherapy.' *American Journal of Group Psychotherapy, 9,* 661–672.

Schermer, V. L. (1999) 'To know a mind: Freud, Oedipus, and epistemology.' *Psychoanalytic Studies, 1, 2,* 191–210.

Schermer, V. L. (2001) 'The group psychotherapist as a contemporary mystic: A Bionic object relations perspective.' *International Journal of Group Psychotherapy, 51,* 4.

Schermer, V. L. and Pines, M. (1999) *Group Psychotherapy of the Psychoses: Concepts, Interventions, and Contexts.* The International Library of Group Analysis 2. London: Jessica Kingsley Publishers.

Seager, W. (1991) *The Metaphysics of Consciousness.* London: Routledge.

Searles, H. (1965) *Collected Papers on Schizophrenia and Other Subjects.* New York: International Universities Press.

Searles, H. (1975) 'The patient as therapist to his analyst.' In P. L. Giovacchini (ed) *Tactics and Techniques in Psychoanalytic Therapy. Vol. II.* New York: Jason Aronson, pp.95–151.

Segal, H. (1974) *Introduction to the Work of Melanie Klein.* New York: Basic Books.

Segal, H. (1989) *Klein.* London: Karnac Books.

Segal, Z. V., Williams, J. M. G., and Teasdale, J. D. (2001) *Mindfulness-Based Cognitive Therapy for Depression.* New York: Guilford.

Shengold, L. (1989) *Soul Murder: The Effects of Childhood Abuse and Deprivation.* New Haven, CT: Yale University Press.

Sidlofsky, M. (1999) 'The Partzufim, Isaac Luria's revisionist Kabbalah.' In *Resources for Kabbalah and Jewish Meditation.* [Online monograph. http://kavannah.org/partzufim.html]

Smith, B. and Smith, D. W. (eds) (1995) *The Cambridge Companion to Husserl.* Cambridge: Cambridge University Press.

Solomon, A. (2002) *The Noonday Demon: An Atlas of Depression.* New York: Touchstone.

Steiner, J. (1989) *The Oedipus Complex Today: Clinical Implications.* London: Karnac Books.

Stern, D. (1984) *The Interpersonal World of the Infant.* New York: Basic Books.

Stolorow, R. D., Atwood, G. E., and Brandchaft, B. (eds) (1994) *The Intersubjective Perspective.* Northvale, NJ: Jason Aronson.

Storr, A. (1989) *Solitude: A Return to the Self.* New York: Ballantine Books.

Strozier, C. (2001) *Heinz Kohut: The Making of a Psychoanalyst.* New York: Farrar, Straus, and Giroux.

Sullivan, H. S. (1953) *The Interpersonal Theory of Psychiatry.* New York: W. W. Norton.

Sutherland, J. (1989) *Fairbairn's Journey to the Interior.* London: Free Association Books.

Suzuki, S. (1970) *Zen Mind, Beginner's Mind.* New York: Weatherhill.

Symington, J. and Symington, N. (1996) *The Clinical Thinking of Wilfred Bion.* London: Routledge.

Szasz, T. (1985) *Ceremonial Chemistry: The Ritual Persecution of Drugs, Addicts, and Pushers.* Holmes Beach, FL: Learning Publications.

Tart, C. (ed) (1972) *Altered States of Consciousness.* New York: Doubleday.

Thomas, D. (1971) *Collected Poems.* New York: New Directions.

Thompson, J. G. (1988) *The Psychobiology of Emotions.* New York: Plenum Press.

Tiebout, H. (1943) 'Therapeutic mechanism of Alcoholics Anonymous.' In Alcoholics Anonymous World Services (1957) *Alcoholics Anonymous Comes of Age: A Brief History of AA.* New York: Alcoholics Anonymous World Services.

Tillich, P. (1952) *The Courage to Be.* New Haven, CT: Yale University Press.

Tomkins, S. S. and Demos, E. V. (1995) *Exploring Affect: The Selected Writings of S. S. Tomkins.* Cambridge: Cambridge University Press.

Trull, T. J., Sher, K. J., Minks-Brown, C., Durbin, J. and Burr, R. (2000) 'Borderline personality and substance use disorders: A review and integration.' *Clinical Psychology Review, 20,* 235–253.

Vaillant, G. (1983) 'The natural history of male alcoholism: Is alcoholism the cart or the horse to sociopathy?' *British Journal of Addictions, 78,* 317–320.

Waldrop, M. M. (1992) *Complexity: the Emerging Science at the Edge of Order and Chaos.* Carmichael, CA: Touchstone.

von Wallenberg Pachaly, A. (2000) 'Group psychotherapy for victims of political torture and other forms of severe ethnic persecution.' In R. H. Klein and V. L. Schermer *Group Psychotherapy for Psychological Trauma.* New York: The Guilford Press.

Weeks, G. R. (1991) *Promoting Change Through Paradoxical Therapy.* New York: Brunner-Mazel.

White, R. W. (1959) 'Motivation reconsidered: The concept of competence.' In *Psychological Review, 66,* 292–333.

Wilber, K. (1983) *Eye to Eye.* (Third edition 1996.) Boston, MA and London: Shambhala.

Wilber, K. (1997) 'An integral theory of consciousness.' *Journal of Consciousness Studies, 4*, 1, 71–92.

Wilber, K. (1998) *The Marriage of Sense and Soul: Integrating Science and Religion.* New York: Random House.

Wilber, K. (2000) *Integral Psychology: Consciousness, Spirit, Psychology, Therapy.* Boston, MA and London: Shambhala.

Winnicott, D. W. (1951) 'Transitional objects and transitional phenomena.' In *Playing and Reality.* New York: Basic Books, 1971.

Winnicott, D. W. (1956) 'Primary maternal preoccupation.' In *Collected Papers: Through Paediatrics to Psycho-Analysis.* New York: Basic Books.

Winnicott, D. W. (1960a) 'Theory of the parent–infant relationship.' In *The Maturational Processes and the Facilitating Environment: Studies in the Theory of Emotional Development.* New York: International Universities Press, 1965.

Winnicott, D. W. (1960b) 'Ego distortion in terms of true and false self.' In *The Maturational Processes and the Facilitating Environment: Studies in the Theory of Emotional Development.* New York: International Universities Press, 1965.

Winnicott, D. W. (1963a) 'The capacity for concern.' In *The Maturational Processes and the Facilitating Environment.* New York: International Universities Press, 1965.

Winnicott, D. W. (1963b) 'Communicating and non-communicating.' In *The Maturational Processes and the Facilitating Environment.* New York: International Universities Press, 1965.

Winnicott, D. W. (1986) 'The theory of the parent–infant relationship.' In P. Buckley (ed) *Essential Papers on Object Relations.* New York: New York University Press.

Wolf, E. S. (1988) *Treating the Self: Elements of Clinical Self Psychology.* New York: Guilford.

Wolman, B. and Ullman, M. (eds) (1986) *Handbook of States of Consciousness.* New York: Van Nostrand Reinhold.

Wolters, C. (trans) (1978) *The Cloud of Unknowing, and Other Works.* New York: Penguin Classics.

Woollcott, P. and Desai, P. (1990) 'Religious and creative states of illumination: a perspective from psychiatry.' In D. S. Browning, T. Jobe, and I. Evison (eds) *Religious and Ethical Factors in Psychiatric Practice.* New York: Burnham. [Also available at webpage: http://www.lifwynnfoundation.org/woollcott.html]

Wright, J. (1990) *Above the River: The Complete Poems.* New York: A Wesleyan University Press Edition: Farrar, Strauss, and Giroux and University Press of New England.

Wurmser, L. (1978) *The Hidden Dimension: Psychodynamics in Compulsive Drug Use.* New York: Jason Aronson.

Wuthnow, R. (1989) *Meaning and Moral Order: Explorations in Cultural Analysis.* Berkeley, CA: The University of California Press.

Yalom, I. (1995) *The Theory and Practice of Group Psychotherapy.* (Fourth edition) New York: Basic Books.

Young, A. (1976) *The Reflexive Universe.* New York: Doubleday.

Zukav, G. (1979) *The Dancing Wu-Li Masters.* New York: William Morrow.

Subject Index

Author Index